Essays in Socialism by Ernest Belfort Bax
Prism Key Press | www.prismkeypress.com

ISBN: 978-1463656300

Essays in Socialism
Ernest Belfort Bax

Contents

Preface

THIS book, as its name indicates, comprises essays old as well as new. Rather more than a third of the contents of the volume have already been published in a little book now some years out of print, bearing the title **Outspoken Essays**. As regards this portion of the present work, only those alterations which were indispensably necessary have been made, the author preferring to let the pieces in question remain as far as possible as they were originally written. The consequence of this is, of course, that examples and illustrations impliedly drawn from current events, in reality date some ten years back. The above remark especially applies to the essay entitled *The Monstrous Regiment of Womanhood* and the police and law cases there cited. To have obviated this would have involved complete rewriting, which the author felt was the more unnecessary, as precise parallels to the typical cases adduced may be readily discovered by any one who cares to take the trouble to glance through a newspaper file of the past twelve months. The tone of public opinion and the principle on which the law is administered have not sensibly changed in the matter in question during the last decade.

The suggestions contained in the essay on *Early Christianity and Modern Socialism* may be supplemented to-day by a perusal of some works of recent scholarship that have since appeared, such as Professor Dill's **Roman Society from Nero to Marcus Aurelius**, and M. Gaston Boissier's **La Religion Romaine**. For the rest the author ventures to think the suggestions in question will not have lost any of their point for those who are interested in following up the analogies indicated as obtaining between the modern movement and that of the first centuries of the Christian era.

Concerning the *Natural History of the Nonconformist Conscience*, it may be pointed out that the history of English public opinion during the Boer War has since afforded a sinister commentary on the outline sketch given ten years back of the origin and history of that notorious ethical product. Yet while the mass of British Nonconformity during the war showed up to the old hypocrisy in a luridly odious guise, it would be unfair not to recognise the individual cases of Nonconformist ministers, who were prepared to sacrifice everything and face ruin rather than bow the knee to the foul Jingo idol. These, however, were exceptional men, of whom it may be truly said that, if not "the world," at least the Nonconformist Conscience, was unworthy of them.

The rest of the essays forming the bulk of the present volume speak for themselves. Some of them have appeared already in Socialist and other periodicals, others now see the light for the first time. In putting them forward in their present form, the author hopes that, amid the wide range of subjects he has briefly touched upon from the point of view of modern Socialism, readers may be found who will gather, at least here and there, a hint or suggestion which may fertilise in their own minds and yield useful results to the progress of Socialistic thought and the spread of Socialistic doctrine in this country. If such is the case, his object will have been attained.

Socialism, What It Is and What It Is Not

IT may seem at first sight almost superfluous to add one more to the already sufficiently numerous definitions and brief expositions of Socialism. It can hardly, however, be deemed so, when one takes into consideration the misconceptions still existing, in spite of all the current thought and writing on Socialism going on around them, among all save those who have given themselves especial trouble to study the subject. To take only one or two obvious absurdities commonly to be heard from the man-in-the-street. Prominent among these is the extraordinary notion that Socialism to be consistent, in some mysterious way, involves a squalid way of living – that the great antithesis of Socialism is luxury. Another is, that Socialism presupposes a saint-like self-abnegation on the part of the individual. Even the old idea of the general liquidation and dividing up, as being the economic goal of Socialism, is by no means yet extinct, while that of the grinding tyranny of a regulative power ordering production and distribution for the good of all, still holds the place of honour among the weapons in the arsenal of individualist opponents of Socialism among the old political parties. But before saying a few words on the things Socialism is not, it may be well once more to rehearse the (by the present writer) oft-repeated story of what Socialism is.

The word Socialism dates from the early decades of the nineteenth century and was first used, I believe, by Robert Owen. It implied from the beginning a state of society based on Communism, though in the three great Utopian systems of Saint Simon, Fourier, and Owen, the stress was still laid rather on the communism of the product than on that of the means of production. These systems were all based on the notion of the voluntary reconstruction of society on a preconceived plan. All classes were to co-operate in the re-construction on becoming convinced of the reasonableness of the said plan. This it was held, must inevitably be the case as soon as the reasons were adequately laid before them. Hence all that was required was a thoroughgoing and vigorous propaganda. These systems of Utopian Socialism insisted on a complete transformation in all the departments of human life. The change of moral and speculative ideas formed part of the scheme of human life as put forward by the three great Utopian theorists. Other analogous schemes, the most important of which was, perhaps, that of Etienne Cabet towards the middle of the nineteenth century, also followed on similar lines.

The difference between modern scientific socialism and these fanciful speculations and crude attempts at artificial social reconstruction, is wide, but wide as it is, it is no wider than the difference between the guesses of alchemy and the conclusions of chemistry. On the other hand in either case, the later and scientific form is, in a sense, the child of the earlier. Utopian Socialism and Scientific Socialism, have so far, the same content and aim, namely a revolution in human life involving the change in matters economic, of individualistic or private property holding, to communal property holding, in matters political from the government of men to the administration of things, in matters intellectual from tradition and authority, as such, to science and criticism, as the test of belief. But while the Utopian Socialist thought to achieve his aim solely by an effort of conscious will on the part of mankind individually, irrespective of all that had preceded, the notion of evolution being unknown to him, the modern Socialist is well aware that the most the individual man can do is to hasten and, at best modify, in points of detail, the realisation of a given direction of progress – that the will of mankind in general follows certain determinate laws in economical as in intellectual matters, laws which cannot be altered fundamentally by any conscious determination on the part of the individual. These laws the Utopian Socialist ignored, being himself unaware of their existence, just as the alchemist, in seeking to modify according to his will, the constitution of bodies, ignored the laws of chemistry of which he likewise was ignorant. The modern Socialist knows that success is impossible until the time is ripe, but in recognising this he no less recognises that an analysis of modern social conditions shows him that the time is quickly ripening.

Modern Socialism lays especial stress on the economic revolution which is, indeed, the central point of Socialism. The direct aim of all practical Socialism to-day is the transformation of private ownership and control by individuals or syndicates of the means of production and exchange into their public ownership and control by the Community at large. Hence it is, that we not infrequently find Socialism described as a purely economic doctrine, implying no more than an economic change in the fabric of society. This, of course, is only true on the hypothesis that the economic change would suffice of itself to bring about those other changes which Socialism from its Utopian phase onwards, has all along been understood to involve. But even were this conceded the description of Socialism as a purely economic doctrine, and the social revolution as solely having reference to a purely economic change, is none the less calculated to mislead. And, indeed, to this source is traceable not a little of the misconception prevalent as to the true significance of the term Socialism. The word Socialism has come to be applied to any activity of the state or municipality in an economic direction, irrespective of what the nature of the activity or the state concerned is. Hence any industrial or commercial enterprise undertaken by a governmental body is labelled Socialism nowadays. The mere form is here confounded with the content. Mere Statification, as we may term it, does not mean Socialism. The state of to-day is mainly an agent of the possessing classes and industrial or commercial undertakings run to-day by governmental bodies are largely ran in the interests of these classes. Their aim in all cases is to show a profit, in the same way as ordinary capitalistic enterprises. This profit accrues to the possessing classes in the form of relief of imperial or local taxation, mainly paid by them, interest on loans, etc. In other words these industrial undertakings are run for profit and not for use and their employees are little, if at all, better off than those of private employers.

But this is not to say that Socialists do not approve of a policy of the concentration of industry as far as possible in the hands even of the present state or municipality. Such a policy necessarily prepares the way for Socialism, even though it is not Socialism itself, in addition to the fact that such a policy usually redounds to the interests of the working-classes as a whole even to-day in their capacity as consumers. The organised community, presupposed by modern Socialism or Social-Democracy, is however something very different from the existing class-state. And herein, we may see the fallacious tendency of assertions as to Socialism being a purely economic doctrine. For here it is clear that a political change is involved concurrently with the economic change. Indeed without the political revolution, sometimes spoken of as the "dictatorship of the proletariat," the economic revolution itself, as implying the reduction of the whole means of production and distribution into the possession and under the control of the people themselves, would be impossible. The non-recognition of this fact has led to much foolish talk by "practical" prigs, Fabians, and others anent Socialism "from above," the possibility of Socialism under existing political forms, monarchical, constitutional, or what not. As a matter of fact, Socialism as embodied in the writings of its chief protagonists, Utopian and scientific, as well as in the aspirations of the disinherited of modern civilisation, is radically inconsistent with any form of class-domination, economical, political, or otherwise. The directive power of the Community which, as Social-Democrats contend, is destined to supersede the state of to-day, will be simply the organ of a Community politically and economically free and not, as to-day, a bureaucracy representing a governing class distinct from the Community. Even where you have an elective representative

12

system, as in the most advanced constitutional countries, it is well-known that the possession of wealth is – quite apart from bribery proper – in nine cases out of ten, the determining force which decides elections. This is the direct economic power behind politics. But this is not all. Even were the power of wealth entirely inoperative in directly or indirectly determining the results of elections, you still have the political and administrative power of class to contend with in the shape of the bureaucracy which is the real and direct governing power in the modern constitutional state. Every one who knows anything of the inner working of the governmental machinery of modern times, knows that it is the permanent officials of departments who really govern and administer the affairs of a nation. A bureaucracy, that is, a body of permanent officials, intrenched in government departments, according to whose piping ministers themselves have willingly or unwillingly dance, is totally incompatible with the very elementary conditions Socialistic administration. Any change which has Social-Democracy as its end must begin by a clean sweep of all departmental officials above the simple harmless penman-clerk. For the interests of a bureaucracy are always opposed to change of any sort whatever, and there is nothing in nature which hangs together so closely, where its interests are threatened, as a bureaucracy.

The aim of the modern Socialist movement is, of course, primarily economic, since the material conditions of life, the mode in which the wealth of the community is produced and distributed, constitutes in a very crucial sense, the basis of everything else. The intellectual, emotional, aesthetic sides of human nature can none of them escape the influence of this, their material environment, and their dependence on it. Even though up to a certain point, intellectual development may follow an independent line of causation of its own, yet this obtains only up to a certain point. In the long run the points of contact with the material conditions of life assert their importance in modifying the so-called "spiritual" side of things human. Of course they, in turn, are reacted upon. Intellectual progress modifies material progress just as much as *vice versa*. Hence the fact remains that a deep-lying organic change in the material side of human life, that is, in the modes of the production and the distribution of wealth, is inconceivable save as in conjunction with corresponding changes in men's habits of thought, and ways of looking at life. Direct causation between the two sides maybe only imperfectly traceable, but their concurrence and mutual determination is undeniable. The whole of human development is concrete. It is a synthesis of different elements, but if there is one element at least in the present stage of evolution, more fundamental, more implicating the entire synthesis than another, it is incontestably the economic element in human society.

Let us take as an instance of the close connection between the material and economic bonds of human society, and the immaterial relations which bind it together, the question of ethics. It is a commonplace with modern thinkers that morality is conditioned by the structure and circumstances of a given community. Scarcely anyone contends in the present day for an absolute morality independent of the circumstances of a definite social environment. Those principles of morality, that are applicable to all conceivable states of human society, without denying their importance, so far as it goes, obviously resolves themselves into a few general maxims too vague to afford of themselves a guide for conduct in many concrete cases. It is quite clear that a society for which the individual, as an isolated entity, is the unit of social life as regards the possession and control of property, cannot have the same rules of conduct as regards property, as the society for which the individual is not a self-regarding unit in this respect, but, on the contrary, for which the community in some form or shape stands as the unit for property-holding. Then again as to the question of sexual ethics. To the anthropologist and the student of the history of institutions, it is well known that forms of marriage and the family are intimately connected with the prevailing modes of property-holding. Under primitive communistic conditions various forms of the family prevailed which appear grossly immoral to the man who has grown up among modern individualist conditions. Hence arises the tendency in the present day of many convinced Socialists to shirk this question. They are, in their own minds, perfectly well persuaded that in a society such as Socialism implies, based on the communal production of wealth for social use and enjoyment, and hence where private property-holding has either ceased to be altogether, or at least has lost its importance – while they are, I say, quite aware that in such a society the principle of rigid monogamy enforced by law and public opinion, as at present, must break down before a freer conception of human relationships, yet they are extremely chary of admitting this in so many words. The current point of view of marriage as a legally enforced bond and not a free-relationship depending for its continuance on the will of the parties concerned, has acquired an absolute character with many persons who otherwise consider themselves emancipated, and hence there is a tendency either to deny the obvious implications of Socialism in this respect, or at least to fence with the question in a disingenuous manner.

Let us take another department of ethics. Under existing individualist conditions, where every man is for himself, the Christian virtue of charity or philanthropy obviously has a distinct significance and many applications. But equally obviously in a society based on communistic conditions the occupation of the charitable soul and the philanthropist, in the sense in which it exists to-day, would most certainly have gone. Now the special ethical duty devolving upon Socialists, as such, is to hasten, by every means in their power, the advent of the state of society which shall render philanthropy unnecessary and obsolete. As regards the exercise of personal charity at the present time the Socialist stands in the same position as any ordinary good and humane man who, maybe, has never heard of Socialism – neither more nor less. His obligations to the exercise of personal charity are, indeed, not so strong from the point of view of his principles as those of the Christian believer, for whom private property-holding and its ethical counterpart private charity are a part of the divinely-ordained system of things. Yet when shall we cease to hear from the lips of non-Socialists and anti-Socialists stale twaddle to the effect that the first duty of the consistent Socialist must be to straightway distribute all his possessions in indiscriminate alms-giving? They little reck that for the Socialist, whose motto is "justice, not charity," such a procedure would be positively inconsistent with the principles he professes. No! emphatically – alms-giving, whether good or bad, right or wrong, under existing conditions, not only *is not Socialism* but has *nothing to do with Socialism*.

Yet again, the notion that poverty and squalor have some mysterious virtue in themselves, expressed in a modified form in eulogies of "plain-living and high-thinking," etc., is still prevalent among many who might be supposed to know better. For Socialism, poverty and squalor are unmitigated evils, and a rationally conceived and directed luxury in material things for all alike, is its direct aim. This notion of asceticism, of the virtue of mortifying the flesh, of self-abnegation on the part of the individual, derived from Christian doctrine as interpreted by the Puritanism of the rising small middle-class of former days, is attributed to Socialism as a part of its ethics – is arbitrarily foisted, that is, on to a system of thought for which it has no meaning and in which it has no place.

The saying of Tridon, subsequently repeated by Bebel and others, to the effect that Socialism stands for a system of life and thought expressing itself in economics as Communism, in Politics as Republicanism, and in Religion as Atheism, embodies in a few words a large measure of truth. It may be convenient for Socialists, with a view to election-expediency to seek to confine the definition of Socialism to the economic issue abstracted from all the other issues of life and conduct. But the attempt to limit the term Socialism within the four walls of an economic definition is, in the long run, futile. Such a limitation is justified neither by historic usage nor, as above pointed out, by the implications involved in the economic change itself.

The conviction that Socialism involves a complete revolution in all departments of human life, and that though beginning with the economic change it does not end there, is ineradicable alike with friend and foe because founded in the nature of things. Socialism as implying the emancipation of mankind from economic thraldom implies also his emancipation from every other thraldom, from political thraldom, from intellectual and moral thraldom, from domestic thraldom. Hence all the existing forms of these things – founded as they are, on convention and tradition, having their roots far back in the past, but in their present form moulded to meet the exigencies of present-day capitalistic society – must necessarily go by the board. Political institutions having their basis in class- or caste-rule, religious beliefs founded on arbitrary dogma, tradition, and inherited sentiment, domestic institutions originating in social necessities no longer obtaining, and supported in their holds on the minds of men to-day mainly by convention and custom-clad sentiment – all these things must pass away as a tale that is told. It is no use then, pretending that while the economic structure of society is undergoing a fundamental revolution, other aspects of social life are to remain unscathed. They too must go, the only question is how, and this question it is that really troubles people. When Socialism, for instance, is said to be incompatible with religion in its traditional sense, as involving belief in supernatural dogmas and sanctions, many persons conjure up to themselves visions of an attempt to forcibly repress the practice of the Christian *cultus*, or a drastic inquisition into private beliefs. Again, if one speaks of a modification of the marriage relation in the direction of greater freedom than at present, their horrified imagination at once portrays to them the violent rupture of all domestic relations, the hearth in ruins, etc. For them the present condition of nominal asceticism in sexual relations tempered by hypocritical licentiousness, is the only conceivable form of the relation between the sexes. They do not see that in all these things the change inaugurated by Socialism would be of a purely permissive character and would, at first, at all events, consist, in all probability, solely in the breaking down of barriers in law and public opinion by which these institutions acquire a of privilege that enables them to tyrannise over the lives of men. The Socialist administration will in religion be purely secular and hence it will recognise no form of supernatural belief or cult. Similarly it will recognise to the full individual freedom in "self-regarding" matters. It will not, therefore, presume to regulate the purely private concerns of individuals, sexual or other, as is done by the existing marriage laws and by the unwritten law of public opinion. Alike law and public opinion in a Socialist state we have no reason to doubt would confine themselves to enforcing duties, of whatever nature they may be, towards offspring. The *question of offspring* is the *only one with which the community is concerned as regards the sexual relations of individuals*; all else is a private matter only concerning the individuals themselves. This, I take it, will be the attitude of a Socialist community towards these matters. As will be seen, this implies *no compulsory abandonment* either of current superstitions or of current domestic relations, but merely *leaves the way open* for the supercession of traditional ways of thought and traditional modes of life by others more consonant with human freedom and more adapted to the human nature of the time than those that have been left behind.

Of one thing let us beware in our attempts to envisage the "world-rebuilded," (to use William Morris' expression) of Socialism. We are only too prone to interpolate into our conceptions elements drawn from the present or the past. The result is very much the same as though Lord Bacon or Sir Thomas Gresham had attempted to give a picture of the world of modern London. We should indeed have had a curious amalgam of mediaeval survivals, combined probably with shrewd anticipations of the real future. It would be well were all content to recognise the truth that though the attempt to picture our future of Socialism may be an amusing pastime, or even give rise to interesting products of artistic romance, yet for practical purposes it is unprofitable. We can define and appreciate tendencies, we can give the main lines on which the society of the future must build itself up, but this is all we can do towards forecasting the time to come. Of one thing, however, we may be sure, and that is, that we have rather to fear the slowness of the tempo at which fundamental changes will take place, than to dread the violence of the wrench that the world is destined to undergo in the transformation of the old into the new order.

The Materialistic Doctrine of History

THE materialistic conception of historic evolution may be defined generally as meaning the view that the social life of mankind on all its sides, including its moral, intellectual and aesthetic, is either the direct or indirect outcome of the psychological reflection of its economic conditions, i.e., of the conditions under which its wealth is produced and distributed.

According to this view in its most extreme form, morality, religious conceptions and art are not simply modified by economic conditions, but are merely the metamorphosed reflection of those conditions in the social consciousness. In short, the substance of all things human is *wealth*, *qua* its production and its distribution. Religion, art, morality, etc., are its accidents, i.e., each and all of their manifestations are traceable directly or indirectly to economic causes.

That this doctrine contains an infinitely larger element of truth than the previously accepted one, that the dominating influence in human affairs is the speculative theories holding sway at any particular time, is, I take it, incontestable. But this fact by no means necessarily entitles us to regard economic condition as the sole determinant of progress – for such is practically the position taken up by certain exponents of the "materialistic conception of history." Those who adopt it seem to me to deny or ignore the fact that human nature always implies a synthesis, and, as such, more than one element. They further seem to think that in the reduction of any given psychological or social phenomenon to its earliest expression – it may be back to an earlier animal form or even to simple organic tissue – they have thereby disclosed the essence, the "true inwardness," of the phenomenon in question. The mere tracing of a thing back to its beginning in the order of time does not, however, necessarily disclose its intrinsic import, or affect its ultimate significance. An illustration of the fallacy here referred to is to be found in the debate on the subject of this article between M. Jaurès and M. Lafargue held some years ago in Paris. M. Jaurès maintained (whether rightly or wrongly does not affect my present purpose) that in the earliest psychological stages of humanity the notion of Justice and Equality can be traced, and that all subsequent popular movements have simply represented progressive manifestations of these ideas, though of course, as modified by the economic conditions of the period in question. To this Lafargue suggests that his opponent should carry his argument further and demonstrate the existence of such ideas in the ape and even the oyster. The answer to Lafargue is, to my thinking, perfectly simple. In the first place, Jaurès was not dealing with oysters, or even with apes, but with human society. His contention was that certain ethical notions or tendencies are first clearly and definitely manifested as such in the earliest stages of man's development as a social being; that, often obscured, they have been never quite lost throughout his subsequent development; and that they reach their full fruition in Socialism.

The saying *natura non facit saltum* is doubtless true in sociology as elsewhere, and therefore no one has right to say that, assuming M. Jaurès's assumption to be correct, something corresponding to these ethical tendencies, Justice, Equality, etc. might not be found in the ape bearing an analogy with the same tendency displayed in man. The like observation may be carried further back even unto the oyster, or possibly if one likes, to inorganic matter. In the "irritability," the reactive response to stimulus, of the body of the mollusc with the sensibility we infer to accompany it, we have the direct precursor of the conditions presupposing man's moral, intellectual and artistic impulses. The merely sensitive "reflex action" of the mollusc represents unquestionably at its stage of evolution the "higher," no less than the lower, consciousness of Humanity – it contains all these tendencies implicitly – so to say, in *potentia*. But the mere fact that in the time-sequence the one is preceded by the other does not enlighten us as to the nature either of "higher consciousness" and "conscious volition," or of mere blind sentiency and reflex action, still less as to the ulterior forms of human consciousness lying hidden in the future.

The endeavour to reduce the whole of human life to one element alone, to reconstruct all history on the basis of economics, as already said, ignores the fact that every concrete reality must have a material and a formal side – that it must have at least two ultimate elements – all reality as opposed to abstraction consisting in a synthesis. The attempt to evolve the many-sidedness of human life out of one of its factors, no matter how important that factor may be, reminds one of the attempts of the early pre-Socratic Greek philosophers to reduce Nature to one element, such as water, air, fire. With Plato and Aristotle, the Greeks gave up their efforts to trace back even external nature, much less experience in general, to any single factor within it. Now the more extreme partisans of the *Materialistische Geschichtsauffassung* would make of economic basis their "source and origin" of all things in the manner of the old Greek Hylozoists. In disputing this pretension on one occasion with an eminent partisan of the extreme view, I was maintaining that there were things in the heaven and earth of human affairs that were not dreamt of in his philosophy – that there were moral, intellectual and aesthetic facts of life which could not be traced back even remotely to purely economic causes. His reply was significant. "Where do they come from then?" he said, "they don't fall down from heaven." The impossibility of any alternative between their being the psychological reflection of economic conditions and their "falling down from heaven" struck me as extremely naive. The possibility of declining to accept either horn of the pretended dilemma never seemed to present itself to my friend.

As a matter of fact the theory under discussion would seem to require correction in the following sense:– "The speculative, ethical and artistic faculties in Man exist as such *ab initio* in human society, although undeveloped, and are not merely products of the material facts of man's existence, albeit their manifestations at any given time throughout the past have been *always* slightly and *often* considerably modified by those facts. The total evolution of society, thus far, has been in a far larger degree determined by its material groundwork than it has by any purely speculative, ethical, or artistic cause. But this is no equivalent to saying that you can resolve any such "ideological" factor back into a *purely* material condition. I maintain that no sort of demonstration has been given of the possibility of resolving any single epoch-making speculative, moral or aesthetic conception into being the product of *mere* economic circumstance. This may enter into it and modify it in its realisation, but it has never been shown that it can explain it more than partially. The same remark applies to any historical period or event. This too has never been *exhaustively* explained as a product of past or present, material conditions, although in certain cases I admit it may be sufficiently so for practical purposes, just as society has a distinct economical development, so it has also a distinct psychological development, the interaction of these two lines of causation giving us social evolution in the concrete.

An important distinction is, moreover, usually ignored by exponents of the theory, to wit, that between negative condition and positive cause. New material conditions of society which have merely removed previous hindrances to the development of an idea cannot be treated as the cause of that idea. The removal of those hindrances may be an antecedent condition inseparable from the realisation of the idea or the ideal, but it is no more its cause than the removal of a mechanical hindrance to the straight growth of a tree is the cause of its normal form or stature. Instances enough of this must occur to the reader from the domain of history. The precise form a movement takes, be it intellectual, ethical or artistic, I fully admit is determined by the material circumstances of the society in which it acquires form and shape, but it is also determined by those fundamental psychological tendencies which have given it birth. For example, the reasoning faculty, the power of generalisation, the bringing of events into the relation of cause and effect, can certainly not be reduced to the "psychological reflection of economic conditions," even though the earliest stimulus to its exercise might be shown to have been due to them or its results to have been modified by their influence. The reasoning faculty generalises certain external perceptions, i.e., it reduces them under a rule of universal application, or in other words *explains* them. Its subject-matter is primarily the phenomena of the world as perceived. The earlier hypotheses in which it envisages natural occurrences may be crude, but the fact at their foundation is a naive observation of external nature, rather than reflection of economic conditions. Again philosophy is the outcome of, at first, observation of nature, and later, of the analysis of the elements of consciousness in and through which nature is given. Undoubtedly by way of unconscious analogy, the social life of the society in which the mind has grown up has a tendency to modify the conclusions arrived at. But this does not constitute the total result the *mere* "psychological reflection of economic conditions." There is a great deal beside this to account for, that cannot he so explained.

Indeed in some cases the hypothesis of economic cause is superfluous, as for example when a speculative belief arrived at directly or indirectly by simple inference from observation, by reflection, or by analogy, has come to be held as an article of faith – not merely as a "pious opinion," but as something which is to him who holds it as real as the facts of his everyday life. Its influence on action and on the course of human affairs in such a case is absolutely certain and may be quite as powerful as that of any form of economic circumstance. Thus, the early Christian communities among whom the belief in the approaching miraculous "end of the age" or (later) in personal immortality was absolutely undoubting, unquestionably had their whole mind and action determined by these beliefs. The latter developed of course upon lines which to the then existing social and political condition of the Roman world were those of least resistance – but these external conditions did not create them.

A plant presupposes certain conditions – soil, climate, moisture – in order that the seed may take root and grow up. But soil and climate are not the plant, the seed itself is the plant (potentially) and this notwithstanding that soil, climate, and other outward circumstances play a part small or large in modifying the plant, and this again in modifying that plant's subsequent seed, and so on to infinity. But all the same, trace back as far as we can go, follow modification after modification indefinitely, we yet never get to a stage at which soil and plant become one. The double element of germ and soil remains throughout. So in Human Evolution, go as far back as we may we never can eliminate one of the two ultimate elements. We are always driven back upon the reciprocal determination of outward material condition and inward "ideological" spontaneity. These two elements are found in inseparable interaction in every concrete human society, even the earliest and the simplest. The elimination of either one of them leaves you with an abstraction.

We now come to the important question, in what relative proportion they operate at different periods. That one sometimes preponderates very considerably, and that this one throughout the historical period been the material element, I regard as, nowadays, incontestable. But that even within the period covered by historical records there have been exceptional occasions when the "ideological" has overweighed the former, is unquestionably also true – viz. when a speculative belief has become so real to a considerable body of believers as to dwarf the importance of the material interests of life. The first beginnings of Christianity as already stated, are a case in point. The tendency has been of course for the material and (especially) economic factor to reassert itself the moment large masses of men are concerned, and this was to an increasing degree the case with Christianity after the first century. A similar remark applies also to the religious movements of the Reformation. In the evolution of Christianity during the first two generations material conditions played a very minor role, and, such as it was, almost purely negative. In the early period of the heretical movements of the Middle Ages the speculative factor was likewise dominant.

But apart from the special case of a speculative belief firmly held, we can discover considerable variations in the relative distribution of influence between the "ideological" and material sides of life throughout history in different periods. The question here arises, Can we formulate any law of those variations? Can we show the principle on which they depend? I think we can, and that it is to be found in the relative security or the reverse of the necessities of life for large sections of the population. The basis of social development is obviously material, since human beings consist of animal bodies dependent for their existence on food, shelter, clothing, utensils, etc. Hence, the securing of these things is the first concern, the *sine qua non* of all societies. When therefore these means of existence are inadequate or are placed in jeopardy, their attainment plays the primary role and occupies the foremost place in human consciousness. The higher human activities in the long run presuppose the satisfaction of the lower. So long as the lower animal wants remain unsatisfied, they must always fill the whole horizon of thought and action. The mind must be ceaselessly pre-occupied with them. This applies as much to the ascetic as to the ordinary man, only in an inverted form. The ascetic is concerned with his animal nature which he endeavours to suppress quite as much as the ordinary man is with his animal nature which he endeavours to satisfy. There is no possibility of evading this natural basis of all things. Now, as already said, given the want of the material necessaries of life, or given difficulty in their procurement, or insecurity in their tenure, you are *mutatis mutandis* bound to have the economic factor predominant. And it has been the case throughout history that for large classes of society, in most cases for the majority, one or all of the above mentioned conditions have obtained, though in varying degrees in different periods. Hence throughout history "ideological" products have been largely coloured and in many cases entirely moulded by economic causes. In this connection I may quote what I have said in another place (*Outlooks from the New Standpoint*, pp.127-8), to wit, that, to put the matter shortly, "for economics to be the primary motive power of progress, we must have (1) a class in a position in which it is either deprived of the average necessities and comforts of life possessed by another class, or in which its enjoyment of them is precarious; (2) a consciousness in the former class of this deprivation, i.e., of its own inferiority and precarious state: (3) a belief in the possibility of attaining the coveted comfort, leisure, or security by class-action. These, I say, are the conditions for the economic movement to make itself felt in history. They are conditions under which when present in a class forming the majority, or even a considerable minority, in the state, it must make itself felt." This may take place unconsciously no less than consciously. In the former case, men will probably think they are actuated by political or religious motives, when they are really moved by consideration of the material well-being and prosperity of themselves and their class. In the past this has often enough been the case. Nowadays, on the contrary, the cloak of religion is seldom anything but a conscious or at best semi-conscious sham.

To sum up the contention I have here sketched out in opposition to the extreme view of the *Materialistische Geschichtsauffassung*:– For the latter human affairs are determined solely from without by the economical causes, just as for the antagonistic view they are determined solely from within by psychical or "ideological" causes. Both these views seem to me to be erroneous, because one-sided, although the former is nearer the truth than the latter, inasmuch as throughout historic evolution up to the present time, the determination from without by physical (i.e., economical) conditions has unquestionably predominated; while at the present day this predominance is so overwhelming as to strike even the most unobservant. This last circumstance it is which has contributed to the spread of what I term the extreme materialist view. Because we are passing through a period in which economic conditions dwarf all other considerations, it is difficult to conceive of a time when they did not do so. The notion that theology should ever have been so undoubtingly believed in by men of the world as to seriously influence their actions, or that chivalry, feudal devotion, or tribal sentiment should ever have been so strong as to subordinate all else in life, seems inconceivable to the modern man. I know I shall be told that all these things were themselves in their origin the outcome of material (economic) conditions, to which I reply by a reference to the theory that Tenterden steeple was the cause of Goodwin Sands, both having appeared together. Of course "ideological" conception to bear fruit must be planted in suitable economic soil, but this economic soil, as such, is merely a negative condition. The active, formative element lies in the seed, i.e. the "ideological" conception. And this is the case even in Socialism in so far is it is a conscious movement. That, to continue our metaphor, the economic soil is not alone enough to produce a change, however ripe it may be for such a change, is aptly illustrated by the fact that it is Germany and not England or the United States (where the great industry has been longer existing and is much further developed) that has produced the most powerful Socialist party up to date. In Germany the "ideological" or psychological factor, to wit, the Socialist theory working on an educated population, was present under economic conditions, relatively unfavourable, at least in its earlier stages, and a great result followed; in the other, the psychological factor was absent or but little developed, and though the economic conditions were ten times as favourable, both a very much later and a very much less powerful result followed. This is very significant in an age and in a movement where economic condition plays, and must necessarily play, a role of the first magnitude. Here you have a doctrine based on economics and proclaiming the necessary ultimate evolution of the great industry into Socialism, which is nevertheless weaker in those countries where economic conditions are most advanced, such as England and the United States, than it is on the continent of Europe where the great industry is a comparatively recent importation. The proletariat is larger, and probably greater misery exists in the cities of Britain and America than in most parts of Germany, yet Socialism in Britain and America is as yet struggling with an imperfectly class-conscious working class. Economic conditions, let them press never so hardly, require the fertilising influence of an idea and an enthusiasm before they can give birth to a great movement, let alone to a new society.

I have already pointed out how the proportionate share of either of the two elements in the total result varies at different periods, and have indicated what I deem to be the law governing this variation. We have admitted that in the present day economic conditions so far dwarf all others in men's minds as to seem on a cursory view the only factor in human progress. But even despite this actual overwhelming predominance we have seen that what I may term the original psychological spontaneity – the ideological faculty within man – has first of all to seize and transform the results of the economic pressure from without into the form of an Ideal, before the progressive movement can really make headway. When it does not do this the progressive movement, and therewith the general social advance, spreads itself aimlessly, like a river passing through marshy country. That because hitherto the economic factor in progress has been the leading one throughout most periods of history, it does not follow that it always will be so. On the contrary, assuming the correctness of my statement of the law governing the proportion in which one or the other of the two reciprocating elements of social evolution – the outer or economic and the inner or psychological – enters into the social synthesis of any given period, it follows that once you get rid of class-society, i.e., the monopoly of the necessaries and comforts of life by a limited section of the population to the exclusion of the rest, you abolish the leverage which mere material circumstance has hitherto had in determining the trend of human affairs. Hitherto when class-conditions have prevailed, the outer has overpowered the inner, the material circumstance has moulded the psychological determination. This, as already stated, must always be so when you have an unstable economic equilibrium, in other words, when a possessing class confronts a dispossessed class and the consciousness of the dispossessed class is dominated by the want of material necessities and the desire to obtain them. Every idea emanating from such a class will then necessarily bear the impress of this fact. Similarly the possessing class will likewise *per contra* have its consciousness dominated by the economic necessity always present to it of defending its position.

On the contrary, when classes have ceased to exist, – where all society forms one class – the specific economic pressure disappears and the spontaneous psychological movement has free play. It may be true that you can never completely eliminate the economic element. Nature herself must sometimes exercise a pressure, although with the advance of technical knowledge and invention such pressure, common in primitive times – when man's power over nature was limited, when the social group was limited and more or less isolated, and hence when a bad harvest, a hailstorm, or the predatory incursion of a neighbouring tribe meant a dislocation of all existing social conditions – would tend to disappear. Yet notwithstanding that with our greater power over natural forces this direct influence of external nature might be reduced to the minimum, it would scarcely vanish entirely, still less could the friction arising from disturbances due to changes incidental to the internal development of society be got rid of completely. But in spite of all this, the economic factor in progress would henceforth be definitely subordinated and never again dominate the movement of social or intellectual life. Those social modifications which were previously determined *unconsciously* by material conditions, methods of production, distribution, and the like, will henceforward be *consciously* shaped by the will of man.

My object in the foregoing has been to point out the completely reciprocal action of the elements of social dynamics – that like every real synthesis they include at least two main factors, that the one is not and cannot be directly or indirectly the *cause* of the other, however unequal may be the respective preponderance in the total result in different phases of development, but that they are alike cofactors whose united action and reaction creates the reality which is their synthesis. These factors in social development are outward material circumstance (mainly economic in its character), in its widest sense, acting on what we may term (relative to the more mechanical determination of the other factor) the *spontaneity* of human intelligence, and reacted upon by it. The latter like the former follows its own distinct line of causation up to a certain point, but history consists in the unity of these two lines in their action and reaction. The separate syntheses which evolve themselves and acquire a relatively independent existence and development of their own within the great synthesis of social life (the wheels within wheels) are practically infinite. The mode in which economical forms are continually throwing off new offshoots and a life of their own is admirably touched upon in a letter of the late Friedrich Engels, published as a supplement to the **Leipziger Volkszeitung** for the 26th of October, 1895. The same applies *mutatis mutandis* to the other and ulterior departments of human activity. The religious, political, scientific, philosophical, moral, aesthetic sides of life also have a tendency to develop subsidiary forms, each of which acquires a relatively substantial and independent, though subordinate, life of its own. All alike are in varying degrees the products of economic development acting on psychical initiative and psychical initiative reacting on economic development. But at each stage this action and reaction becomes more complex than in the preceding stage, there being no economic form absolutely the product of external forces, nor any intellectual, moral, or artistic form absolutely determined by psychical initiative. Human evolution is a product of these elements. Abstracted from each other they have no causal existence. Their only reality as *causes* of progressive *change* in society is as distinguished in their total result.

The hope for humanity under Socialism consists in the fact that then for the first time will the psychical initiative of man be freed from the distorting and crushing weight of economic conditions and material environment, and will hence, in its turn, dominate human life. Of the incalculable magnitude of the revolution this will imply, none can doubt who have once grasped the meaning of historic development in the past.

The Futility of Holiness

A Study in Ethics

The common opinion that the results of metaphysical analysis are barren hair-splitting, destitute of all practical value, is nowhere more conspicuously refuted than in the deeper aspects of ethics. Here we see what are strictly speculative issues assuming a guise which has determined the whole current of men's views on life and conduct. By this I do not mean to say that it is as philosophy that they have operated on the practical world, or that the philosophical side of the issue has, except in very few instances, and then only partially, been present to men's minds. But it is none the less certain that there is a definite speculative and logical connection between a certain type of ethical ideal and a certain position in philosophy, even although it may never have been very distinctly formulated. The popular line drawn on this point is between Materialist and Spiritualist. This antithesis, however, only represents a very crude phase of speculative thought. In that more developed stage of philosophical analysis in which consciousness, as such, is recognised as the basis of all – beyond which there can be nothing save the meaningless and the self contradictory – at this stage of the philosophic intelligence the distinction appears as between the Material and the Formal, or (as I have elsewhere expressed it) between the Alogical and the Logical, from one point of view, and between the Potential and the Actual, from another. The tendency, as I have shown, has, from Plato and Aristotle downwards, been to hypostatise the Formal or the Logical (and at the same time the Actual) at the expense of the other and deeper principle constituting the complementary element in the synthesis of Experience or Reality. This is no less true of the moral consciousness than of any other aspect of Reality. Here, too, one element of the synthesis has been hypostatised at the expense of the other. I might point out how this particular phase of the moral consciousness has been historically connected with certain stages in the economic and political development of Human Society. My object, however, in the present essay is to analyse the philosophical aspect of the doctrine referred to, rather than to trace its practical evolution in the concrete world. As a consequence I merely refer to this side of the question briefly and where unavoidable.

The metaphysical distinction between Alogical and Logical which interpenetrates the whole sphere of experience, in the region of Ethics assumes the form of the so-called lower and higher nature, the "brute nature" and the "divine nature" in man. Now this latter distinction came into prominence concurrently with another, to wit, with the distinction between the individual man as such and the Society or Stock – the kinship group – to which he belonged. The distinction, once made, tended, as is the wont of such distinctions, to develop into a separation and thus to give rise to a pair of hypostatised abstractions, each of which was regarded as in absolute and eternal hostility to the other. As the individual man began to assume an independent, economical and political value apart from his tribal kinship, a further distinction arose and grew clear within his own personality, the distinction between his intellectual or moral nature and his animal or material nature. The identification of the former in essence with the great spiritual power of the Universe, and of the latter with the Sensible world around him, followed in due course. The first became the hypostatised formal Principle. We have, therefore, in the crudely-expressed antithesis between Body and Soul, the World and God, the earliest form of the philosophical antithesis of Matter and Form, of Alogical and Logical. The foregoing is the historical genesis of the notion.

The hypostasis of the formal principle, or the idea of the divine in man being separable from the animal, the notion that man as individual can by a voluntary act, so to say, slough off the brute and become absorbed in the divinity – formal principle to formal principle – has been the basis of the whole introspective morality on which the so-called "universal" religions of the world are based. Now this idea belongs to what in philosophy I have termed the theory of Pallogism for wherever formal principle is set up in opposition to its material base, and given an independent reality of its own, there you have Pallogism. In philosophy Pallogism takes various shapes. It starts with the conception of the primitive unity of the consciousness as purely formal. In its "theory of knowledge" it proceeds to oppose the category to the sense impression as the only True, the universal in contradistinction to the particular, as the only Real. Its Metaphysic postulates the Absolute as the totality of the system of Categories in which the Material and Sensible are abolished. Its psychology similarly founds on the absolute absorption of feeling and will in reason. Thus, as will be seen, in each department the formal principle is proclaimed as that which is alone valid, the material being a dross which has to be got rid of – the matter of sense blurring and confounding the "Platonic idea." It is therefore not surprising that in Ethical theory the "material" is identified with Evil, and the "formal" with Good. The absurdity of this is apparent when we reflect that, in reality, Evil falls quite as much on the side of form as Good. The "Material" here, as elsewhere, is the element of indifference which *becomes* indeed one or the other, but which as distinguished *per se* is neither one *nor* the other. Viewed more closely, the "Good" of a pallogistic ethic takes the form of the hypostasis of certain imperfectly defined aspirations which are collectively termed the Divine or the Higher in man – i.e., in short, certain *differentia* of Man as such – and their opposition to the purely animal instincts, or to what I may term the *mixed* instincts, namely, those into which the real instincts enter, but which are not exclusively animal. Now the notion of killing off the animal with a view to living the Higher or Divine life with the abstract residuum preparatory to some sort of union with the Divinity after death, has been the aim and ideal of the prophet and saint for more than two thousand years past, and has been termed "Holiness." This ideal, therefore, I regard as the practical

37

side of the same fallacy which in speculative philosophy appears as Pallogism, viz., the abstraction of one element in a synthesis and its treatment as an independent entity. For the notion of cutting adrift a certain formal aspect of human nature from the parent matter of which it is the form, is the sign-manual of Pallogism, and forms a part of the time-honoured scholastic fallacy called "Realism" or *Universalia ante rem*.

All the truly human emotions we find spring out of the animal, and are inseparable from the animal. Sympathy, love, friendship, generosity, good-heartedness, all have their root in the animal life; the mere nerve-vibration which is the material basis of sympathy, the responsive echo in one personality, of suffering in another, is the source of all the higher concrete emotion. To separate these from the animal is impossible; but there are certain conditions under which the reflective moral consciousness we term conscience claims the violation in our own person of what are otherwise the primary dictates of our being; for example, the "ought" of conscience may point to the duty of our facing personal pain, or even destruction, for the sake of an ulterior extra-personal object. The extra-personal object (viewing the matter historically) was originally concerned with the material things, affecting the life of the race, viz., with the continuance and prosperity of kindred and tribe, as is familiar to every student of early religious thought and of the religious ideas of primitive races. Now with the gradual destruction of the old kinship of tribe and clan and the rise of the new morality of introspective Individualism, the notion of the duty under all possible circumstances of crushing the natural or animal instincts becomes detached from its connection as an element of a concrete moral consciousness and hypostatised as the end of all morality and the highest object of man's being. Concurrently with the divorce of ethical sentiment from social life, and the hypostasis of one of its elements, took place similarly the divorce of the Formal principle of the Universe from the Material and its hypostasis in antagonism to the latter. The two sides of the pallogistic fallacy, the moral and the metaphysical, worked into each other's hand, their full fruition, their complete historical development, being realised in the type of the Catholic saint. The majority of mankind, however much they may have in theory given in a nominal adhesion to the principle, were preserved by their healthy understanding, by the "blessed animal" within them, from becoming mere lumps of morbidity, such as a St. Anthony, a St. Bernard, or a St. Theresa. "Holiness," the life of the saint, was nevertheless the ideal of conduct to which men looked up throughout the Middle Ages, and in a debased form the view has survived even to the present day.

With the fall of Pallogism in speculative philosophy, the last shred of *raison d'etre* for its maintenance in practical philosophy is abolished. That apotheosis of pain and of want which is the hall-mark of Christianity, the belief that the Beatific Vision, the union with God – or, however otherwise the ultimate goal of life may be designated – can be attained by the negation of the animal on the part of the individual man falls to the ground. This being so, the whole Christian theory discloses itself as resting on a misconception, on a diseased growth of the speculative understanding. The notion that there is anything intrinsically noble in the struggles of the saint to crush out his animal nature disappears. The higher life that he thinks he obtains is seen to be an illusion – an illusion based upon bad metaphysics. We then become aware of the fact that the detachment of the higher from the lower – that the antagonism between the intellectual and the animal – is not an essential but a merely transient and phenomenal phase in the unfolding of the moral consciousness. The true "higher" includes the lower, it is only the false higher, the pseudo-spiritual, which would violently detach itself from its animal basis.

But does the foregoing imply that the distinction between higher and lower, between intellectual and animal is spurious? By no means. The *distinction* indeed exists, it is only the attempted hypostasis of one of its terms to the exclusion of the other, whereby a mutual antagonism is created, that is spurious. The way to the true, the concrete, higher, will from this standpoint be seen to lie not in the suppression but in the cultivation of the animal instincts, while the mere apotheosis of suffering, the outcome of the former view, will go by the board. But with the rehabilitation of the "animal" as at least the *basis* of all that is best in us, and the recognition of the impossibility of any permanent good existing apart from the "animal," much less in opposition to it, then the ethical idea of Holiness becomes obsolete. By the clear recognition of this, mankind will finally emancipate itself from the *cul-de-sac* in which the moral consciousness has been confined throughout the period of Christian civilisation.

The apparent contradiction which obtains between the animal life as such with its appetites based on sensation, and the higher intellectual and emotional life, will assuredly in the end be resolved in the natural course of things – by the inevitable process of the exhaustion of the lower forms assumed by the animal through these forms themselves becoming repellent – and not by the effort, in the long run for mankind at large always futile, to violently suppress them. The attempt to "rush" what for want of a better word we may term the "higher life" on the part of the individual, by crushing out the animal has been a failure. It is the killing of the goose that lays the golden eggs. You cannot by any act of will on the part of the individual forestall what to be effective must be the issue of a determinate social process. So long as the desire for the lower form remains, the time is not yet ripe for the higher; so long as the lower gives pleasure, the lower has still a part to play. The violent disruption of the two sides of the synthesis leaves you with a spurious simulacrum and abstract "higher" manifested in the morbid emotional state called "Holiness." With the fall of this abstract introspective morality falls also its special mark, the apotheosis of suffering as such.[1]

The historical function of the movement represented by Christianity, part of which, at least, was founded on the notion of pity, has received its travesty in the most logical and developed form of that movement, as the glorification of pain, poverty and ostentatious humility. In consequence it has issued in cruelty and the violation of every social instinct in turn.

Antithetical to "Holiness" or the rejection of the animal, is "Sin," or the affirmation of the animal, each side of the antithesis being alike conceived by the Christian ethics as a hard-and-fast abstraction. That the same action may be under one set of circumstances, and under one aspect, a violation of morality, cruel under another set of circumstances or in another aspect, be compatible with the highest morality never enters the purview of the saint.

Now the characteristic of the concrete morality which is gradually supplanting the old abstract, ethical categories, but the full fruition of which it were vain to expect under existing social conditions, is entirely opposed to the ethics of introspection and the morbid ideal set up thereby. For the former the sole standard is social utility, using the word not in the narrow sense in which it has sometimes been employed, but as meaning that which is conducive to the needs of human society, at once static and dynamic. Morality is thus brought down from heaven to earth. The extra-personal for which the individual may be called upon to sacrifice himself casts off the form of an abstract Divinity and takes on the form of a concrete Humanity. Mere personal self-sacrifice finds its proper level, as, in certain stages, indeed a most important incident in morality, but yet as no more than an incident. It is in fact, under present moral conditions, like gold coinage under present economical conditions. Just as coined gold, though possessing no economic utility in itself, is nevertheless the ultimate measure and standard of all economic utilities, – so self-sacrifice, though having no ethical utility in itself, is nevertheless the ultimate measure of all ethical utilities. But the function in either case is not absolute, but strictly dependent on the social order into which it enters. Most persons, at present, as regards their ethical conceptions, are in a position equivalent to that of the "mercantile theory" in Economics. Just as the mercantilist believed gold and silver to constitute the only riches of a nation, so the current moralist believes the whole of morality to be summed up in mere self-sacrifice, as such.

The mere suffering of the Individual no longer appears as good in itself once we have got rid of Introspectivism, but, on the contrary, is seen to be in itself an evil which only assumes another aspect in a special relation to the total conditions of which it is an element.

The moment we reinstate the "animal," the moment we catch a glimpse of the real synthesis of human life, the fallacy of the Christian apotheosis of pain becomes apparent.[2] The only meaning the word *Evil* has is that of pain, want or suffering. There is no other real evil. From the mere nerve-vibration, which is the physiological basis of what we term sympathy – the point of connection between ourselves as individuals and ourselves as element of the social body – springs our whole ethical life and consciousness, just as from simple sense-perception springs our whole aesthetic life and consciousness. Contrary to the theory of introspective moralists, the individual now ceases to embrace the self-sufficient end of all within his own personality. The notion that we can achieve the goal of all consciousness, as it were, *per saltum* by a voluntary act, or a series of voluntary acts, and thus become absorbed in the Beatific Vision, attain union with the Divine, disappears. Even now there is universally present a feeling, vague it may be, but none the less persistent, that somehow or other the most important ideal with which the modern man can concern himself is connected with the social life around him. The change in the attitude of the religious sects is sufficient proof of the foregoing. From an exclusive concern for the individual soul as being the one thing needful, they have nowadays betaken themselves to schemes, good, bad, or indifferent, for the "regeneration of the masses." Even where the old dogmas, the old moral saws, are still preached and still nominally adhered to, it is easy to see that they have lost their old savour. Whatever may be the ultimate *telos* of Reality, there is a consensus of instinct that it lies along the highway of social progress rather than in the *cul-de-sac* of individual purification. For this new attitude, if it be but logical, it is obvious the only true virtues are the social virtues in which the animal plays its part, just as the only ideal is a politico-social ideal. The false "spiritual" of morbid introspection is as much "the enemy" as the lower "brutal" of mere animalism. But it may be objected by the Introspectivist that politico-economic change can affect no more than material conditions, and that the so-called higher interests it must fail to touch. The objection is characteristic of the one-sidedness of Introspection, with its ideal of "Holiness." For the Introspectivist the Higher, the "Spiritual," is absolutely cut off from material things. The former comes from above, the latter from below. The concrete moralist, as I may term him, sees on the other hand that good material conditions are the basis of all that is, truly speaking, higher life. In their absence there is nothing but the lowest and most squalid brutality on the one side and the spurious pallogistic ideal called "holiness" on the other. Which of these is the better or the worse I will not pretend to decide.

I need only point out that these conditions – this material basis – of a higher life has hitherto failed save for a small minority of mankind, and that even this minority, if not immediately sufferers from the general conditions of society, have been none the less indirectly affected by them as regards their aspirations and views of life generally. What, therefore, mankind will attain to when all are freed both *directly* and *indirectly* from the presence of material care and material squalor can at best be dimly imagined, but cannot even be distinctly conceived. It is surely not unreasonable (as I have elsewhere suggested) to assume that we shall hereafter enter upon the first stage in a social life the end of which may be consciousness under a totally new phase. At present the social psyche is dominated by the animal consciousness of the individual human being. It manifests itself directly only in and through the latter. It is but one of the forms or determinations of this consciousness. But who shall say that it shall not, in its turn, obtain a form and substantiality of its own and shall subordinate to itself that individual animal-consciousness, of which in its present stage it is but a mode?

Whatever may be our view on these points of ulterior speculation, the failure of the Individualist introspective morality to satisfy human aspirations is apparent. It is equally apparent that its metaphysical basis is Pallogism, which is in the last resort identical with that theory of *Universalia ante rem*, with that hypostasis of the formal element in every real synthesis, which has, with little intermission, dominated the higher speculative thought of the world since Plato. (1) The introspective phase of the ethical consciousness postulates two hypostatised abstractions, it abstracts the individual from his social environment, and gives to types of character a value in themselves which they only possess in synthetic union with that environment. (2) Again, it abstracts the higher life (real or supposed) of the individual from his animal life and postulates a spurious antagonism between the two which is fatal to all concrete moral progress. It assumes, in a word, *that the Individual as such stands in a direct moral relation to the Universe or to the Absolute nature of things*. It declines to accept the obvious truth, that he has no direct, but a purely indirect relation thereto, i.e., one existing only in and through man's social growth, and that hence in a social connection alone can morality exist. Hence I say, the ethics of the future must inevitably involve a rehabilitation of the social against the spurious abstract individual, and a rehabilitation of the animal as against the spurious abstract-spiritual. Such a rehabilitation must indeed be the next stage in the evolution of the moral consciousness of humanity.

Footnotes

1. The infamous Christian dogma of the atonement is based upon the notion of suffering as something good in itself. The suffering must be there, even though it be the just that suffer. It has entered into Catholic asceticism. The scourgings and macerations of the monk were conceived of, as so to say, the filling up of the cup of the atonement by voluntarily increasing the sum of suffering in his own person with the view of being the more acceptable to the Deity. In the last resort asceticism meant of course the doctrine of the inherent evil of matter. Pain was good as tending to destroy matter. Pain was the enemy of the "natural man" and therefore the friend of the "spiritual man."

2. It is a cheap sneer of the champion of the ethics of "holiness" to urge that his opponent is incapable of understanding the mental attitude of its votaries. The answer to this insinuation is obvious for one who regards "holiness" as a morbid state, to wit, that there are many morbid conditions, animal no less than intellectual or moral, which he is incapable of entering into sympathetically. For example, the impulses of a lunatic, or, again, certain aberrations of sexual psychopathy; but this incapacity does not necessarily argue any intellectual or moral inferiority, but rather, on the contrary a healthiness of mind.

Early Christianity and Modern Socialism

We are now in the midst of a great popular movement for the emancipation of human life from the oppression of its material conditions. The first century of the Christian era also saw a movement, mainly popular in character, for the emancipation of human life from the oppression of its material conditions. We have thus a parallel between the circumstances under which Early Christianity arose and those under which Modern Socialism has arisen. Both represent a protest against the dominant civilisation. Both are alike in this; they are also to some extent alike in their methods and in the nature of their agitation. But there is also a vast and a radical difference between Modern Socialism and Early Christianity, a difference which suffices to place them to some extent in opposition to each other. We will first of all consider Early Christianity, the struggling movement of the first century.

At the Christian era nearly the whole civilised world had become definitely united under the sway of Rome. The independence of the provincial cities with their old civic patriotism and their old civic religion was undermined or abolished. At the same time every great centre could show in addition to its slaves a vast vagabond, "free" population, dependent for its means of subsistence on the donations of wealthy patrons, and in Rome itself on the largesses of the Emperor. The polarisation of wealth at one end of the social scale and poverty at the other, with the gradual extinction of the intermediate stages, was in full progress, more especially in Rome and the larger cities. The development of ancient civilisation had issued in politics in a centralisation of the most pronounced character, and in economics in a crude form of capitalism based on slave production without the aid of machinery, and manipulated to a large extent by a tax gathering bureaucracy. As the century advanced all these symptoms increased in intensity. The provincial cities more and more lost their old municipal patriotism. The last remnants of independent peasant holdings anywhere near the great centres of civilisation became merged in the latifundia, or big farms worked by hordes of slaves, under a *villicus* or overseer. The old village community melted away in and around all the main arteries of the Roman power. The corruption and sensuality of the wealthy classes which under the republic reached its climax in the reigns of the first Caesars. It was then that the Roman military organisation, the Roman jurisprudence, and above all the Roman fiscal system made an end of the ancient world in the form in which it had hitherto existed. The old basis of ancient civilisation had been the group – the gens, the tribe and the city, originally a league of tribes; the largest group known to the ancient world. Up to the last, ancient civilisation bore within it traces of the primitive communal group-society out of which it arose. But with the advent of Roman imperial power the old local autonomy disappeared as it had not done under any of the older oriental empires, which were little more than loose confederations.

The Roman Empire was the first instance in the world's history of a bureaucracy on an extended scale. The Roman or Romanised functionary slowly but surely destroyed all independent local life. Add to this that although production never of course reached the machine state under the crude capitalism of the Roman Empire, and even division of labour was very rudimentary, yet that the associated production of a number of slaves belonging to one owner was not only prevalent as above-mentioned in agriculture, but also in many branches of handicraft, so that the competitive power of aggregated capital undoubtedly made itself felt. The Roman who had enriched himself by tax-gathering the spoil of the provinces was not always above investing in an industrial or commercial enterprise, in spite of the traditional aristocratic prejudice against such methods of gaining wealth. Thus no less a man than Sallust made a large revenue out of his "*Insulae*" or blocks of buildings let out in small dwellings on the Esquiline hill.

The conditions described, political, economical and otherwise, which reached their full development under the early Caesars were the conditions under which Christianity was born and grew up. The practice of emancipating slaves , which the master could not always afford to keep in the old way as appendages of his family, had become common. The poor freemen who, driven by altered circumstances, flocked from the various provinces to the large centres, formed a motley crowd, having, as already said, a precarious economical footing in a society where labour was mainly carried on by slaves, and hence whence the poor freeman was largely dependent for his existence on the crumbs which fell from the rich men's tables of the more favoured classes. The demand for money now made itself felt in districts where before exchange had exclusively been carried on under the forms of barter. Finally there was the vast army of actual slaves employed in agriculture or in other forms of productive labour. All these classes as Friedrich Engels has said (**Neue Zeit**, No.XIII 36), "had their paradise, their golden age behind them." For them there was no more hope in this life. The old conditions of their existence were gone while for them, as for all other classes, the old enthusiasm for the life of their native city had disappeared before the Roman eagle, the symbol of the great centralising power, which had carried away their municipal gods, and had deprived them of an independent political life. What wonder that men abandoning their old ideals of civic patriotism, of the worship connected with their social group, should turn within and seek comfort in their own soul and in meditating on its relation to the supreme soul of the world! This life it is true could offer nothing to them, but this fact did not affect the possibility of an existence after death – an existence which had been vaguely admitted by all popular tradition and had been enlarged upon and decked out in imaginative colouring by the later poets.

The "mysteries," i.e., secret religious ceremonies and doctrines whose original Pagan meaning had probably fallen into oblivion, had become schools where the aspirant was initiated into dogmas relating to God, the soul, and immortality. It was an age when the thoughts of all thinking men were turned on these theosophic and mystical questions, just as today the thoughts of all thinking men are turned on questions of economics and of social reconstruction. The theory that Christianity was a doctrine that burst upon the world with a new light is directly contradicted by history, which discloses it as simply the popular and democratic formulation of tendencies already present in the Paganism and Judaism of the time. The old social relations and ideals connected with the group-society, the tribe, or the city (as already said the largest political unit of the ancient world) had or had been undermined by the Roman ascendancy, and the whole trend of the age was towards finding compensation for the loss of the old life with its earthly immortality of the social group by a heavenly immortality of the individual soul in the presence of the supreme deity – no longer the mere god of the family, the tribe or the city, but the great spiritual, power of the universe. We must not forget that it was an age when throughout all the Roman provinces, in Italy, Greece, Asia Minor, Syria, Egypt, there was a mad rage for new superstitions of all kinds, when magic and jugglery of every description flourished, and miracles abounded on all sides. Such was the social atmosphere of the time. Now the philosophic sects and the Pagan religious "mysteries," whose theological doctrines were discussed or taught, were mainly the appanage of the learned or the wealthy, the education or initiation in some cases being only open to persons of family, and in well-nigh all cases involving expenditure of time and money, impossible save for those in a good social position. All society was more or less dissatisfied with current conditions, each section in its own way. For large numbers of the rich, as already stated, the public, life, and the religion of local and civic patriotism, with the worship of, their guardian divinities, which had occupied their forefathers, was dead. But the rich could at least plunge into pleasure and profligacy, or where they took the matter seriously they could devote themselves to the platonic or stoic philosophy, or they could get initiated into one of the numerous mystical Pagan cults then prevalent. But for the poor, the disinherited, and the ignorant there seemed no future. The pleasures of life were not for them, philosophy was only for the learned and the leisured, the Pagan "mysteries" were similarly for the honourable, the rich and the "virtuous," and not for outcasts. And now appeared a sect which offered, to all alike "the promise of happiness "and the answer to those problems with which all serious men were then concerning themselves – secrets which had hitherto been revealed only under severe conditions to closed corporations of initiates; such was the state of affairs during the first century of the Christian era. Present mundane existence was deprived of its ideals and hopelessly bankrupt for large sections of the population, the thoughts of all turned towards something beyond the present life and outside mundane interests – in other words, turned in upon the individual soul and its fortunes. Under these circumstances the new sect offered a doctrine and ceremonies freely to all, the acceptance of which should at once ensure the eternal happiness of the individual and satisfy all his questionings. All were here invited to come and "know of the Mystery."

Prominent among the various eastern religions which were obtaining adherents over the Roman world was the Jewish. The national divinity of the Jews had long been raised by the Hebrew race to the dignity of supreme ruler of the universe, while at the same time the doctrine of a future life was popular among a large section of them. Still Judaism, as such, remained a national, or rather, tribal religion, of which one of the leading tenets was at this time the belief in the approaching advent of a divine agent or Messiah who was going to raise the Jews to the chief place among the tribes and peoples of the earth. In this connection Judaism possessed the characteristics of all ancient tribal religions, its main concern was the future of its race, of which, its god was the protector and guardian. Christianity, it must be remembered, was at first no more than a Jewish sect which believed in a special Jewish teacher as the promised Messiah. This was the point which differentiated the earliest form of Christianity from its parent Judaism. But with this point was involved another, namely, its opposition to the current order of things both at home and abroad; and, as a consequence of this, that it was mainly recruited from the "common people," i.e., from the impoverished peasantry and outcast population before spoken of. It was opposed in Palestine by the respectable adherents of the old religious parties and their official representatives, who also succeeded in making unpleasant elsewhere for, the adherents, of the new heresy by stirring up the Roman authorities against them. Thus it came about that while old respectable Judaism was tolerated by the Romans, Christianity was persecuted. Early in the movement a schism sprang up, caused by the accentuation of certain points in the programme, especially of the proselytising side and the individualist-introspective side, at the expense of the Judeo-ceremonial side. From the first, Christianity, like other forms of Judaism, as it then existed, recognised proselytising as one of its functions; it also from the first regarded ceremonial as subordinate to the inward devoutness of the individual, but even in the latter it was not new. Judaism had for long, begun to be introspective, and many perfectly orthodox Jews were tending in this direction, especially as their immediate hopes of national independence grew fainter. But nevertheless the points from which Christianity was to start in its career as the future world-religion were precisely these two: (1) the conception of the relation of the individual souls and of a future life, and (2) its definite transcendence in the religious sphere of those tribal and racial limits (I will not say *national*, because nations in our sense did not exist in the ancient world), which the Roman Empire had already transcended in the political sphere. There were then during the second half of the first century the following elements present or latent in Christianity: (1) its cardinal dogma, according to which Jesus was at once the predicted Messiah, and was also identified with the one voluntary sacrifice, that, according to the theory of Philo of Alexandria, should ultimately supersede the ceremonial system of sacrifice; (2) the traditional Jewish rites and ceremonies (3) the notion of proselytising, of making converts to the Jewish religion outside the Hebrew race; (4) a vague idea of the future life of the individual and his preparation for that life by faith, holiness and religious devotion (5) the traditional Jewish patriotic aspirations. Such and such only were the principles which we may, without hesitation, assert to have been common to the first churches or definitely organised Christian bodies. Respecting the earliest beginnings of Christianity we know nothing that is with certainty authentic. The attempt to disengage the historical elements in the comparatively late documents which have come down to us called gospels is obviously hopeless of success, often as it has been tried. The only possibility of ascertaining any fresh matter of fact concerning the first origin of Christianity would seem to lie in the discovery of some new document or inscription at Cesarea, the headquarters of the Roman government in Palestine.

The first undeniably authentic glimpse we get of Christianity is in the second half of the first century when it was already an established sect, and had undergone its first serious persecution by Nero. This is to be found in the so-called *Apocalypse* or *Book of Revelation*. This document has been proved by internal evidence to date from the year 68 or 69 AD, the five kings referred to as having fallen being the first five Roman Emperors, Augustus, Tiberius, Caligula, Claudius, Nero, the one spoken of as then existing being Galba, and the seventh that was yet to come being an allusion to the current belief known to have existed among certain sections of the population at the time that Nero was not really dead, but was in hiding among the Parthians, and would return to take vengeance on his enemies. Nero who was the anti-Christ, i.e., the persecutor of the followers of Christ, is also referred to according to a common practice of the age by the number 666, which in Hebrew letters spells Nero-

Caesar. In the Johannine *Apocalypse*, then, we have our earliest known Christianity.

Engels remarks that the writer invariably addresses his readers as "Jews" never as "Christians," which would seem to indicate that the latter epithet was still regarded only as a nickname bestowed on them by their opponents, and that they still deemed themselves merely aspect of the Jewish religion. The writer is, moreover, presumably himself a Jew, as the Greek is that of a foreigner and ungrammatical to boot. Of the five elements spoken of as immanent in the Christianity of the time, and all of which are traceable in the "Revelation," those belonging to Judaism proper are, with exception of the first cardinal point, by far the most prominent, and it is not difficult to see that some, at least, of the strictures directed against the churches which in the view of the writer had "gone astray" refer to the new "Hellenistic" or anti-Judaistic movement which was destined to develop into the Christianity of history, and which is associated with the name of the Apostle Paul. Some critics, in fact, have regarded the whole attack as directed against the rapidly-growing Pauline influence.[1] The gist of the whole book turns on the current belief, among the first votaries of the faith, in the approaching triumph of the new Christo-Judaism and the end of this age, when the world shall be ruled by the elect of the twelve tribes of Israel, and of the new heaven and new earth, which is to arise on the ruins of the old one after the lapse of a thousand years, and after the final destruction of "the world, the flesh, and the devil," which are to be judged by the supreme divinity himself (not, as was afterwards imagined, by Christ). The whole document belongs to a class of writing not uncommon in that time of religious exaltation. The series of visions which repeat themselves very much in substance are not very original. The imagery is borrowed largely from older Jewish writings of the same class, e.g., from Ezekiel, etc., though there are some touches of local colouring, e.g., death on the pale horse, a piece of folk-lore still obtaining among the peasants in some of the

Greek islands, also the allusion to certain natural phenomena still prevailing in the Aegean sea, as, for example, the water having the appearance of blood. The whole book breathes a ferocity against the powers that be, and all who are "not of the fold," contrasting strangely with the later Paulinised Christianity which strove to be reconciled as far as possible with secular authority, and with the world in general. But the most interesting point about the Apocalypse is not so much what we find there as what we do not find. As before said, we find most of the notions proper to the Judaism of the time coupled with the apotheosis of the person of Jesus as the redeemer and atonement, who, however, is placed second to Moses. We read of the "song of Moses and the Lamb." The strict Jewish monotheism of the book is very pronounced. Of the dogma of the Trinity there is no trace. The "lamb" is the servant of the one Jewish god, whose death had been accepted by the latter as the perpetual sacrifice for mankind in accordance with the popular Jewish theory of the time expounded by Philo. The conceptions which later on, under Alexandrian influence, developed into the "Holy Ghost" appear here in the Judaeo-Mazdaic form of the attendant "seven spirits of God." The doctrine of personal "future life" in the ordinary man, moreover, here takes a very subordinate place, the chief point of interest being the approaching advent of Christ, and his reign with the saints to whom should come "a great multitude whom no man could number," who had accepted him at once as the Messiah and the redeemer, and had presumably become, by adoption and submission to the law, "of the house of Israel." It was not until the second generation, and later, that the idea of the second advent and of the last judgment began to be relegated to the position of a pious opinion. The first generation of Christians seem to have been mainly influenced by a notion which was a kind of cross between the old idea of the eternal life of the race and the new one of the eternal life of the individual – to wit, that of the speedy advent of the Kingdom of God in which the elect should be preserved in an apotheosised bodily form, in a regenerated earth with its New Jerusalem, conceived on a scale of oriental magnificent as built up of gold and precious stones, with God like a gigantic diamond (as Renan has observed) to illumine the whole. Such, interspersed with obscure references to contemporary events of which history has left us no other trace is the main purport of the Johannine *Apocalypse*.

In the second generation of the Church, the Pauline or anti-Jewish party, began to acquire strength and ascendancy; new dogmas came in: justification by faith, the logical consequence of the doctrine of the atonement, before long the Alexandrian theory of the *logos* appears, and soon afterwards the Trinity, not as yet in the fully fledged form of the Nicene Council, but still sufficiently recognisable. But most important of all was the definitive enthronement of the individual conscience, the individual soul and .individual immortality after death, as the central pivot on which all turned; and as the logical consequence and complement of this was the definite abandonment of all notions derived from the old racial, tribal, or civic clannishness, whether Jewish or otherwise, or from distinction of outward circumstance, and the proclamation of the doctrine of the equality of all men, "barbarian, Scythian, bond, or free," before God. These were the two points which constituted Christianity a revolutionary creed.

But even here Christianity did not stand alone. Stoics like Epictetus, Platonists like Plutarch and others, preached the worth of the individual as such and the fatherhood of God, and in some cases the tone of their writings is very difficult to distinguish from that of the Church fathers. Yet although Christianity in a sense only formulated the ideas which belonged to the common mental atmosphere of the time, it nevertheless won over them all, because it succeeded in finding the suitable formula and the suitable policy in and by which these ideas were to become the official expression of the conscience and belief of mankind for ages to come. With the philosopher or pagan mystic these doctrines hung together in a manner at once vague and obscure. Again, while the philosophical sects, it is true, proposed in theory the doctrine of equality, they very often in practice retained the old exclusiveness, or, at the least, took no trouble to propagandise. It was only the Christian sects that took the new doctrine of equality seriously, and accordingly made it their lifework to go forth into the highways and hedges and preach to all, and agitate and organise among all. Thus Christianity created the social organisation which was to be for ages the rival of the secular power. Before the end of the second century the last echoes of the old and bitter quarrel between Petrine or Jewish and Pauline or Gentile Christianity died out, and the reconciliation begun earlier in the century was completed – the canon of our New Testament, which represents the amalgamation of the two hitherto hostile tendencies into the "one Catholic and Apostolic Church," becoming fixed. The main battle of the Church for the next century was between Christianity and the various Gnostic heresies, but this does not specially concern us here.

Now the general analogy between early Christianity as a popular movement and modern Social-democracy as a popular movement is obvious. Early Christianity was essentially a creed offering salvation from existing ills for the disinherited. So does Socialism. Christianity, like modern Socialism, found itself in antagonism to the whole established order of things. Christianity called upon all, irrespective of race, language, or condition, to embrace its teaching and its practice. So does modern Socialism. Christianity proclaimed a higher life for mankind. So does Socialism. Christianity preached brotherly love. So does Socialism. These five points are the chief resemblance in principle between the early Church and the Socialist party. There are plenty of resemblances in the development of the two movements, in the tactics employed, the nature of internal dissensions, etc., which we shall consider presently. First of all let us discuss the question of principle. Most of the points of resemblance, it will be remarked, are somewhat negative in charaxter. Christianity professed to be a gospel of salvation for the oppressed of the world, it is true. But how? Not in this life and not as a class, but in a super-sensible sphere, and as individuals, who by "grace" and a change of heart have become "born again." The reward is to be reaped by the individual in a future life, and not by the class or by humanity in this life. It is to be effected by an operation between the man's soul and his God. Every man shall work out his own salvation, in spite of the complementary proposition "of His grace ye are saved, not of yourselves." Christianity is therefore a doctrine of Individualism and of direct personal self-seeking. It is true it may lead the individual to sacrifice even life itself, and naturally, since in as far as he sincerely believes his creed, he feels convinced he is passing into a better life. Socialism, on the contrary, teaches that there is no salvation for the individual save in and through society. The future life of himself as a particular individual is of comparative indifference to Socialism. It is the future of society, of the working-class, and of humanity through the working-class, with which Socialism is peculiarly concerned.

The solution of the ills of the world for Christianity was, from our point of view, negative, since it lay in the renunciation of all hope or joy here and in the fixing of the attention on a future life. Respecting the political or social conditions of this life, Christianity had nothing to offer. Neither at that time did the serious part of the world want to know anything about them. Earnest men for the most part, and above all the poor and the outcasts, had ceased to take any interest in public life. What they were interested in was their own souls. So much was this the case, as already remarked, that every Pagan rite and ceremony, and every Pagan legend, which originally referred to some social function, to something concerning the life of the tribe or the city was beginning to be explained as symbolical of the life of the soul. Now, of course, we see exactly the opposite. Men have begun to get tired of fidgeting with their own souls. They are looking for salvation, not in a shadowy, individual life beyond the tomb, but in a social life on earth. As a consequence, we see churches and religious bodies, like the Salvation Army, interpreting "Christianity" as meaning the solution of the problem of "darkest England," and Anglican clergymen explaining away the doctrines and precepts of the Church in a non-natural and also non-theological, quasi-socialistic sense. Yet in spite of all this Paganism remained Paganism and not Christianity, just as Christianity to-day in spite of every effort remains Christianity and not Socialism. There is an unbridgeable gulf in both cases between the two theories of life, the decaying theory and the growing theory.

Then, as to the brotherly love of Christianity, this meant as its practical expression the assistance by one individual of another individual in distress, such as the voluntary surrender by A of a portion of his property to B, in other words Charity – Christian Charity. Socialism sees that this individual Charity in a society based on private property is a remedy which "doth but skin and film the ulcerous place, while rank corruption mining all within infects unseen." The brotherly love specially enjoined by Socialism is the renunciation of the desire for the supremacy of the privileged class to which one belongs or to which one may hope to belong some day – in other words, the desire for, and the endeavour to bring about, true social liberty, equality, and fraternity – to bring about a society in which class have ceased to exist. Finally, as to the internationalism of Christianity. This again was rather negative than positive. Christianity proclaimed the equality of all men before God – i.e., that all might become initiated into the doctrines and the rites of the new faith, and enjoy the spiritual salvation it offered; but how little this spiritual equality availed to prevent rivalry and jealousy between the churches even of different localities, and how little it sufficed to prevent distinctions based on rank and wealth growing up, the history of the Church very soon proved. Socialism, on the contrary, proclaims International solidarity as positive principle, inasmuch as it shows the existing national jealousies to redound simply to the advantage of the common enemy – the capitalist class – by whom they are fomented, and hence it shows that modern Patriotism is an outwork of Capitalism. The international character of Socialism is no merely spiritual "equality before God," it is based on the increasing economic interdependence of peoples, and on its necessity for the final accomplishment of economic equality. The overthrow of nationalism as it exists to-day is, in other words, a fundamental condition of the triumph of Social Democracy.

The resemblance in external circumstances and internal squabbles between the early Christian and the modern Socialist movement is very striking. We find the same tendency to go off on side-issues, the same muddleheadedness as to the ultimate aims of the movement, the same squabbles and internal intrigue, and finally the same tardiness and laxity in paying subscriptions, among the early Christians as we have to contend with to-day in the Socialist movement. The great Petrine-Pauline struggle which shook the Christian movement during the first century of its existence finds a certain parallel in the antithesis between Anarchism and Social Democracy, and this in more ways than one. In its earliest form Christianity, for example, tried to directly carry through its principle of the renunciation of this world and the concentration of the attention on the kingdom of God, which was immediately at hand, or on the future life. On this account it reckoned worldly goods of no consequence, and cursed the then existing political and social order almost in the manner of a modern Anarchist. As against this you had the followers of St. Paul, who maintained the necessity and obligation of living in the world and performing the duties of the world. In the same way we find all sorts of divergent tendencies of various kinds making themselves felt. Just as Socialism is sometimes described nowadays by superficial bourgeois writers as a body of opinion having only a tendency in common, so Christianity might have been described by a superficial Pagan writer of the time of Trajan. In either case, of course, the view taken is wrong, but it is natural for one who only looks at the outside of things and sees a number of persons claiming to call themselves by the same name, but who nevertheless seem to differ even in essentials, and in some cases bitterly oppose each other. In both instances, however, in spite of all the eddies and side currents, there were certain cardinal doctrines which undeniably represented Christianity, just as there are to-day principles which undeniably represent Socialism. These principles are the touchstones by which to gauge the respective positions. They are the doctrines by which to "test the spirits," as saith the Scripture. Behind the doctrines themselves there was a main movement throughout the Roman world, embodying these doctrines and the instinctive tendencies which clustered round them, just as there is to-day in every country a distinctive movement embodying the principles of socialism and the instinctive tendencies which gather round these principles.

There were in the early Christian world all sorts of heresies in opposite directions; there were Judaising heresies, paganising heresies, Montanist heresies and Gnostic heresies, but there was one movement which held fast to the main dogmas of the Christian creed against them all, which became the Catholic Church, and which succeeded in establishing Christianity as a world-religion for ages to come. So in our Socialist movement to-day we have in this country Fabian Socialists, Labour-party Socialists, Sentimental Socialists, various groups of Anarchists, in short, all sorts and conditions of persons calling themselves Socialists, and making use of one or other plank in the Social Democratic programme as a shibboleth but who are either unclear on the whole question, or who are at variance with the fundamental articles of Socialist doctrine on other points.

If it be asked what one may signalise as the fundamental theses of Socialism corresponding to the cardinal articles of the Christian faith in its earliest developed form (as dating from the second century – for the form in which we find it in the Apocalypse corresponds to Socialism in its Utopian phase), I should put forward the following: the accomplishment of the communisation of the means of production, distribution, and exchange in and through the modern class-struggle, this being the final issue of an historical development beginning with the dissolution of the primitive communism of the clan, the tribe and the village; the recognition, in economics, of labour, as the ultimate basis of value; and of modern Individualist society, as founded on the class-monopoly of the means of production whereby surplus-value is extracted by the capitalist class from the labouring class; the acknowledgment that our socialistic duty consists in joining with the class-conscious working-class in its struggle with capital, and generally in furthering the realisation of a communist society in which classes shall have ceased to exist (together with the other antagonisms of civilised society); in short of a society in which the *government of persons* shall have given place to the *administration of things*. These points, I take it, are "of faith." They are vital, and in every country there is a movement and a party, large or small, embodying them. This is the true Socialist party. To set up an opposition direct or indirect to such a party is to injure the cause of Socialism. In Germany this is recognised. The "Independents" of fifteen years ago have gone under. The "Revisionists" of five years ago are fast going under. There exists but one powerful Social-democratic party. In France, where unhappily, there have been many dissensions, the movement is concentrating itself on the lines of the so-called Marxist party, i.e., on the basis of modern scientific Socialism, as above stated. The same may be said of Italy. In England, as we all know, we have many Socialisms promulgated by persons who are anxious to show themselves original, and who for this and other reasons are shy of joining the one English Socialist body which is in line with the great Socialist movement of Proletarian emancipation throughout the civilised world.

Although now the predominance of scientific Socialism, or, as it is sometimes called, Marxism, is assured the workmen of the Continent; although old feuds, theoretical and personal, have lulled down before the supremacy of the central Socialist stream – the one and indivisible Social-democratic party – in other European countries, yet that this was not always so the following extract from Friedrich Engels will show. Speaking of the great classical sceptic of the second century, Lucian of Samosata, who has left us an account of an adventurer named Peregrinus, who became a teacher in the early Christian Communities, and was subsequently turned out for eating forbidden meat, Engels says:

> "All who have known from experience the European workman's movement in its early beginning, will call to mind dozens of such occurrences. Nowadays such extreme cases have become impossible in the great centres, but in remote places, where the movement is occupying new ground, a Peregrinus may even still have a certain limited success."

Engels goes on to observe that as with the revolutionary movement of classical antiquity, Christianity, so with the modern revolutionary movement, Socialism, all elements are attracted to it "that have nothing to expect from the official world, or that have played themselves out therein." He gives among other instances "free church parsons whose congregations have fallen away from them, unfortunate inventors, sufferers from real or imaginary wrongs, characterised by the official bureaucratic world as 'insufferable nuisances,' honest fools, and dishonest impostors." All elements set free by the disintegration of the old world tend to gather round a movement which is consciously or unconsciously felt to contain within itself the germs of a new world.

> "There was no folly, no chimera, no imposture," says Engels, "that did not force itself upon the young Christian Communities, and that did not, at least in some places, find open ears and willing believers. As with our early communist workmens clubs so with the early Christians."

63

He continues, "they possessed an astounding credulity for things which it pleased them to believe – so much so that we can be by no means sure that some fragment or other of the numerous writings compiled by Peregrinus for the edification of the Christians, has not found its way into our New Testament." Ernest Renan once observed that the best modern analogy of an early Christian Church was a local section of the (at that time still-existing) "International." This is so true, Engels observes, that it is impossible for any old member of the International to read the Second Epistle to the Corinthians, with its complaints direct and indirect of the laxity and delay with which overdue subscriptions came in, without feeling old wounds break out in him afresh. I have no doubt that many branch secretaries of the Social Democratic Federation will be prepared to echo Engels' words as regards the latter body, and may find some consolation from a perusal of the Second Epistle to the Corinthians.

Such a parallel as I have sought to elaborate will not be without its uses if we bear in mind the Latin proverb *crimine ex uno discant omnes* (from the fault of one, let all learn), and also if we remember what led the Christian movement to success. It was not the heresies of brilliant geniuses. It was not the bright original idea of some local preacher who thought to start a brand-new Christianity of his own. It was the steady development of the main stream of Christian thought and organisation on lines well-fixed, at least, from the second century onwards, which led Christianity to victory over the Roman world. It will assuredly be only by a similarly strong and definite adhesion to principle and organisation that modern Socialism will accomplish its far, far more difficult task of conquering the world of modern capitalistic civilisation. Christianity, which was essentially a religion of the other world, left the economical and political side of things with little immediate alteration. It definitely established the great anti-thesis between sacred and profane, church and world, spiritual and temporal, priest and layman, an antithesis which was undeveloped throughout antiquity, when religion being

64

essentially social there was no marked distinction between it and politics, every religious act being also social or political, and every political or social act also religious. Thus Christianity, owing to its solution of the problem of human life involving the transference of the sphere of religion (1) from society to the individual, and (2) from this world to the next, was able to come to an agreement with the powers that then were, by which it reserved to itself the spiritual and left the temporal pretty much as it had been. The fact of its involving these distinctions also subsequently enabled Christianity, especially in its most extreme individualist form of Protestantism, to become the appropriate religious expression of an economically individualist society.

Socialism, on the contrary, knows no such convenient separations. Its aim is primarily the effecting of an economical change, the greatest which history has known, in the conviction that a complete revolution in human relations and conceptions must follow upon this change. Christianity proposed to solve matters by revolutionising one side only of human affairs, and that the easiest to move. Socialism, on the contrary, formulates the principles underlying the coming revolution in the whole of human life, in and through the side involving the deepest and most tenacious of all interests, in and through its very heart and marrow, its economic constitution. The immense task of realising this change will assuredly demand a full measure of the energies, intellectual, moral, and physical, of the "Proletarians of all countries" who unite themselves, and of those who join with them in this noblest of all unions.

Footnotes

1. The doctrine of the personal immortality of the soul as distinct from bodily resurrection was unquestionably introduced or at least brought into prominence by the ex-Pharisee Paul and his party. The oldest Christianity which the "Revelation" in the main represents was completely dominated by the conviction of the approaching advent of the Jesus Messiah and the "end of the age." Those "believers" who died were expected to rise again in bodily form in a few months, or, at most, years, to join in the reign of the saints on

earth in the New Jerusalem. It was only as time wore on, and that the first generations of Christians *did* pass away without any of these things being fulfilled, that the Pauline doctrine of personal immortality came universally to the fore, replacing the older belief in the approaching advent of a millennium. The latter, henceforward, became relegated to the subordinate position of a "pious opinion" as to what would happen in an uncertain and possibly remote future of the world's history.

Century Ends and Mid Centuries

THE observation is often made that the phrase "*fin de siècle*" is absurd since it implies a special character as attaching to an arbitrarily-fixed point of time. The truth of this proposition seems unimpeachable, since no reason can be assigned why the first or last decade of a century reckoned from such arbitrary point of time should mark an epoch more than any other decade. This may be so; yet by a possible coincidence, or owing to deeper causes, as yet imperfectly investigated, there does seem a certain definite period when the cycle of changes – the specifically new elements in life associated with a given century – do reach their given maturity and that this period is approximately the same in each century. The first half presents few prominent characteristics beyond those present in the second half of the preceding century. New developments and new tendencies are then germinating and have not as yet subjugated the old, the old are still dominant. It is about the middle of a century that they begin to acquire an independent life and to assert themselves at the expense of the old. They continue to expand and to deepen in intensity till the close of the century when they have attained their zenith.

The first fifty years of the succeeding century presents chiefly the "backwash" (as we may term it), or the settling-down, of the characteristics just spoken of. In some cases the backwash is so strong as to produce a temporary reaction. The forward wave of the previous fifty years is met by a counter-current which for the time being seems to annihilate it. But this is merely temporary and superficial. The new development receives a fresh impulse at or about the turn of the century and another wave of change, with its new developments and new tendencies, sets in. The dividing period of time is, I submit, in short, to be found at mid-centuries, rather than at the beginning or the end of centuries. The last and the first half of any two successive centuries, I contend, belong together and form a coherent cycle of time. But the first and the second half of the same century are sharply distinguished. When we speak of the characteristics of any particular century we usually have in our mind those of its second half.

The above will be found to hold good as regards all sides of social development – industrial, commercial, political, religious, artistic, literary or customary. It will be found to be true of almost every century respecting which we have sufficient information since the Christian era. A few instances will illustrate what is meant.

Beginning with the first century, we find Christianity entering the arena of history in the persecution of Nero, *anno* 64. It was at that time already a well-known sect of Rome, and the celebrated passage in Tacitus would point to its having been introduced, or at least become noticeable, a few years before. Thenceforward, during the next hundred years, took place that great development of the new faith which found its expression in the writings constituting our New Testament, the completion of which is placed by most critics somewhere about the year 150. The next hundred years of ecclesiastical history was occupied with the conflict between Catholic Christianity on the one side, and the various forms of Gnosticism, and of Manichaeism. About and after the year 250, an enormous material development took place in the Church, a development but little affected by the short periods of the Decian and Valerian persecutions; catacombs and private houses were abandoned as places of worship for the purpose corresponding to our churches began to spring up. The Church now distinctly assumes the character of a wealthy corporation. The old Gnostic and even the later Manichaean controversies quickly lost their importance before the new disputes concerning the nature of the Trinity. It is true that early in the next century took place the formal establishment of the Christian religion by Constantine, but this was only a stage in a success which reached its culmination in the second half of the fourth century. It is not till the time of Theodosius that the triumph of Christianity over Paganism became definite and assured.

A similar and synchronous line of epochs may be traced in the political development of the Roman Empire. With the reign of Nero, shortly after the middle of the first century, was struck the death-blow of the Imperial system in the form inaugurated by Augustus. As M. Gaston Boissier has shown, the opposition-movement, of which Seneca and Tacitus were representative, gained its great impetus from the fall of Nero, maintaining itself throughout all changes for the next hundred years, and achieving realisation during the second half of the second century under the Antonines. No essential change in the political condition of the Empire took place before the middle of the third century, when the true condition of things became apparent – the internal instability of the giant fabric and the first serious inroads of the Barbarians on its frontiers – which led to the reconstruction of Diocletian in the last decade of the century. The vast machine held together in its partitioned form after a fashion, but the turn of the following, viz., the fourth century, disclosed the barbarian with a firm footing inside the frontiers, as a staple element in the Roman armies, and even an important factor in court intrigues. As the century drew to its close all frontiers were threatened, and the incursions had begun on many sides. The great period of the barbaric inroads was of course the first half of the fifth century, but their result, i.e., the establishment of the Germanic kingdoms which formed the basis of mediaeval Europe, was marked by the dividing line of the century, which coincides within a few years with the establishment of the Vandalic Monarchy in Africa, the Visigothic in Spain, the Frankish settlement in Gaul, the Anglo-Saxon in Great Britain and, last but not least, the fall of the Western Empire and the Conquest of Italy by the Ostro-Goths. In short, the turn of the fifth century shows us distinctly the first beginnings of mediaeval Europe. The barbarian now is master everywhere throughout the West. The consolidation of the new Northern and Western nationalities proceeded apace during the first half of the sixth century, and these were not regained for the Empire, notwithstanding the brilliant reign of Justinian. The second half of the sixth century was signalised by the final extinction of the pagan religion, by the dissolution or transformation of the old classical forms in literature, art and architecture, even within the limits of the Eastern Empire. The Byzantine period now begins.

The few indications given from the later classical and early Christian world, which could be multiplied indefinitely by the industry of the reader, will be sufficient to illustrate the general meaning of the, point dealt with. Turning now to modern history we find the same tendency if anything still more strikingly exhibited. The turn of the thirteenth century saw the rise of corporate towns, the first great development of mediaeval industry, the success of the mendicant orders, and altogether the beginnings of what we may term the second period of the Middle Ages. The year 1350 and the subsequent decades saw mediaeval township, trade guild, mediaeval handicraft, mediaeval art at their zenith. In England the same period is remarkable for the Lollard movement, and the first serious blow struck at serfdom.

The principle or coincidence here dwelt upon is, of course, in no century more strikingly illustrated than in the fifteenth. With the taking of Constantinople in 1453, and the dispersal of the Byzantine scholars and artists, consequent thereupon, dates the period known as the Renaissance. A few years later saw the overthrow of the Old English nobility in the "Wars of the Roses," and the beginning of the uprooting of the people from the soil in this country; in England (Edward IV), in France (Louis XI), and in Spain (Ferdinand and Isabella), the beginning of Absolutist Monarchy. It also saw the invention of printing and the earliest forms of modern commerce. In other words, the second half of the fifteenth century was distinctly the "beginning of the end" of the Middle Ages. The Reformation, the dramatic opening of which took place early in the sixteenth century might, at first sight, be supposed to contradict the point we are here insisting upon. But a closer view will show this to be a mistake. The outbreaks during the earlier part of the sixteenth century were really only the continuation of a movement which had begun in the latter decades of the fourteenth century with the English Lollards, which was carried on in the next century by the Hussites on the continent of Europe, and, at least, the *negative* side of which, i.e. the hatred of the Catholic hierarchy and contempt for the dogmas and rites it represented, had become common, one might almost say universal, amongst the educated classes of all countries. This movement, although the struggle was going on throughout the first half of the sixteenth century, was not in any sense completed before the Council of Trent – the definite establishment of the Protestant principalities in Germany, and the accession of Elizabeth in England. Not until the second half of the sixteenth century, therefore, was Mediaeval Europe noticeably giving place to the Bureaucratic Europe which lasted till Napoleon, and under cover of which the new middle classes, and with them the modern world of industry, commerce, and science grew up.

In England one of the most conspicuous products of the declining sixteenth century was the Puritan movement. This continued gradually to permeate the English middle-classes, till in the middle of the following century it overthrew the Monarchy. But underneath the Puritan movement, in truth the development of it, though in some respects antagonistic in its form, was the movement trending towards modern England. The victory of the Puritan was short-lived. Puritanism in its old form exhausted itself in the Civil Wars and the Commonwealth. The reign of Charles II (i.e., the declining century) is signalised by the birth of modern science in various departments, of modern commerce, and of modern finance. At this time the so-called "manufacturing system" became general in English industry. In place of the more simple methods of production, the combination of a number of workmen under one roof and the system of division of labour which accompanied the latter became now the rule, and formed

71

the transition to the machine or "great" industry of modern times.

The political configuration of Europe, which lasted in its main features up to the end of the last century, was fixed by the Treaty of Westphalia in 1648. During the second half of the century, Louis XIV and Mazarin perfected that centralisation and bureaucratisation of France which held together for over a century, and which paved the way for the French Revolution and the Modern France which resulted from it. Finally, while the first half of the seventeenth century was conspicuous for its belief in magic and witchcraft, the second half saw the decline and practical extinction of that belief, among the governing and educated classes generally. The first half of the eighteenth century presents few prominent characteristics over and above those present in the later decades of the seventeenth century. On the other hand the undercurrents of a new thought and life and of new economic conditions were stirring.. But, as usual, they did not bear fruit until after the turning-point of the period in question. Taking France as an example, we find during the early part of the century the public mind occupied with controversies started in the preceding century, with disputes between Gallican and Jesuit, between *Parlement* and Court; we find the first crude forms of modern commercial finance developing into schemes like the "Mississippi," which had its counterpart in England in the "South Sea Bubble." But there are no essentially new developments. On the other hand, no sooner does the century pass its meridian than the doctrines of the *Philosophes* begin to pervade all classes of society. In England, where these doctrines had their source, but where they had no immediate practical effect on the public mind, we have, on the other hand, the beginning of machine-industry in the invention in 1760 of the spinning jenny. The rapidity in the progress of invention and improvement which succeeded and which by the end of the century had begun to transform the whole character of English industry, only requires to be barely mentioned. The French Revolution, occurring at the close of the century, was the summing up of the new conditions, intellectual and material, which had begun to manifest themselves three or four decades earlier. Their economic basis was, of course, the struggle of the new middle class – the third estate – to emancipate itself.

The early decades of the nineteenth century present, it is true, a vast undercurrent of new tendencies and ideas, but they were not yet recognised, the dominant tone was indeed, distinctly reactionary. Another half-century had to elapse before the middle-classes succeeded in completing as to essentials, the movement to conquer the political power, and even to emancipate industry from its remaining mediaeval trammels. The great inventions which had established in this country the modern phase of production – the machine-industry – before the close of the preceding century, increased in variety and in number at a prodigious rate. The typical achievements in invention of the nineteenth century are, of course, the Steam Engine and the Electric Telegraph; though strictly speaking they are merely special features of the general industrial development. In any case, steam as applied to locomotion on the railroad has, without doubt, directly tended to metamorphose human life more than any other single invention in the world's history. But although the first short railroad was built in 1830, it was not until a quarter of a century later that the whole of even the main trunk lines of the European system were complete, and hence that mankind at large had begun to realise the enormous nature of the change in all human relations imported by the steam-engine and by the "great industry" generally. Until the fifties, the majority of mankind were still living, so to say, in a bygone age. Similarly in intellectual matters. The bulk of the thought of the first half of the century, its science, its philosophy, its art, its theology, its free-thought, were the "backwash" or the mere continuation of results and movements essentially belonging to the eighteenth century. Even the reactive elements saw their foes in the old eighteenth century theories. To take one example of the continuity of the later eighteenth and earlier nineteenth centuries from literature, the great German literary and philosophic development up to the forties was a direct development without a break of the movement associated with the names of Goethe, Schiller, Herder, and above all Kant, dating from the previous century. Again, up to the middle of the century the middle-class parties led the advanced movement as in the previous century, in their opposition to the aristocratic and land-owning classes, but with the Revolution of 1848 a new element appeared distinct from, and even in antagonism to, the old Liberal and Radical factions. It was the party of the new proletariat which has to-day become the Social-Democratic party. As if to accentuate the position taken up in this essay, the Chartist movement, the product of an earlier period of the nineteenth century, not only proved abortive as regards its immediate ends, but died completely out. On the contrary, the corresponding proletarian movements initiated in the decline of the century are growing larger and more important day by day.

The foregoing illustrations are only culled at random from an indefinite number which might be taken. Perhaps they are sufficient, however, to make out a case for an "empirical law." Any student of history who cares to take the trouble will find it easy to discover further facts to reinforce those given, to any extent he pleases. It is curious, if nothing more – this perpetual recurrence of a coincidence if, declining the hypothesis of the "empirical law," we must perforce regard it as such. It seems, indeed, at first sight, absurd enough that human affairs should regulate themselves in any fixed manner, so as to coincide regularly with the arbitrarily fixed points of time we call the beginning, middle, and end of centuries. We must not forget, however, that the recurrence of periods of change at regular intervals may be traceable to some law of rhythmic motion in the manifestation of social, as of other classes of phenomena, notwithstanding the purely accidental nature of the particular relation they bear to our time-reckoning. If the arbitrary date fixed as the starting point of the latter had happened to have been made fifty years earlier or fifty years later, the periods of change referred to would have obviously fallen during the first half, and not the latter half, of the ensuing centuries dating therefrom.

If there be any truth in the theory of historic pulsation referred to, the implication as regards the future is plain enough. The great achievements of the nineteenth century, together with those impulses and movements connected with them which have given to that century its character as a time-marking epoch of historic evolution, will continue their development for the next fifty years or thereabouts on the lines they are now doing or may even in some departments succumb to a temporary movement of reaction, but the realisation of the ultimate issue of the changes now going on will not take place in the lifetime of the present, or hardly indeed that of the rising generation, though they will do so none the less surely and none the less fully in their own time. The earlier portion of the twentieth century will probably show us new developments and an accentuated character in the great class-struggle between capital and labour now going on. There may, and probably will, be many sharp conflicts and many subordinate crises. It may be that many will succumb on both sides, but if there is any truth in the assumption here suggested on the strength of the movement of past history, the final decision will not be taken, the new world will not be definitely entered upon till the twentieth century has passed its meridian and is beginning to descend into the place where all centuries (good and bad) go to when they die. Whether or not by that time we shall have acquired another time-reckoning starting from a more recent epoch than the so-called Christian era is a question which may be left for the reader's imagination to decide.

The Rule of the Small Middle Class

The word Democracy covers a multitude of false conceptions. Democracy is supposed by many to he necessarily progressive and Socialistic in tendency. It is often thought that were the Democracy supreme, one would at once have made the great step towards Socialism or Social-Democracy. This idea, of course, lies at the basis of the belief in the referendum. Now, those who hold the view as to the perfection of the Democracy and its counsels, if only uncontaminated by the evil influences of the aristocrat and the wealthier bourgeois, would do well to pause and ask themselves of what the Democracy, as at present constituted, consists. For the Democracy is like the ten commandments – a "rummy lot."

The Democracy is generally supposed to consist of all outside the traditional governing classes the aristocratic and plutocratic sections of the community. The position of the professional and intellectual classes, as a whole, might be considered doubtful; but as, to a large extent, hangers-on of the extreme wealthy section, in the shape of lawyers, higher functionaries, fashionable doctors, journalists – it is, for the sake of the argument, safer to exclude them in the lump (notwithstanding that many of them do not answer to this description) from the Democracy, or the "people." There remains, therefore, only that portion of the community whose academic education has been limited, or *nil*, and whose means, generally speaking, are equally limited – during, at least, the greater part of their lives. Now, what is the nature of the main body of the population – called, and properly called, *par excellence*, the Democracy or the People? It really consists of several classes, all having an economic tendency to gravitate towards a centre, it is true, but often having present aspirations tending in quite different directions. We have within the pale of the Democracy (1) the clerk class; (2) the small shop-keeping class, (3) the domestic servant class, (4) the struggling artist, musician, actor, author, journalist class – or, in other words, the Bohemian class, (5) the Lumpen Proletariat or quasi-vagabond class, (b) the labouring or producing class proper – the skilled and unskilled workmen, including the agricultural labourers.

The Democracy, or the "people" is made up of, at least, all these elements. They all tend to gravitate economically towards the proletariat proper, but their actual sympathies are various. The peasant proprietary class, such an important factor in many parts of the Continent, fails, of course, in Great Britain altogether. The proletariat proper, the class which bears the future Socialist world in its womb, by no means at present everywhere outweighs, numerically, all the other classes. On the contrary, so far as I am aware, this is only the case in Great Britain and some of the North American States, and even in these countries the majority is not large. Now, as before said, the bulk of the non-proletarian sections of the Democracy are by no means proletarian or Social-Democratic, even in their instincts, let alone socialistic in their convictions. The predominating – or, at all events, most influential – elements in the non-proletarian democracy is what, for brevity, I have, rather loosely, termed the clerk and shop-keeping class; in other words, they who are, or who hope to become small capitalists, the small middle-class (*Petite Bourgeoisie, Spiessbürger*). This last section of the "people," or the "democracy," is, as such, the most formidable, because the most subtle, enemy the Socialist movement has to contend with. The snobbery of the Lackey class is obvious; the class itself is not so numerous, and has little influence. The Lumpen-proletariat class, that class which has no regular calling or means of livelihood, has, properly speaking, no politics. Danger from it can only arise when any considerable number of its members tack themselves on to the Socialist movement as Communist-Anarchists, making foolish, would-be extreme revolutionary, speeches, and still more foolish terrorist attempts. In this case its treacherous and unstable character makes it the mine from which reactionary parties dig their police-spies and provocative agents, and an element on which they can generally rely as buyable in any revolutionary crisis.

The "bohemian" class, in its various grades, though also non-political in general, is, as far as it goes, revolutionary in tendency, though without any definite aim. But the small capitalist class, in its various ramifications, has a more or less instinctive, but none the less definite, political and ethical creed. This creed, needless to say, is the outcome of its economic position. The latter presents it with an enemy behind and an enemy in front. The enemy behind is the remains of aristocratic or land owning privilege, together with most forms of bureaucratic (official) and plutocratic privilege. This enemy is common to itself and the rest of the democracy, including the proletariat. But it has also an enemy in front, the kernel of the working-classes to wit, the social-revolutionary proletariat, with the aim of which its own position is no less irreconcilable than that of the aristocratic-plutocratic section. The aim of the small capitalist, and of him who hopes to become one, is security and free play under the most advantageous conditions for his small capital to operate. On this account the little bourgeois constitutionally hates landlords and all forms of aristocratic and bureaucratic privilege as absorbing his profits, and as parasitic on the only class which for him has indefeasible rights to existence – the small middle-class, as incarnate in the "respectable tradesman." For the same reason he looks with no very friendly eye on very big capitalists, especially the big financiers, the Jay Gould and others who make him lose his money. He is, in short, a thoroughgoing Radical if he is plucky and thorough, if he gets timid he is a Liberal, who thinks things must go slowly, or possibly a Tory-Democrat.

But what you may know him best by is his religion and ethics. In this country he is generally a Nonconformist, and always a moral man – that is, he has a nonconformist conscience – who goes in for the closing of public-houses, the suppression of the male sex, the prohibition of gambling, and the general abolition of all that is not business or the kind of edification productive of men like himself. He objects to the Prince of Wales, not so much as such, but on the ground that he plays baccarat (about the most harmless occupation on which he could be engaged). He believes in thrift, and in strict economy in administration. He is eminently practical in his politics, the mainspring of his action being the reduction of the rates and the promotion of trade in the district. Now this is the type of creature of which consists what is called the nonconformist vote, the vote for which the parliamentary candidate is prepared if necessary to sell his immortal soul. Owing to its numerical diffusion, democratic measures have at present a tendency to throw the weight of power into the hands of this class. And here lies the danger spoken of. For the sake of winning working-class support, it is possible the small capitalist may make certain concessions to the proletarian movement, but as a class the small bourgeoisie will never be anything more than "Nonconformist conscience." It has as much reason to dread Socialism as any other possessing class, while its lack of education and of ideal aspiration of any kind makes it the one class outside the proletariat which furnishes least individual recruits to the cause of Socialism. The professional classes have supplied plenty of individual sympathisers and workers for the movement, but the "respectable tradesman," how many of him join the SDF?

Varnished over with hypocrisy which finds its expression in ostentatiously favouring every ascetic movement that does not touch the root principle of profit-mongering, with its head in its day-books, and its soul in its till; the small middle-class in its various sections is the great obstacle which will have to be suppressed before we can hope to see even the inauguration of the Socialist world. It must be destroyed or materially crippled as a class before real progress can be made. In many parts of the continent the Jew has been a useful aid to evolution in helping to make mutton-broth (economically speaking) of the "respectable tradesman" and his congeners. But on the continent the peasant proprietor, who may now be reckoned as part of the *petite bourgeoisie*, just as the landlord with us may be reckoned as part of the big capitalist class, is a potent factor in retarding the process. Agriculture in Europe is not sufficiently developed to be carried on otherwise than almost entirely on a small scale, and thus the peasant class continues, in spite of usurers Jew and Christian.

With us here in England, however, it is somewhat different. We have no peasant proprietary class, and the small middle-class stands practically on its own feet. Hence the crippling of this class, the reduction of its members to the position of proletarians would abolish an element in our midst which, while with a show of reason claiming to be "advanced" on one of its sides will, in the long run always join with capital as against labour, and is, especially dangerous owing to its capacity for drawing red herrings across the track of Socialist progress.

The truth of what is here said is illustrated is :he case of a country like Switzerland, where the small middle-class is in complete possession of the political power. There you have none of the evils incidental to larger bureaucratic and plutocratic political systems. You have juridical and political equality in theory perfect. You have a humane and excellent penal system. The big capitalist by no means monopolises all the influence in public life. If he becomes too big public opinion rather frowns on him than otherwise.

But is Switzerland, until quite recently, Social Democracy has been a mere tolerated tail of the Democratic movement, that is, the movement of the small middle-class and peasantry. Now that the town proletariat is increasing, and above all, is becoming organised, matters are of course looking up. But it is still very difficult for the Swiss Socialists to act efficiently in the political sense, independently of the Democratic party. In fact, considering the disproportion of the proletarian population to the small capitalists and peasants, it speaks wonders for the organisation that Social-Democracy holds the position in Switzerland that it does.

For the rest, one has in Switzerland, the *beau ideal* of the small middle-class state the side on which it has advanced beyond the great bureaucratic states where the big Bourgeois dominates, and the side where it becomes reactionary, and is as anti-socialist as the most retrograde monarchy. The "people" is sovereign in Switzerland, but the "people" is predominantly "small middle-class." "Respectable tradesmen," and commercialised peasants, or the friends and relations of "respectable tradesmen," and commercialised peasants, fill nearly all responsible positions. As a consequence the power of the tradesman is practically unlimited. For a customer to successfully dispute an extortionate claim made by a tradesman is undreamed of. The law gives the house landlord powers which make him a small despot over his tenants. One of the ruling passions of the small middle-class, personal gossip of the back-biting description, permeates society. Everybody knows what his neighbour is doing, and often what he or she is not doing. Persons in a responsible position do not disdain to become "old women" (*klatschweiber*) in this respect. Like opium eating with the Chinese the passion for this becomes so strong with the small middle-class mind as at times to completely dominate the whole man. We see the same phenomenon *mutatis mutandis* in the *espionage* of the non-conformist conscience in our provincial towns. The "respectable tradesman" and his class will never put off the "old woman" in this respect so long as he remains a "respectable tradesman." Again, just as the parsimony of the "respectable tradesman" is seen in our own local governing bodies and school-boards in refusing public libraries, etc., so in Switzerland you find it in a curtailment of expenditure, in a slipshod judicial procedure which in some cantons to save the expense of producing witnesses allows a deposition to be taken at a distance and dispenses at the option of the judiciary with that great and only safeguard of accused persons, cross-examination.

I would urge in short, on Socialists, the desirability of not forgetting that in spite of its use at times as an auxiliary in the attack on aristocratic, plutocratic, and bureaucratic privileges, the small middle-class democracy, as a distinct factor in political and social life; is quite as much "the enemy" as the more obviously hostile classes. Unfortunately, many labour leaders are themselves immured in small-middle-class ideas. The revolutionary democracy, it must never be lost sight of, is, properly speaking, the organised working-class.. In the centre of this class, the whole of which is, by virtue of its economic position, Socialist in tendency i.e., unconsciously Socialist, stands the modern Social-Democratic or Socialist party, the party which alone has attained to a clear consciousness of the economic goal of labour action – political and trade union – and of its ultimate aim in the entire transformation of human society.

Luxury, Ease and Vice

Superstitions die hard. Even among Social-democrats we sometimes hear echoes of the peasantly and small middle-class denunciation of luxury as though it were the most heinous crime of the possessing classes – the implication being, of course, that asceticism is the ideal of human life. The stump-oratorical criticism of the corpulency of the man of wealth, depreciatory allusions to champagne, turtle-soup, and other evil things of this nature, still sometimes heard at Socialist meetings, are legacies from this order of ideas. Such sentiments never fail of a certain effect in "fetching" a popular audience by their familiar tinkle and by the appeal they make to the small-tradesman element it comprises. The notion that the luxury attendant on the institution of private property is its worst feature is a very old one, and its economic basis is very easily traceable. Its *raison d'être*, however, in so far as it has ever had one, has disappeared almost completely since the era of Bourgeois ascendancy, as I shall endeavour to explain presently. The poor peasant, the handicraftsman, and the beggar or vagabond, has always and naturally viewed with envy, hatred, and perhaps excusable malice, the sight of the enjoyment of good things from which his own economic position debars him. On the principle of the fox and the grapes, these things being unattainable by him, his tendency is to regard them as evil. Such is the economical basis of asceticism put in a sentence.[1]

The hatred of the sight of luxury has always been particularly strong among a class whose economic foundation was slipping from under it. This powerfully contributed to the success of Ebionite Christianity, that form of Christianity which laid special emphasis on poverty, and which, perhaps, was the earliest form of primitive Christianity. The small cultivators and handicraftsmen of and around the Roman provincial cities, were the first to embrace a faith which among other things proclaimed the righteousness of misery and the wickedness of luxury.

This we find drastically expressed in the parable, obviously emanating from an Ebionite source, of the Rich Man and Lazarus. The Rich Man "gets it hot," not because he has done anything particularly wicked, but because he has been "clothed in purple and fine linen and fared sumptuously every day." Lazarus on the other hand is comforted with the blessings of Abraham's bosom. – as a reward for any good useful work done in his lifetime or on any theological ground but on that of his rags, which, it appears, were of themselves a sufficient passport at the gate of Paradise. As far as appears, both the Rich Man and Lazarus for that matter belonged to the idle class at opposite ends of the scale: the one to the idle rich, the other to the Lumpenproletariat of the period. We find the hatred of luxury and of the wealthy not on the ground of their exploitation so much as on that of their wearing fine clothes, feeding well, and living in well-furnished houses as a charateristic of all the popular reform movement of the Middle Ages, not to mention peasant insurrections. That this was so is explained by the fact that in former ages, with their more obvious and direct motives of conduct, the "rich man" consumed, i.e., spent, in personal adornment and luxury, the wealth he possessed. He was emphatically not a business man. He liked being rich not for the sake of acquisitiveness per se, but because he could dress in damask, silk and velvet of splendid dyes, could purchase costly perfumes and spices, could drink exotic wines, and also on occasion enjoy exotic women.

Such was the ancient and mediaeval "rich man." The lust of the eye and the pride of life, whether gross and sensual or artistic and intellectual, as the case might be, was for him the end of the possession of wealth. The acquisition itself and the process of the acquisition were merely Means to this one end – the palpable enjoyments of life. He hoarded his cash and his gold and silver treasures against emergencies, but he only in exceptional cases thought of *investing* his money if he did so at all. He was, moreover, for the most part prodigal in his generosity with all and sundry, for without investment there is little temptation to parsimony. The modern rich man, the Capitalist, is a totally different being. He dresses like everybody else with the dowdy ugliness that Bourgeois civilisation exacts of all classes which it compels to don its machine-made uniform. He takes his pleasures sadly, as if something almost to be ashamed of. His one serious aim and interest in life is "business" and sound investments. Likely enough he is personally abstemious; he may be, perhaps, a social-purity man, a teetotaler, a non-smoker, member of the anti-gambling league. He does not exact unseasonable delicacies at his table, but does not disdain the mutton-chop, the beef-steak, or the cut off the joint. All of us know this particular type of exploiting scoundrel, of virtuous private life, whose soul is in his business, who is absorbed perpetually in the problem of how to cut down wages, who tries to break up unions, to minimise expense by not safe-guarding machinery, and other methods, and who generally exhibits all the steady, plodding habits and business-capacity so much esteemed by the small middle-class mind. He despises the man devoted to pleasure – does this plain-living and hardworking man of business.

This class of man who has his prototype in the English Puritan of the seventeenth century has practically accepted the Ebionitic ideal of the mediaeval sectary in so far as the condemnation of pleasure and luxury is concerned. The "poor man" of old, living in much closer contact with his rich neighbour than is the case nowadays, was made wild by the contrast between the silk, velvet, and cloth of gold of the latter and his own humble homespun; between that neighbour's peacocks' heads, well-spiced dishes, and wines flavoured with the essences of Araby and Ind, and his own plain and (possibly, though not necessarily) scanty fare; between the patrician's palace or the noble's castle and the peasant's homestead or the craftsman's dwelling. Now we have changed all that. The modern Bourgeois has gone far towards realising on one of its sides the ideal of the early Christian and of the mediaeval Christian-Communist sectary, in the dethronement of pleasure and beauty as the end of life. But he has done so in favour of "business" and bald "utility," and the reduction of all things to a dead level of sordidness. In the matter of clothing the only difference between the rich and poor consists in the snobbery of the top hat, and a more fashionable but not more beautiful cut coat. No one new dresses in richly coloured silks and velvets or in cloth of gold. The modern bourgeois, even if he wanted to, could not. He is himself under the thumb of a public opinion, the creation of his class, which rigorously enacts thaet every one shall dress like everyone else – which ordains that we shall all dress in shoddy uniform of hideous pattern. Bourgeois fashion strains to maintain the ideal of cheap ugliness as far as possible in ordinary life; and on festive occasions, to make quite sure that no chance ray of taste shall creep in, it exacts a special uniform – otherwise the peculiar badge of the waiter and the undertaker. For the rest, while shoddy broadcloth is so cheap, even the beggar need not dress in picturesque rags.

Again, in the matter of architecture, the model lodging-house and the West-end mansion or the suburban villa are about equally ugly. Not only does the modern Bourgeois, unlike the ancient "rich man," not "clothe himself in purple" or even always in specially fine linen, but he does not necessarily fare sumptuously every day, for if "business" requires it, he is quite prepared to satisfy himself with a hastily-swallowed "stand up" luncheon and a half a pint of "bitter." He grudges the time if not the money spent in pleasure. His one passion in life, I repeat, is just "business," which means the extraction of surplus-value from labour in one or other of the varied forms of that art, or the acquisition of profit from one or other of the multi-form operations connected with the shifting of the realised surplus value after extraction, between sections and individuals of the middle and upper classes. He, it is likely enough, will join with you or any one else in aspersions on the scanty survivals of the old life of the "rich man," on Lord Mayor's banquets and such like frivolities.

Was it not the **Times**, the organ of the "City," of the great gamblers (i.e., *business* gamblers) of the stock-exchange and high finance, which in lofty moral tone lectured the present King when Prince of Wales on the wickedness of playing Baccarat? This Baccarat business may be regarded as the survival of a time when "dicing" was the daily amusement of the "rich man" and hence when there was no opportunity of covering gambling up under the mantle of "business," when that "blessed word" itself even had not yet acquired its mystic flavour – hence Baccarat seems unspeakably shocking to an age in which all are turned Puritans because their only serious pleasures in life are the modern forms of profit-grinding. The absurdity of Socialists making a fuss about Baccarat among the *haute volée* in manifest when we consider that it merely means the shifting about of already extracted and realised surplus-labour among individuals of a wealthy class, and hence is of no conceivable moment to anyone except those immediately concerned in it.[2]

No, it is not the occasional idleness or "pleasures" of the modern capitalist that specially deserve our invective, it's the daily round of his accursed "industry." This it is which is the mainstay of the misery in modern society. "It ain't the 'untin' as 'torts the 'orse's 'oofs, it's the 'ammer, 'ammer, 'ammer, on the 'ard 'igh road." The character of the polemic must of necessity logically change with the character of its object. The modern Socialist, unlike the ancient and mediaeval communist, has for his aim the communisation not directly of the product, i.e., of articles of consumption (the latter is of no importance, and will come of itself in good time), but the communisation of the *means of production*. The ancient and mediaeval communist, who only knew the small handicraft and *petite culture* modes of producing wealth, naturally did not conceive of the communisation of the means of production, which could not, such as they were in his state of society, be effectively communised. All *he* thought of, therefore, was the more obvious communisation of the products designed for consumption, hence his particular *bête noire* was that luxury and idleness on the part of the few which he imagined would be impossible for any were these products equally at the disposal of all.

Now, in the present day with the means at the command of an organised commonwealth for the indefinite production of luxuries (if desired), and the indefinite reduction of the arduousness and duration of daily labour, there is no particular sense in a polemic against ease or luxury as such, neither is there any special point in attacking the capitalist on the ground of his sometimes indulging in leisure and luxuries. He is a fool if he does not. Moreover, as I have just shown, these things are with the modern capitalist not as with the "rich man" of old, the dominating object of his life, but are, as a rule, quite a subordinate matter with him. His main interest centres not so much in the *enjoyment of wealth* already obtained, as in the *processes and methods by which he obtains it*, and which constitute his "business." For example, it is related of the deceased Jay Gould, that when on a holiday tour in Europe, he spent his whole time in the Bourses of the various capitals, pulling off odd twenty thousands at the game of bulls and bears, disdaining altogether the "lust of the eye and the pride of life." How commonly do we see the spectacle of a man, the manufacturer, the merchant, or the banker, who having made his pile wants to retire, but finds he is miserable and has to go back to business again, because, forsooth, he knows no pleasure like it. This is a phenomenon which may be looked for in vain in any previous state of society.

Talk of vice, forsooth! Why, the present age isn't in it. Consult a mediaeval menu of the fifteenth century, or read your Petronius for a description of a Roman "rich man" banquet, and say if the city corporation dinner (which we suppose may be taken as the high water-mark of modern gluttony) is a patch upon it! Then as to drinking, what have we to show nowadays in the way of "cups" to compare even with the after-dinner orgies of the Squire Westerns of the eighteenth century, not to go farther back. Take adultery again. All the adultery and sexual vice of the wealthy classes to day are summed up in a few miserable aristocratic divorce suits which swell to the proportions of *causes célèbres* because they are the best things of the kind modern society has to offer! But for real sexual vice in cultivated luxuriance commend us to the noble palaces of Renaissance Italy, to the court of Alexander of the Borgias, the Sforzas, and the Medicis, or at the very least to the entourage of Charles II. Once more, in place of the perennial "dicing" of the "rich man" of old we have nowadays to make as much as possible out of a paltry Tranby Croft scandal. And so on with the rest of the "deadly" seven which went to make the staple of the life-interest of men of wealth in earlier ages. No, we must admit that though they undoubtedly exist still, the deadly sins are in a parlous way, viewed in comparison with former times.

The vices of the noble and ecclesiastic contributed to the fall of the feudal system; it will be the virtues of the bourgeois which will contribute to the fall of the Capitalist system. It's not his idleness, it's his industry, it's not his "pleasure" for which probably he cares very little; it's his business, for which he undoubtedly cares very much. This is the thing that defiles the modern man. Out of "business" come Panama scandals, Liberator swindles, Southern Railway conventions, and not out of pleasure. The pride of the "rich man" of old was in being a "gentleman," i.e., in having no occupation and living for amusement on money he had not himself made; the pride of the rich man of to-day shows itself in pretending to be living for business and on his earnings, or on wealth which he *has* himself acquired even when he has not done so. Thus the supremacy of the Bourgeois has insensibly and gradually but materially modified our whole views of life. The "backwash" of the old aristocratic "gentleman-at-large" sentiment extended even some way into the nineteenth century, and I believe even still lingers on in Ireland and other industrially-backward countries.

To me it seems inexpressibly feeble to hear a man ranting against the poor survivals into modern times of the luxury and even vices of the "rich man" of old, which no class or body of persons is concerned seriously to defend nowadays – when the real enemy lies in quite another direction. "It ain't the 'untin'" It's not in a high life adultery. It's not in an occasional orgy. It's not in Tranby Croft and Baccarat that the real class-vileness of the Bourgeois lies. "It's the 'ammer, 'ammer, 'ammer." It's in the factory office, it's in the counting-house, it's on the Stock Exchange that we have to seek it. The very qualities which gave the Bourgeois his strength in his fight with Feudalism, absolutist Monarchy, and the old Clericalism, will doubtless in time work out the contradiction of their own results, and prove themselves the instruments of his downfall. They have helped him to develop modern industry and commerce to a point at which he can no longer control them. The cant and hypocrisy this small-middle-class morality engendered having been made the nominal standard for all human life will help the destruction of the society of which it is the outcome.

I have endeavoured to show the inappropriateness of the class of polemic which attacks aldermen or others for eating turtle-soup or drinking champagne, or doing other things of this nature, without formulating some theory as to why they should not. To my thinking, as already said, if these good things are within his reach, the man, whoever he be, is a fool who doesn't consume them. It may fairly be doubted if many of those who in popular harangues deprecate the practice, would, if it came to the point, themselves be such fools. In fact, it seems to me that the Bourgeois who devotes himself to pleasure and consuming wealth nowadays is often less objectionable and certainly more rational than the one whose whole soul, from youthful manhood to the grave, from early morn to dewy eve, is wrapt up in profit-grinding or what he calls "business." The way I should put the matter from a Socialist point of view would be thus: – Ye

Bourgeois (i.e. some of you), eat turtle-soup and drink champagne, ye do well, and what we propose to do is to educate the proletariat into such a taste for turtle-soup and champagne or other things equally commendable, that they shall find life intolerable until they are in a position to do the same! As it is, they are for the most part well content to eat inferior "cagmag" and to drink cheap and nasty beer and spirits, or, if teetotalers, London water or some other vile temperance decoction. Should they once acquire the taste for refinement in eating, drinking and amusement, the present system of society will very soon go by the board.

The foolish because inaccurate attacks on the modern wealthy classes as specially vicious (in the conventional sense) are also to be deprecated. In the first place it might be difficult to prove that *mutatis mutandis* the "seven deadlies" were better represented among them than among the working classes. But, even if this were the case, the fact remains as already shown, that as against the wealthy classes of former times, the modern capitalist is in the conventional *petit bourgeois* sense, a moral being. It is by the Puritanical standard the Bourgeois has himself set up, in some things doubtless justly, in others with as little doubt unjustly, and outward conformity to which he enacts as the condition of his respectability, that the lapses which sometimes come to light are judged – and judged by all classes. The question Socialists have to ask the defenders of the present system is: What has all this increased sobriety of life, whether it takes the unimpeachable form of aversion to conventional vice, or the less unimpeachable one of the denunciation of pleasure and luxury and the cultivation of sordidness in general – what has it all done for mankind? Is the Bourgeois world, in which we are all "puritans," despising pleasure as frivolous and waste of time, all thrifty and industrious or pretending to be so, is it intrinsically better and happier than (say) the Classical world, the Feudal world, or the Renaissance world? Can any one assert in view of the modern factory hell, the East end slum, the struggle at the

93

Dockyard gates, the yearly increasing army of the starving unemployed, that there is less human misery in our world than in its predecessors. The sordid, industrious, profit-grinding shopkeeper, merchant, manufacturer, financier, who "scorns delights and lives laborious days," is he really a more estimable man than the gay Florentine of the fifteenth century? If so I fail to see why, though we have been taught to believe so.

The Socialist who wastes his powder and shot on unessential survivals reminds me of the virulence of that distinguished novelist, Mr. Hall Caine, against those relics of the past, the Sultan and the Paellas of Morocco. Mr. Hall Caine, in his novel **The Scapegoat**, in which he declaims against the surviving old-world oppression of the Pachas or local Governors of Morocco, speaks complacently of a plot to get the late Sultan Abd-erRahman and his Pachas into a palace to a banquet and afterwards on a given signal to lock the doors and fire the building, so that they all might be roasted alive. To attack a more than half-dead system surviving in an obscure country, which no one cares to defend, is cheap but scarcely heroic. What would Mr. Hall Caine say to a proposal – not treacherously to burn alive, we set aside such horrors as that – but painlessly to blow up or electrocute some of the bulwarks of modern aggressive Capitalism, say, for instance Mr. Cecil Rhodes and the Directors of the British South Africa Company?[3] Would the bare suggestion not evoke in him a shudder of horror throughout his whole frame? It is easy to win the applause of the modern market-hunter by scathing attacks on an old-fashioned despotism which stands in his way. But it is not so pleasant to court unpopularity with the same person by denouncing in similar terms unprovoked and cowardly raids on Matabeleland and elsewhere, with their accompanying treachery, slaughter and misery; by attacking, in other word, the real living, visible evils of the present day, by which the very man who is loudest in howling at the decayed despotisms of Morocco hopes to make money and strengthen his class-position. Now I maintain that the Socialist who devotes energy to blazing away at the perfectly immaterial practices of some rich man, even though vicious in themselves, is doing much the same thing unconsciously and without ulterior object (beyond perhaps that of winning a momentary cheer from his audience) as Mr. Hall Caine has done in his novel, though in his case it may be with the definite intention of currying favour with those to whom the existence of the ancient system of government in Morocco is inconvenient. No man wants to defend the crimes of oppressive Pachas; and no one wants to defend the evil vices of the wealthy. But to dissipate your onslaught on vital ills by fulminating against mere survivals or symptoms, is at least tantamount to drawing a red-herring across the track of the quarry of progress.

It remains to say a few words on the probable future of leisure, ease, luxury, and finally what is conventionally tensed "vice" under Socialism. The attack upon luxury as such even at present I hold to be pointless unless it can be shown that luxury among the well-to-do classes directly enhances the misery of the working classes. In a Socialistic state, the question of luxury is one of degree merely and not of kind. When all will equally participate in the advantages gained by social labour it is for society collectively to decide the amount of labour to be expended in the production of luxuries after having defined what may be deemed to constitute luxuries. Assuredly much that to the Proletarian of today would be the most extravagant luxury will under a reasonable state of society be viewed as necessary to a decent life. As to undoubted luxuries (e.g., champagne and turtle-soup), Whether they will be freely produced or eschewed altogether, it is impossible to say. Probably in a matter of this kind different Socialised communities will hold different views, and act accordingly. In the present day when a limited portion of the population has the monopoly of the means of production and distribution, and when the whole social system is based upon this monopoly, whether the well-to-do classes spend their unearned increment on luxuries, or whether they "invest" it, is a matter of indifference, speaking. economically, to the working classes.

Whether the "surplus value" goes in payment of wages for the production of champagne and turtle or of railways that are not wanted, must be a matter of absolute economic indifference to the wage-earners collectively.

There is no special virtue, as such, in converting money into constant capital or directly even into variable capital (i.e., the payment of wages), rather than into articles of consumption, since the consumption itself, it cannot be denied, has indirectly the effect of employing labour. This I know is an old saying, but it is none the less true in spite of the Manchester economists. I am now speaking, of course, solely from the standpoint of Capitalist society. In a Socialist society the matter would be very simple, the question being decided in each particular case as it arose. The basis of the decision must be whether the strength of the social desire for the particular luxury outweighed the expenditure of time and social labour in its production. There are many things an average well-to-do man has now, and is glad enough to have since they are there, but which, nevertheless, he would not sacrifice the time or labour necessary to their production to obtain if they were not there, in other words, which he could easily do without. And although under a properly-organised system of social production, the time and labour required for the creation of all forms of wealth would be reduced to a minimum, yet the principle of measurement of the relative amount of time and labour as against the amount of the enjoyment derived from the consumption of its product, would, I take it, have to be applied in some form or shape, in order to determine the reasonable limits of the production of luxuries. It is, in fact, the only rational standard that can be applied at all. There is no intrinsic virtue in abstinence from the consumption of champagne and turtle, and under Socialism it will be for the majority, either simple or proportional, of the community, to decide whether it prefers to set aside a certain amount of time and labour for their production rather than not have them, or to set aside the turtle and champagne rather than not have the time and labour for other purposes. Probably, as above said, the decision would not be uniform throughout the Socialised world.

Now as to actual vice. Will vice disappear under Socialism or will it be modified? It depends, I take it, on what we mean by vice. By vice I understand the indulgence in excess of the average man of any natural appetite or its indulgence in bizarre forms. If we mean sensuality, drunkenness, and gambling, for example, in the forms in which we see them to-day and know them in the past, then decidedly vice must disappear under altered conditions. But for all this I see no reason why we should all turn social purists, teetotalers, or even necessarily forswear the amusement of gambling altogether. Under Socialism the mercenary element in sexual relations must necessarily disappear, and with it the essential degradation connected therewith. All else resolves itself into a matter of individual taste. That the consumption of alcohol even in excess of the average would be less harmful both to the individual and less of a social nuisance in a society where all alcoholic beverages like everything else were not produced for profit but for use, is obvious. One chief cause of the present injurious effects of alcohol is admittedly its inferior quality, and the poisonous ingredients of its adulteration. Moreover with a fair average of mental culture throughout society, the effect of alcohol on the brain will be so modified that at least its socially unpleasant results will disappear. How often do we not see a rough, ignorant labourer get noisy, and even "drunk and disorderly" on a dram of whisky that would scarce warm the inside of a reasonably cultured man. Want of cerebral development often has quite as much to do with liquor "getting into the head" as the amount consumed. Again, as to gambling. The passion for watching the play of chances is a very ancient quasi-animal appetite, and most of us have it in one or other of its forms. As exhibited in the form of gambling, when it is connected with the idea of gain it might be supposed it would be impossible in a communistic society. Yet even here there are circumstances in which such a thing is conceivable. For instance, in case of a scarcity-supply of any article (say of a rare vintage wine), it would be surely possible that an allotment might be staked on an even chance against another similar allotment (on the principle of double or nothing) or against some other scarcity-value.

Taking the question of vice in general, i.e., of the excess of some special appetite or aberration in its manifestation, it is noteworthy that most men of strong character have been possessed of some vice, and that where they have had no vice, in the conventional sense, an unscrupulous greed or ambition has taken its place. Dehumanised monsters, such as Calvin, Robespierre, or Torquemada, can scarcely develop out of men who have a safety-valve in some reasonable human vice. The advantage in strongly-marked individualities of a dash or seasoning of vice (in the conventional sense) has not been the subject of sufficient study. It seldom seems to occur to any one that the enforcement of a dead uniformity in the measure of indulgence of the animal and quasi-animal appetites is as absurd as it is in other things.

The upshot and true explanation of the current opprobrium attaching to ease, luxury, and even some manifestations of vice, is this:- It is the offspring of the reaction of Capitalism against Feudalism, i.e., not necessarily against the aristocratic life in particular, but against the whole life created by feudal or non-capitalistic society. Ease, luxury, and vice, which were pre-eminently the offspring either of an ancient tax-gathering, slave-holding, and non-industrial state, or of a developed mediaeval community, were abhorrent to the rising middle-classes. The embryonic proletariat, still umbilically attached to the Bourgeoisie, especially the small Bourgeoisie, shared the same antipathies and aspirations as the latter – and even after having, at least in a measure, attained to an independent class-consciousness of its own, the old leaven still clings to it and it applauds the moral catch-words of the class which on other issues it combats. Of one thing we may be perfectly certain. The Bourgeois will never place on his moral "index" any pursuit or course of action which is in any way essential to the system by which he profits. Before he condemns anything as immoral he will take good care that in so doing he is not helping to impede the working of that Capitalist system in which he lives and moves and has his being.

Those who remember the American Civil War will recall how divided was Bourgeois public opinion on the subject of slavery, for the most part siding with the Southern State slave-owners. At that time it was not quite clear that slavery was not merely non-essential to the cotton interest, but was actually a stumbling block in the way of an industrial and commercial expansion in general. *Now* with one consent middle-class public opinion from top to bottom of the scale fulminates against the bare suggestion of slavery under that name and in its old forms, even in communities like those of Central Africa, where it is undoubtedly less hurtful to the natives than the (so-called) "free" competition of Capitalism would be. Again, the Bourgeoisie is all agog for abolishing public gambling tables, lotteries, and even horse-racing, but no one has yet proposed the closing of the Stock Exchange. The whole system of Capitalism is one great gamble in which oftentimes a man's whole existence is metaphorically placed upon the tables. What business, what investment is there nowadays to be found not involving that element of risk which is of the essence of gambling? That is all right and as it should be. This is *business*. To make up for it, your smug Bourgeois piously denounces all gambling that takes the form of a mere occasional pastime, the latter of course, in no way affecting the working of the capitalist system as such. This is *pleasure* and vicious, or at least frivolous, only good for men who have nothing better to do, just as if the Bourgeois who says so were himself doing anything intrinsically better.

"Timeo Danaos et dona ferentes." I say, beware of the Bourgeois when with the severe countenance and mien of righteous indignation he preaches morality to you! Turn your back on his preachings. Follow the advice of Pilate's wife, O

Socialists, and "have naught to do with this just man," even when he seems to make for your side, since you may be sure there is something in him more than meets the eye or ear! But look at the question (whatever it may be) fairly and squarely in the face and decide it on its merits, unswayed by middle class public opinion and its press, and uninfluenced, as far as possible, by your own prepossessions, derived as they are from dead or dying social conditions.

Footnotes

1. It is true that asceticism has also a speculative or metaphysical basis with which I have elsewhere dealt, i.e., one founded on a particular theory of the universe, and the two have worked into each other's hands. But we are here concerned with the one mentioned in the text, which is the sole explanation of its attraction for the down-trodden and oppressed among mankind.

2. Our Fabian friends in a manifesto (issued by them the same year as the Baccarat scandal), whose stock of wits was apparently running low at the time, had to fall back upon some cheap conventicle moralising on the subject, in the course of which they perpetrated in their eagerness an economical *lapsus*. They spoke of the shuffling of money in gambling as the way in which the upper classes "*spend* their money" forgetting that "spending" means the exchange of money for articles of consumption. Shaw's name was appended to this production, which surprised me as I should never have thought him capable of such very cheap playing to the gallery, and the chapel gallery too!

3. Written in 1896.

The Natural History of the Non-Conformist Conscience

The Nonconformist voter and his conscience as a product of Anglo-Saxon civilisation has a distinctive and peculiar history in the social development of these islands which is worthy of a short exposure.

At the present day the Nonconformist element in the country (using the word "Nonconformist" in its widest sense) comprises the bulk of the middle classes, and such of the working classes as are desirous of being their hangers-on, politically or otherwise. It comprises the so-called "religious world", barring the Catholics, Roman or Anglican, and is in the main co-incident with the old Evangelical Party, of which it is indeed a mere modern adaptation. To understand the power which the modern "Nonconformist conscience" has in influencing British public opinion, it is above all things necessary to recall what the old "Evangelicalism" was to which the " Nonconformists" look back with such profound reverence, and to understand the at times somewhat indistinct line of demarcation which separates the new type from that of a generation ago.

The disruption of feudal relations, the modified village-community of mediaeval England, the decay of the guilds, and the rise of the independent craftsman, merchant, and trade syndicate, was expressed in the region of religious thought by what is known as the Reformation. But the rising middle-class took the Reformation differently from those of the other classes who nominally protected or supported it, but who really wished to save as much as suited them of the traditional system of Christianity.

It must be remembered that at this time doubt as to the fundamental articles of Christian theology had never entered the heads of the enormous majority of the inhabitants of

Christendom. They were as axiomatic to most men then as the commonplaces of science are to us to-day. The feudal classes, although often like the rest desirous of being " shot" of the Papal supremacy and of certain sides of ecclesiastical domination, were determined to hold back the movement at this point as far as possible, and not to let it get "out of hand". The new middle classes, on the contrary, were bent upon driving the rupture with Catholicism to its logical conclusion, and getting a thoroughly individualistic form of Christianity established, in which each man as an individual should work out his own salvation. As soon, moreover, as the whole movement in Elizabeth's reign ceased to have to struggle for its bare existence, the two strains within it began to break out into open antagonism, which issued later in the victory of the middle classes in the Commonwealth. Hence Puritanism on the one side, and high Anglicanism on the other. The Puritans wanted in the ecclesiastical sphere no hierarchy, but free play for individual enterprise in religious matters, just as they wanted in the secular sphere no nasty feudal privileges, but the opportunity for the commercial expansion of the individual by his own efforts.

In both cases, however, the free play of the individual was, of course, to be limited by the exigencies of bourgeois' supremacy as a class. In politics the Puritan wished indeed to get rid of the arbitrary power of king and nobles, and were even not indisposed to get rid of the king himself. But the political and social doctrine of Anabaptists and Levellers was a thing to hold no parley with. Similarly in religion they zealously championed freedom from tradition and priestly control in the interpretation of dogma, but only to insist upon subservience to the dogma itself with more pitiless ferocity. Mariolatry was to be superseded by Bibliolatry, slavery to Pope and Church by slavery to the **Authorised Version**. Again, the new movement had no words strong enough to condemn the special religious life of the old religious orders, with its asceticism, but it was only to bring a sordid asceticism into the whole of human life, without distinction. Pleasure itself was an evil, all bodily satisfaction more or less vicious, and to be deprecated even where not positively condemned. Still, whatever our view of them in other respects, the rank and file of the old Puritans must be absolved of the charge of conscious hypocrisy. They really believed in their Bible, and the arid and unlovely dogmas they founded on it. The old genuine and militant Puritanism died before the end of the seventeenth century. Its tradition, however, slumbered on through the earlier part of the eighteenth century, and towards its close it had entered upon re-birth in the movements associated with the names of Whitfield and Wesley. Now the spread of these new Puritan movements was coincident with the rise of the great industry, and the new development of the middle-class consequent thereupon. The latter seized eagerly upon the latest religious revival – which soon found its counterpart in the Established Church – and the cancer of Evangelicalism took root in English society, ramifying in all directions, and gaining strength from the reaction in religious as in political matters succeeding the French Revolution. Without denying a measure of sincerity and enthusiasm in some of its earlier votaries, difficult as it is to see what there was in it to be enthusiastic about, it may be safely said that it soon sank into the festering mass of hypocrisy out of the womb of which has come the " Liberator " as the last-born among many brethren.

The two salient dogmas of Evangelicalism were always Bibliolatry and Sabbatarianism. Family prayers and punctilious church-going followed as a matter of course. The essential dogmatic structure was the old Catholic theology, as somewhat clumsily pruned and awkwardly innovated upon by the reformers of the sixteenth Century.[1] Again, while the hierarchical order of beings, which the mediaeval theology took over from the pseudo-Dionysius, and he again from the last of the Pagans, Proklos, was got rid of; the quasi-neo-platonic dogma of the Trinity was still retained. Prayers to saints, and prayers for the dead, were abandoned as superstitious forms; but the belief in prayers as in some way or other altering the course of things, provided the alteration was like the illegitimate baby of fiction "only a little one", was strenuously held to. Purgatory was thrown overboard, but Hell was retained. Miracles, i.e., great and palpable violations of natural law, were pronounced by the fiat of the Evangelical mind to have ceased. But, of course, to doubt the Biblical miracles, so long back in the past, was impious. All this arbitrary tangle of illogical positions it was the duty of the British "Evangelical" to hold intact, at once against the more logical Catholic theology, and against the inroads of modern science and criticism. The condemnation of Catholicism as superstitious by orthodox Protestants is exceedingly naive all round. The Protestant condemns the reverence paid by the Catholic to the pyx or to relics, but the Protestant finds so much sanctity in the brick and mortar of his churches that it would shock him to use them for everyday purposes as the Catholic churches of the Middle Ages commonly were.

But there was another side to Evangelicalism, also derived from Puritanism – *viz.*, its practical side. This consisted in the carrying out of an ascetic life. Theatres, dancing, card-playing, the pursuit of every amusement beyond a very limited point were forbidden to the man "converted" to Evangelicalism, who must devote the whole of his time to two objects – making money (called "attending to business"), and saving his own and other people's souls. If it was forbidden to do many things on week-days, it was forbidden virtually to do anything on Sundays. Many regarded even the exertion of the legs in walking as a breach of the Sabbath. Certainly a peal of laughter was unsuited to the character of the day. Altogether the God of the Evangelical seemed to find a singular amusement in watching his creatures boring themselves. There was a fourth aspect of Evangelicalism, and that was philanthropy. Philanthropy was a kind of adjunct to the soul-saving. Evangelicalism as the ideological expression of the English bourgeois Philistine was up to the tricks of its trade. Philanthropy was a plausible cloak for proselytism. As a matter of fact, it is certain the English middle classes gained more in the end by their proselytism than they lost by their charitable donations. For the indigent man who became "a new creature", and received the "gospel" tidings at the hands of the city missionary, the district visitor, or the charitable society, backed by a more substantial somewhat, was understood from that moment to abrogate his independent class interests and instincts as one of the proletariat, and to become a humble retainer of the middle class in his new character of "Christian man". Henceforth no more going out on strike, no more militant trade unionism, no more class-struggle! Although it is true Evangelicalism may never have made many converts among the organised working classes, there is no doubt the general influence of Evangelicalism was strong in retarding the class-struggle at certain stages.

In accordance with the class-influence it represented, it played its part in distracting attention from the economic situation, and its character of a "red herring" was indeed hardly concealed. For the Evangelical, with all his ostentation of charity and sympathy for the poor, became ferocity itself when it was a question of the working classes bettering themselves at the expense of the capitalist class, to which he belonged. The attitude of the various religious bodies to Chartism, and even the earlier trade-union movement, is a sufficient illustration of this. What really *in foro conscientiae* underlay the Evangelical horror of Infidelity often came out in the course of discussion. "If men all turned infidels, what would become of society, where would be the security for property?" It was the same spirit which led the **Times** reviewer of the **Descent of Man**, in 1871, to admonish Charles Darwin of his grievous responsibility for putting forward such doctrines when the outcome of irreligious teachings was being shown in the subversive aims of the Paris Commune. It was the same spirit which has made the statesman everywhere welcome religion as an ally. The only difference is that the Britisher has a special relish for hypocrisy. He regularly enjoys it as a sweet morsel. Other nations take their hypocrisy more or less sadly, as a conventional lie of civilisation, get it over as quickly as possible, like a black draught, and say little about it. The Anglo-Saxon chews it, and gets the full flavor out of it. Hence the Anglo-Saxon race alone in the nineteenth century has produced an Evangelical party. (I need scarcely remind the reader) that the German word "Evangelisch" does not connote the same thing as the English "Evangelical".)

How far the "Evangelical" of a generation ago was a sincere fanatic, and how far he was a conscious imposter, with his zeal against Catholicism and his unctuous horror of Atheism, it is difficult to determine. Probably he was in this respect like the rain-maker of the savage tribe, who is alleged to be at once dupe and cheat. Hypocrisy had been so part of his education from his cradle, that he perhaps succeeded in persuading himself that he believed in the dogmatic sweepings which formed his stock in trade, and that his moral sense was so blunted by custom as not to revolt against them. Did he or she, for example, really believe that *sotto voce* mutterings called prayers really affected the course of nature? This is a difficult question to answer. Be this, however, as it may, the exigencies of society as understood by the dominant class of the century required some religion, and it was obviously desirable that that religion should be the one selected by that class as best adapted to its nature and objects. This meant that Evangelical Protestantism had to be jealously maintained against "Popery" and "Infidelity". For "Popery" implied subservience to an absolute head, and a foreigner at that; it implied the abrogation of the individual before a corporate entity, the Church, notions which stirred up the chauvinist and individualist bile of the great commercial class. Then again the amount of time allotted by "Popery" to devotion, the setting aside of a large portion of the community in a religious life where they consumed but did not produce wealth; the holidays and feast days when the work of the world stood still, all this was eminently unsuited to the *regime* of competition, *laissez faire*, and the new middle class.

Accordingly Catholicism was scathingly denounced as the "scarlet whore", and a keen scent was kept up for "Papistic" tendencies. Beauty in churches and art in services were banished, and the uglier these things were the more evangelical did they become. The Evangelical parent and teacher had the brazen impudence, moreover, to paint the mediaeval church black to the rising generation for its persecution of Galileo, when with the next breath they were themselves denouncing Darwin or the geologists, and to hear them one would have thought they only stopped at the stake for lack of power. They well knew that the Inquisitors of the sixteenth century were merely anathematising a doctrine contrary to the "Bible". Of course, the Evangelical declared it not at all contrary to the Bible – after it was useless to deny it longer – just as his descendant has now found out that "Darwinism" is perfectly consonant with that very accommodating body of writings. But the fact remains that the Inquisitors were only doing what they themselves were doing when they placed the **Origin of Species** on *their* Index, or tried to hunt Dr. Colenso down. The latter, we may remind the reader, a simple-minded, earnest man, who was not in the "swim" of his trade, was sent out to Natal as the ordinary Evangelical church parson, became convinced on a point of Biblical criticism, and was naive enough to proclaim the fact. The evangelical clericate, backed by its retainers, the religious middle class, determined to leave no stone unturned to destroy the man who was too unworldly to know how to play their game properly, and they only failed after some years through working their cards badly with the ecclesiastical judges. There was an additional incentive to persecution in the fact that Colenso was the first official Englishman whose conscience rose in active revolt against the oppression of native races, and hence he was by no means a *persona grata* to the religious and philanthropic speculator with a little spare capital locked up in South Africa, who wanted missionaries of another kidney. The economic basis of Evangelicalism is nowhere more plainly shown than in its foreign missions, those preliminary canters for the purpose of surveying new markets for the reception of the cheap cottons and other delectable products of the deacon's or church-warden's factory.

The defence of Evangelical dogma took the three forms of *suppressio veri*, something more than the *suggestio falsi*, and of *personal scurrility*. The *suppressio veri* was sedulously cultivated by the Evangelical parent or instructor of youth in the teaching not merely of history and opinion, but even of such a subject as physical geography. To take one trifling example. It is now generally recognised that one of the few successful hits of the old Biblical school of Paulus, technically known as the "rationalistic" school, was in indicating the reference to well-known natural phenomena in certain of the narratives in Exodus. Now it might have been too much to expect that this should have been pointed out in the course of Biblical instruction, but it was surely hardly too much to expect that in the ordinary course of physical geographical instruction the fact might have been mentioned (without comment, of course) that under the influence of strong East winds the Red Sea becomes fordable at certain times, the waters being, as it were, cut in two by the force of the gale; that the serpent and stick trick is a of the repertory of every modern Egyptian juggler; that the red appearance, resembling blood, of the Nile and Its tributaries at certain times is a natural phenomenon, familiar to travellers, and so on with the rest. Yet it would have gone badly with the teacher who had dared to state facts to his pupils, the inference from which was so obviously "agin' Scriptur'." For the Evangelical parent and guardian was a strict disciplinarian these matters. A semi-conscious hypocrite himself, his object was to train a race of as far as possible unconscious hypocrites.

The *suggestio falsi* took protean forms. One of the favorite ones was manipulating geological facts so as to square with Genesis. It seems almost incredible now-a-days that men at that time, of a certain scientific standing, did not disdain to prostitute their pens and their names to this vile and contemptible "pious fraud"'. Recent discoveries in oriental archeology were impudently "adapted" not to clash with the "Bible". The results of foreign scholarship in Biblical research were of course ignored. But the great *coup* in the name of "bluff" was over the Sabbatarian dogma. Here it was the practice to represent to ingenuous youth that Sabbatarianism was a fundamental article of Christian faith, not only concealing the fact that it has never existed outside the races inhabiting the British islands and their colonies, and that even there it has been but a growth of two hundred years standing, but averring at the same time that all those who refused to abase themselves before it (e.g., the entire body of non-Anglo-Saxon Christians, Protestant no less than Catholic) were worse than "Infidels". For Sabbatarianism was no mere matter of opinion, it was a vital point in the Evangelicals' system. So much was this the case that among the stock of pious lies by which it was sought to strike terror into the heart of the "godless", and which the not very fertile evangelical imagination worked up again and again in the form of tracts, the case of the boy who went out on the river on a Sunday, and either got drowned for doing it or else ended with murder, played a very large part.

Scurrility was the third means by which it was sought to damage the opponents of the precious "gospel" which the Evangelical professed it his mission to proclaim. That all "infidels" were counted wicked men goes without saying; and as one cannot expect scrupulous integrity from the upholders of any system of arbitrary dogma, it is perhaps hardly fair to be too severe on our Evangelical for this. But the elaborate and very excogitated lies which were invented to damage particular reputations were really a little strong even for religious men and theologians. One noteworthy case of this was the vilification of Thomas Paine, who was represented as a drunken, swearing monster, with every shade of coloring a malicious imagination could suggest. Of course those who made the assertion knew well enough that it was a direct lie, and that it had been refuted. But it was good enough to serve their purpose, since at that time no one dared to defend the character of a well-known "infidel", ands no "respectable" publisher would then have ventured to publish any statement anent such a one that was not scurrilous. Thus it came that a poor man who had written a somewhat crude essay suggesting in mild language a reconsideration of certain current theological tenets, and whose worst offence was voting for the life of Louis XVI in the French Convention, at the risk of his own, labored under a libellous and false imputation for well-nigh a century. The late Mr. Bradlaugh was similarly vilified by the whole religious middle-class until they found out he was an anti-Socialist.

Now such has been the history of the Evangelical party up to less than a generation ago – lying, hypocrisy, calumny, and social ostracism were the only weapons known to this band of successful counter jumpers, cheesemongers, *et id genus omne*, turned theologians, who terrorised the whole intellectual and social life of the English-speaking race. It may possibly be alleged that even in suggesting at any measure of conscious fraud on the part of the zealots of Evangelicalism have been unjust to honest bigotry. But I ask the charitable soul who thinks thus to remember that the men who were loudest in denouncing the exponents of (evangelically-speaking) inconvenient truths, were shrewd men of business, men keen enough to detect the smallest point which told in favor of or against their interests in a worldly point of view, but who yet fought to the knife the most obvious scientific facts or critical commonplaces which seemed to jeopardise the dogmas they regarded as essential to their interests, and were prepared to maintain or to accept the most childishly transparent fallacies in favor of those dogmas. Does anyone affirm that these individuals would have taken a cheque, a bill, or any negotiable instrument on a week-day, on the strength of such evidence as to solvency of the parties to it, as was sufficient to convince (?) them, let us say, of the Mosaic authorship of the Pentateuch, or of the consonance of the facts of geology with the Hebrew cosmogony, or of the practical utility of prayer on a

Sunday? No, the plea for complete honesty is too thin. For these things involved no subtle points of metaphysics, but the mere ordinary science and commonsense Philistine.

I have spoken throughout this paper of Evangelicalism and Evangelicals in the past tense, as I did not wish to lay myself open to the charge of accusing the modern world of orthodox Protestantism of views and practices which it may be said are no longer obtaining among them. But I have not the least doubt that there are still existing religious circles to which the above remarks will fully apply. And even those who are prepared to explain away or modify the more flagrantly immoral or irrational dogmas of the old "gospel" still maintain without shame the tradition of their disreputable past. The tendency, however, is not to be denied for the sects to lie low as to theology and to turn on the "moral" tap. Finding theology very much at a discount all round, Nonconformity plays out its last card – its conscience. "Out of the eater came forth meat." Out of the Nonconformist conscience came the Liberator Building Society. "Orlando in the old chains!" The old hypocrisy still! Board-meetings opened by prayer. Veritably that prayer was answered! Veritably was the "Liberator" a Nemesis for the small British middle-class that battens on chapels and cant! Hoist they were worthily with their own petard! They wanted piety in the capitalist syndicate to whom they entrusted their savings – and they got it. "Vous l'avez voulu, Georges Dandin!" May all those who entrust the products of their parsimony to boards of directors who open their meetings with prayer fare similarly!

Let us remember that this class in placing their savings with the "Liberator" were only carrying out the principle which a generation ago would boycott men who did not bow to their shibboleth, would make it impossible for a man who labored under the suspicion of religious heterodoxy to earn his living in any provincial town in Britain, and would harry those who did not frequent one of their "places of worship" till they found themselves driven to choose between moral dishonesty and social ruin. The latter was the Evangelical substitute for the stake.

For the rest, as above said, the Nonconformist conscience to-day occupies itself largely in the attempt to maintain intact and keep alive enthusiasm for the conventional class-morality of the bourgeois system. This morality is a compound of the old Christian or Puritan individualist asceticism, and the exigencies of an economically-individualist state of society. But the Nonconformist conscience pretends to find in it the power of God and the wisdom of God to all eternity. Sexual abstinence, euphemistically called "social purity", is its great *piece de resistance*. In the present social and legal restrictions to the formation of free unions between the sexes, which are based on the natural but perfectly prosaic desire of the ratepayer not to be saddled with the maintenance of his neighbours' children, it pretends to see absolute moral laws, irrespective of social and economic circumstances. But even apart from this, any breach of the conventional ethics of middle-class society is sure of the reprobation of their specially constituted guardian, the "Non-conformist conscience" – whose methods are spying, eavesdropping, and other edifying practices of the amateur detective. It would seek to avert the abuse of any particular thing by forcibly suppressing its use. Thus it has no idea of getting rid of the evils of drink by opening up the Sunday, the only rest-day for the masses, to higher means of recreation; it has no idea of mitigating the present evil effects of cheap alcohol by enacting and enforcing laws against adulteration. Oh dear, no; it would do as it has done in the United States, suppress all consumption of alcohol by force of law! In fine, the Nonconformist conscience remains like its forbears, the eternal quintessence of the hypocritical type of bourgeois philistinism.[2] Always bitterly opposed to liberty for others, it has known how to whine loud enough when its own liberties have been infringed by some equally bigoted High Church vicar, with whom, *bien entendu,* it has been only too willing to join hands to oppress the Freethinker. To the latter it was, until recently, if possible, more merciless than

112

any Roman or Anglican Sacerdotalist.

Such is the pedigree of that "Nonconformist conscience" which now arrogates to itself to dictate the character and general walk and conversation of every man holding a public position, and as far as possible the whole public policy of the country. These be your gods, O middle-class Englishmen!

Footnotes

1. The pretence that the traditional orthodox dogmas of Protestantism had their justification in the theory that the Hebrew Scriptures and the New Testament were the ultimate courts of appeal, is almost too thin to be worth noticing. Of course, the "Evangelical" and Protestant generally read *into* the Bible all that he wanted to find there, and read *out* of it all that he did not want. For instance, the Trinitarian dogma and the incarnation are not to be found in the Bible, yet he professes to discover them there. Again, Sabbatarianism is precisely one of the Jewish religious rites (about the only one) which the founder of Christianity, is reported as having expressly abrogated. Yet this has not hindered the English Evangelical from attempting its tyrannical enforcement on the *wrong* day!! On the other hand ancient astronomical theories not consonant with modern science, and quaint survivals of early sexual morality, equally inconsistent with the *morale bourgeoise* in such matters, are conveniently passed by, or explained away

2. There are two prominent types of British bourgeois Philistinism, the one embodied in the "religious world", the hypocritical type: and the other embodied in the "sporting world", the blatantly coarse type.

The Economic Conception of Value

The conception of Value has always been regarded as the corner-stone of economic science. By Value in economics is meant the common measure or standard regulating the exchange of commodities. It is our purpose to-night to confine ourselves exclusively to the discussion of the theory of Value as a fundamental principle of economics, without entering into its applications, which may naturally be made to range over the whole ground of political economy. The first sense of the word "Value" sense not peculiar to economics, is what is called "Use-Value." Value in-use, or utility, denotes the pleasure derived from, or the pain or discomfort obviated by, the use of any article. As just said, this may or may not be a conception entering into economic science; thus we have the familiar illustration of "air" as affording an instance of a Use-Value which is extra-economic, that is to say which is outside the scope of the science dealing with the production and circulation of wealth. The conception of Value, which, on the other hand, belongs exclusively and specifically to the science of political economy, is that of Exchange-Value. Use-Value may exist in an object considered by itself, but Exchange-Value presupposes a relation between Use-Values as commodities, or between their equivalents.

In the simplest form of Exchange-Value, or barter, the Value of a given commodity is expressed in the substance of another commodity. In this primary phase of Exchange-Value, quantity and quality are undifferentiated; in the second or more advanced phase, the given commodity is placed over against the whole world of commodities remaining, i.e., which are not the commodity itself. Homer, for example, expresses the Value of an object by enumerating a long string of other objects. In the seventh book of the **Iliad**, wine is mentioned as exchanged for brass, iron, cattle, slaves, skins of beasts, and other things. Here we may see the beginnings of the differentiation of quantity and quality in Exchange-Value. The Value of the wine is conceived as expressed in a number of things of different qualities, so that quality can no longer determine the general expression. The element in which it can be expressed must be, therefore, something considered quantitatively.

At a later stage still, the Value of all commodities is expressed no longer in all other commodities, but in one specific commodity, as their equivalent, which in the course of time becomes gold or silver. This is the transition to the complete expression of Exchange-Value in *coined money*, or as *price*. In this final, or completed form, the Exchange-Value of all commodities, or Use-Values created for exchange, is expressed in a *tertium quid*, which has practically no Use-Value in itself, but which becomes, by convention, the recognised equivalent of all exchangeable Use-Values or commodities.

Now, it is evident that the specific utilities being eliminated in the process of exchange, and the Value being expressed in terms of quantity, it must be a *quantum* of something, and the question remains, what common element do all these qualitatively-different exchangeable Use-Values contain? A thing is not constituted a commodity by mere Use-Value itself, as witness the case of "air," alluded to already. The obvious answer is that the only common element contained in all these exchangeable Use-Values, in other words, in all commodities, is that of expended human labour. They represent, as Marx expresses it, "congealed human labour." Hence the only measure of their exchangeability is the *quantum* of this human labour contained in them, which can obviously be determined only on a time basis, i.e., by the average amount of average labour which in a given society is expended within a given time. To constitute an object, a commodity, or an economic thing, in the strict sense of the word, there must be a synthesis of human labour and Use-Value. Either element taken by itself is, viewed from the standpoint of economics, an abstraction. Use-Value that does not embody labour in its procurement has no Economic-

Value. On the other hand, labour, to become the measure of Value, must be embodied in an object which has a social utility. The synthesis of these two elements issue in Exchange-Value, which, in its most perfect expression, constitutes Economic-Value in the concrete, or (as realised in the world of the production and distribution of wealth which we see around us), its *price*.

To sum up this argument, the concept Value as used in political economy may be viewed under three aspects. It is a synthesis of three elements. We have first that primary element which all Economic-Value presupposes at all times and places, either actually or ideally, namely, a determinate *quantum* of human labour. This we may call Economic-Value in the abstract. Secondly, it is not enough to have an article merely embodying human labour, but of no use to any one, for that article *must supply a social want*. Thus the simple embodiment of labour, taken *per se*, and the simple Use-Value, taken *per se*, are *quoad* the subject-matter of political economy, that is the actual world of production and exchange, pure abstractions. But their synthesis supplies us with the unit of economic reality – the commodity. Use-Value merely concerns quality, whereas, Value *per se*, that is embodied human labour, possesses economically nothing but *quantitative* difference. We have finally the concrete expression of Value, that is to say, the Value of a commodity against the whole world of commodities, itself excepted. This latter, in its developed or completed form, is represented by a universal equivalent, *money*, and is called its *price*. This conventional representative of Exchange-Value, coined money, has no utility in itself, and is merely the embodiment of a determinate amount of human labour. That gold and silver should have been chosen by social selection to serve the purpose of the universal equivalent is owing to more than one cause. First and foremost, because the relatively great amount of labour required to procure them makes a small portion serve the purpose in view. Secondly, because they can be melted and re-coined, while precious stones, which would answer equally well to the first condition (that of portability), cannot be so treated. In other words, they embody a proportionately greater amount of labour, as regards commodities in general, than other articles that have also been used at different times and places as the universal equivalent, as, for example, cattle (*pecus*), iron, possibly salt, and other things, which, owing to their bulk, are inconvenient.

In the same ratio in which the transformation of labour into commodities is accomplished, the commodities are transformed into money. Hence the proper Value of money is, like that of any other commodity, the amount of labour embodied in it. Old Sir William Petty saw this point as he saw many others, and well expressed it in his **Treatise on Taxes and Contributions**, published in 1667. He there says:

"If a man can bring to London an ounce of silver out of the earth in Peru, in the same time that he can produce a bushel of corn, then the one is the price of the other; now, if by reason of new and more easy mines a man can procure two ounces of silver as easily as he formerly did one, the corn will be as cheap at ten shillings the bushel as it was before at five shillings, *caeteris paribus*."

I may observe in this connection, that the point that currency cranks have invariably forgotten, from Law downwards, is that precious metals embody a determinate amount of human labour like every other commodity, and that it is only by virtue of this that they can serve in the long run as the material for instruments of exchange. As Marx says:

"The money-crystal is a necessary product of the process of exchange, wherein various products of labour are actually equated with each other, and hence are actually transformed into commodities. The historical breadth and depth of exchange develops the opposition of Value and Use-Value, which opposition slumbers in the nature of commodities. The necessity of representing this opposition in a tangible shape, for the purposes of trade, forces on to an independent form of Commodity-Value, which does not rest until it finally reaches the doubling of the commodity into commodity and money." (**Das Kapital**, vol.i. p.65.)

We must always bear in mind that, in the concrete, i.e., in any given case of exchange, the Standard of Value, namely, the equation between the *quanta* of human labour embodied in the commodities, is liable to be disturbed by accidental circumstances which are foreign to economic science proper, and which it is pure quackery to attempt to include therein. But this, of course, does not invalidate the accuracy of the principle, any more than the definitions of geometrical figures – circles, straight lines, points, angles – are invalidated by the fact that such ideally perfect figures are not to be found in nature, and hence, viewed from the standpoint of common sense, might be called inaccurate. The geometrical line or circle may not exist in nature, but geometrical figures constitute nevertheless the standard or norm in the configurations of matter.

The immediate fact that generally strikes one most prominently in any given phenomenon of exchange as that which directly determines the Exchange-Value, or the price of a particular commodity, is the relative amount of the desire for possession on the part of the buyer and his power at the moment of acquiring the article in question. In other words, the relation between supply and demand is the element which seems to determine the price of the article. Monopoly-price, that is to say, the power of exchange inherent in those commodities absolutely limited in number or amount, seems to some persons to be the central principle of Value altogether. Accordingly we have a school of economists which, basing its Theory of Value upon

119

"supply and demand," would deduce all Value from what it terms "final utility," that is, the relative quantity of utility embodied in different commodities, abstraction being made from their specific quality. This point is so plausible that it demands a little consideration. It is quite clear that "final utility," that is, the last article that comes into the market, may for the moment acquire an increased price owing to the special circumstances of the case. De Quincey's illustration of the musical-box in the backwoods of America is a good instance. But this is a matter which is altogether extra-economic. The price given for the musical-box would vary with each individual. If two individuals equally desired it, the price would of course be higher. But this does not affect the intrinsic Value of the musical-box, irrespective of the circumstances mentioned. Apart from the latter, its Value will be always approximately determined by the amount of labour embodied in it.

The same applies to what we may term "unique Values," a Stradivarius, a Raphael, a Caxton, a skeleton of a dodo, a great auk's egg. But these are things which are outside economics, as it is assumed that no possible amount of human labour could reproduce them. They are not like simply rare things, as, for instance, diamonds, which can always be procured by the expenditure of an amount of labour, considerable it may be, but yet on the average ascertainable. These "unique Values," on the contrary, have a fancy price bearing no relation to the amount of labour originally embodied in them, but depending entirely upon the psychological peculiarities of the buyer. Anyone may see this illustrated by consulting catalogues of the different sale-prices of the same rare book. The price is here regulated by convention, caprice, fashion, and other accidents, altogether incommensurable and irreducible to rule. The mere general and elastic principle of "supply and demand," that the competition for an article raises its price, is the only rule or law under which such cases can be brought, and this is so, precisely because the element of Economic, Value, that is, a definite quantity of labour as embodied in a utility, is eliminated. You have Use-Value and Exchange-Value confronting each other without that regulative element of Economic-Value in the abstract which is necessary to constitute a thing a commodity, in proper sense of the word. The price at a given time and place, and under given circumstances, is obviously variable. It is something extraneous to the commodity itself. This element, then, of "final utility," as it is sometimes termed, is plainly not the element which at once enters into the substance of commodities, and at the same time, determines the degree of their exchange-power all times and places.

"When we have nothing else to wear
But cloth of gold and satins rare
For cloth of gold we cease to care
Up goes the price of shoddy"

But though the relative exchange Value of shoddy and of cloth of gold may, under these circumstances be reversed, that reversal will not long continue. It will only obtain until the economic centre of gravity, the relative amount of labour embodied in the cloth of gold and in the shoddy, has had time to re-assert itself. Price is, in short, often adventitious to the commodity *qua* commodity, and may vary indefinitely from day to day, perhaps from mile to mile and from person to person. It is, in other words, in no sense a constitutive attribute of the commodity, but simply its concomitant, an unknown quantity on which we can seldom reckon, unless we have the complete details of an actual case. But this superficial element of "supply and demand" which determines the price at a given time and place is always tending to become extinguished in what may be termed the *natural price* of the commodity, namely, the equivalent in coined money of the amount of labour which it embodies. When supply and demand balance one another, it becomes completely absorbed in the natural price, which is nothing more than the equivalent expression of equal *quanta* of labour. Exchange-Value and Price merely obtain as a relation between commodities, whereas true Economic-Value exists in the commodity *per se*, as the ground-principle of its exchangeability.

There are plenty of instances of things having a price, but a price really extra-economic, as not being reducible to the fundamental laws which regulate the production and exchange of wealth in a commercially free society. For instance, there is the conscience of a candidate for Parliament, which is very often offered for a price, and very often sold for a price. But this transaction obviously lies outside the scope of economics.

The most important example of an object possessing Exchange-Value, as expressed in its adequate form, namely as price, which nevertheless has here no Economic-Value, is land in its natural state. Uncultivated land, though not the embodiment of any human labour, may be bought and sold like a true commodity. The price is acquired by the mere arbitrary act of appropriation. The individual who has the appropriated land in his possession is a monopolist pure and simple. The price he exacts does not represent any Economic value, but it has been arbitrarily imposed from without. Political economy makes abstraction from these temporary and disturbing factors, and assumes a society, commercially free, that is a society free from arbitrary interference with the laws governing the production and distribution of wealth. Now, whatever may be historically the case, it is obvious that the monopoly of land is not a necessary condition of the production or distribution of wealth in the modern, or any, condition of society. While we can assert that, where exchange takes place at all, an hour's labour will not in the long run be exchanged for less than an hour's labour of the same degree, we can see that land may be free or it may be monopolised by individuals. *This does not, of course, alter the fact that when the monopoly of land and its arbitrary treatment as a commodity has been once conceded, the law regulating its rent and price can be dealt by economic science.* On being arbitrarily thrust into the arena of commodities it takes on their colour. The appropriator of uncultivated land or virgin soil says in effect "let it be assumed that this land is a commodity having a Value as though it were a product of human labour"; and thus from being the πρώτ ὕλη the formless matter of things economic out of which the Ἐντελεχεύα of human labour creates values, but without any Economic-Value in itself – it is treated as though it were in itself an embodiment of human labour, and, therefore, as though it had such a Value.

In Economic-Value, the differences of quality in labour are eliminated. The abstract human labour that determines Value is that labour which on an average exists in the capacity of any ordinary individual. "Simple average labour," as Marx says, "varies in character in different countries and at different times, but in a particular society it is given. Skilled labour counts only as simple labour intensified, or rather multiplied, a given quantity of skilled being considered equal to a greater quantity of simple labour. Experience shows that this reduction is constantly being made. A commodity may be the product of the most skilful labour but its value by equating it with the product of simple labour represents a definite quantity of the latter labour alone. The different proportions in which different sorts of labour are reduced to unskilled labour as their standard are established by a social process that goes on behind the backs of the producers and consequently appears to be fixed by custom."

By the economic-labour that constitutes the immanent measure of Value in commodities is to be understood, then, a definite amount of the average labour in a particular community requisite to produce or to procure a given article. If in any individual case the labour should all below this average amount, the article will not be therefore cheaper, and if it should rise above it, the article will not be therefore dearer. A clever workman able to produce some commodity in less time than the ordinary workman will still be able to command the same price as that given for other similar commodities that have taken a longer time and greater labour to produce. On the other hand, a clumsy workman who takes double the time will not, therefore, be able to command double the usual price of the article he produces.

The tendency, however, of the great Machine-Industry of modern times, which is rapidly extending itself over all departments of production, is to actually equate all kinds of labour by reducing them to the average of unskilled labour. The skill required to tend a machine is comparatively slight at most, and approximately the same for one machine as for another. The trend of this modern "great industry" is, therefore, to reduce abstract Value to the sole determinant of price in the real world, by eliminating the possibility of these extra-economic differences of skill, disposition, and other factors already indicated as hitherto modifying the economic principle in its actual manifestations.

Thus it is that the expression of economic categories changes with the changing conditions of society. In primitive tribal society, exchange virtually did not exist. In order that a system of exchange may obtain it is necessary that individuals should be independent holders of property, and this reciprocal independence of the individual did not exist in primitive times. Such exchange as took place at all was between different communities or social groups, not between individuals. As civilisation has advanced, the group (tribe, clan, etc.) has increasingly tended to disappear and individual autonomy to supplant it. But modern industrial and commercial conditions are in their turn tending more and more to break down individual autonomy, and to prepare the way for a form of society in which exchange shall again disappear with its individualistic basis. But this time it must disappear for ever, since there will be no germ of economic individualism, such as was supplied by the exchange between limited groups, which germ, if it existed, might serve as the starting-point for a new development of a similar kind. Civilisation has accomplished its work in the destruction of autonomous groups, and that work is not likely to be undone. We are never likely to revert to the old independent group as a unit. But the autonomy of the individual can no longer maintain itself under the complicated conditions produced by its child, the capitalist system. This system, as we see it to-day, demanding the co-operation of vast bodies of workmen and the delicate adjustment of a highly complex world-market, negates on one side the principle of individualism, and this must completely disappear in a society, which, though the immediate outcome indeed of Capitalism, is yet at the same time a re-affirmation on a higher plane of that principle of Communism whereon the relations of early man were based, and within which neither Exchange nor Exchange-Value had any meaning.

"Voluntarism" versus "Socialism"

That we term human development or historic evolution, implies a progressive movement from the breaking-up of primitive tribal and communal society onwards. This progression – the advance of civilisation as we term it – manifests itself as a development of antitheses which tend to crystallize into pairs of opposites; each member of these claims independence of the other, and becomes embodied in a status or class having interests antagonistic to its opposing status or class. In early tribal society these antitheses did not exist, and even throughout antiquity most of them were more or less latent The one opposition known to the primitive world was that between the social group, whether *gens*, tribe or people, and the alien – that is to say, all humanity outside the particular group in question. It is needless to remind my readers, in a state of primitive communism in which individual or private property was unknown, save, of course, in articles of immediate personal consumption (if by a quibble this can be termed private property), when land and all that was on it belonged to the entire community, there was no question of master and servant, mine and thine. Just as little was there any question of government and governed, ruler and subject. The elders or most experienced members of the community had naturally the preponderating influence in the direction of affairs but there was no *princeps*. Even though he were for the time being chief adviser, no member of the society was more than *Primus inter pares*. Similarly, religion had no sphere of its own, outside and apart from the secular concerns of the society. There was no priesthood, any more than there was a lay power. For ages, even after the birth of civilisation, indeed, strictly speaking, down to the closing period of antiquity, the decadent Roman Empire of the fourth century, the king, *princeps* or *imperator*, was also the chief priest. There was not even any distinction at all for primitive man, or any sharp division for the ancient world generally between the spiritual and the material, between God and the world, between soul and body, between this life and one after death. In short, the period we call history or civilisation in its various stages, has meant the splitting up of the cohesive and uniform fabric of the first phase of human social and intellectual life, into a variety of dualisms, to enumerate all of which would take too long, and would, moreover, be unnecessary for our present purpose. Suffice it to say, all these antagonisms, with their conflicting interests, centre in the cardinal antagonism between Individual and Community.

Now, those persons who, like Mr. Auberon Herbert, view things generally, and especially human life, as made up of hard and fast abstractions, naturally regard the present separation and mutual antagonism between Individual and Community, as a somewhat inherent in the nature of things; unmindful of the teachings of anthropology and history, they regard it as something that "was in the beginning, is now, and ever shall be" so long as human nature lasts. In fact, to read Mr. Herbert's recent contribution to this magazine, would almost lead one to suppose that, like Rip Van Winkle, he had been asleep for a generation, and was, hence, excusably ignorant of what have become the common-places of the historical student. For myself, as for other socialist thinkers, these two terrible entities in mutual hostility, Individual and Community, are but transient phenomena of our passing civilisation. We do not regard "human nature" (that terrible bogey of certain critics of Socialism) as we see it to-day, no, nor even as we know it during the short span of time covered by the records of authentic history, as a thing absolute and unchangeable. We see the marvellous changes it has undergone, even within the period we call history, while modern research into the conditions of prehistoric life, whether it be based on the indications to be found in early literature or early law and custom, or on the analogy of barbaric societies of the present day, point to infinitely greater changes in the period before the dawn of written records; and we believe the "human nature" developed by modern civilisation, familiar though it be to us all, is no more destined to be permanent than that which has passed away.

The adherent of the Manchester school and Mr. Herbert Spencer" founding on the abstraction above-mentioned, cannot conceive of the State as anything else than as the "evil thing," the enemy of the Individual. It may be a necessary evil and they think it is necessary as a matter of fact for certain purposes which we shall hereafter refer to, but it is an evil all the same as the Frankenstein of personal liberty. Now few advanced political thinkers will care to deny, and least of all Socialists, that the State as at present existing, which has for its primary function the *government of persons* rather than the *administration of things*, easily becomes a serious menace to liberty of every kind. In other words we are all prepared to admit that there *does* exist at the present time a natural hostility between the Individual and the State, in so far as the latter is a governing power; but this hostility, itself an inevitable stage in the development of society, the Socialist can explain. It is for him the necessary concomitant of the institution of private property, of the monopoly of the economic factors of social life, the means of production, distribution, etc., by a class or a certain limited number of persons. He is convinced that the hostility spoken of must cease so soon as the State, or to use a preferable phrase, the directing power of the community, ceases to be something over against the community itself, and becomes once again as it was in early society (though on an infinitely more comprehensive scale), a mere function of the community – exercised no longer by a class in the interests of a class, but by the temporary and revocable delegates of the whole social body.

In his juggles with arithmetic I really am unable to follow Mr. Auberon Herbert. He talks a great deal about three men owning two men, and two men not owning themselves. This is beyond me. As Hamlet says, "I am ill at these numbers." "Men either own themselves or they do not," says Mr. Auberon Herbert.

Here we have a beautiful exemplification of what I may term the abstract metaphysical style of argument. I deny both propositions, or rather I deny their mutual exclusiveness. I cannot accept as true unreservedly the thesis that a man owns himself, and just as little that he does not own himself. Every man is a product of the society into which he is born, and of an indefinite series of social formations which have preceded that society. Without society he would not be. Without society, being, he would not continue to be. Hence while admitting as a truism that a man owns himself as against any other man, or any other definite group of men, I can in no sense admit the absolute ownership of himself by a man as against society as a whole. The logical outcome of the attitude taken up by our Individualist champion is to be found in the clever paradox contained in Max Heinze's **Das Einzige und sein Eigenthum**. Mr. Herbert probably does not go as far as this, but his not doing so, starting from the dogma, that men own themselves (absolutely and unconditionally), surely suggests the absence either of moral courage or logical faculty. I would merely point out that on this principle the assumption of any sort of moral obligation is purely arbitrary, since all moral obligation pre-supposes its contrary.

Our Voluntaryist like all his *bourgeois* congeners wants to maintain government for the purpose of guaranteeing the continuance of the institution of private property as at present existing. Hence the thoroughgoing logicality of the Anarchist is distasteful to him. The Anarchist with all his muddle-headedness at least sees the truth with which Socialism is concerned, to wit, that the modern conditions of production and distribution that is, the institution of private property in the means of production, is itself the root and source of the coercion of the individual. To this therefore no less than the Socialist he applies his destructive criticism. The Voluntaryist, the Spencerite, Herbertite, or by whatever other name he may call himself swallows all this in the lump. He begs the whole question as to the justification, historical, economical, or ethical, of the existence in the present day or in the future of the monopoly of productive wealth by a class. He coolly ignores the point urged by the Socialist that this wealth is kept in private hands, is kept from the labourer who produced it, by the monopolist, by dint of coercion, economical, political and other – with the corollary that its justification remains wanting save as a passing historical phase. No. Mr. Auberon Herbert's Individualism is the advocacy of individual liberty for himself and his class. To this end the institution of private property with all its safeguards must be preserved intact, and the Anarchist whose individualism, such as it is, at least aims at being co-extensive with entire society, must be duly condemned.

To speak of the Socialist's leap from nowhere is rather amusing, considering the Mahomet's-coffin-like position of Voluntaryism. If there is a social theory which hangs in mid-air it is surely just this one, cut off on all sides from historic evolution resting on half a dozen neat little abstract saws about men owning themselves or not owning themselves, etc., which possibly have the appearance of the most irrefragable common sense, but which like most similar things that possess this specious quality evince themselves on closer investigation as something very different from what they seem. Socialism on the other hand takes its leap, if we may call it such, not from nowhere, but from that "rock of ages " the sure ground of history. It is at once an induction and a deduction from the facts of human evolution. It sets up no hard and granite-like aphorisms as to what institutions are abstractly right and abstractly wrong; but all its assertions are framed with a view of expressing concrete relations. Hence the Socialist is not taken in as the bourgeois Individualist appears to be by mere external appearances. He does not believe for instance in the liberty of a man to deprive himself of liberty. The liberty he aspires to is not a *formal* liberty which exists in name merely, but a *real* liberty which exists in fact. To take a typical instance of this. Freedom of contract as it is called, appears to be the acme of individual liberty. On the other hand regulation of the conditions

131

of the contract by the State appears contrary to liberty. This case is the one most commonly adduced of the tyrannical action of modern Socialist tendencies. Capitalist advocates can see nothing fairer than that the workman should be able to sell his labour without let or hindrance in the open market. The Socialist sees that the contract in this case, despite its specious *form*, gives no freedom at all to one of the contracting parties, but involves on the contrary the grossest kind of coercion. The Voluntaryist professes to take umbrage at the *form* of coercion involved in the regulation of this coercive contract because it is *direct* and exercised by the community. The Socialist objects to the *real*, though *indirect*, coercion exercised on the workman by the capitalist owing to his monopoly of the means of production. But, says the Voluntaryist, the workman is not obliged to enter on the contract without he desires it. He has the option of not doing so and – starvation or the workhouse!! But no! the Voluntaryist would abolish the poor law and hence the workhouse so that starvation remains as the only alternative. If the Voluntaryist were really consistent he would on the same grounds object to the forcible suppression of highway robbery as it was practised by the gentlemen of the road in the last century. For did not Dick Turpin and Jack Shepherd offer each of their victims the alternative of their money *or* their life? The Capitalist nowadays offers the workman the alternative of his labour or his life. There is freedom of contract in both cases in a sense; but Mr. Auberon Herbert probably does not appreciate it in the one, strongly as he champions it in the other.

The tangle of Mr. Auberon Herbert's sophistry in his lame endeavours to justify on his own principles the existence of the State which he feels bound to defend, in so far as it is necessary to the coercive maintenance of the institution of private property, is amusing. The upshot of the whole is that the State, or as I should prefer to term it, the executive power of the community (which the present state is not, being virtually only that of a section of the community) is to be non-aggressive; i.e., is to defend the individual against aggression from other individuals; but is not to control him in his private and self-regarding actions. "In all matters of liberty," says Mr. Herbert, "in all dealings with his body and mind the individual is supreme." This is the sort of platitudinous mouse, which the mountain of Mr. Herbert's dialetics brings forth as the issue of its labour. Now few Socialists would take exception to this – in a sense at least. Carlyle observes as regards a certain aphorism of physical science "Nothing can act but where it is. With all my heart, only where is it?" Similarly here I say, by all means let the coercive power of the community maintain a non-aggressive attitude as concerns the purely self-regarding action of the individuals. But here is precisely the rub. What actions are we to regard as keeping strictly within the individual sphere without intruding on other individuals? That there are such I do not deny – but I maintain that they are a small and *relatively* unimportant class. (I emphasize the word relatively as I do not wish to under-rate their significance as far as it goes.) But what I do most distinctly deny is that the emphatically *social* functions of *production*, *distribution*, and *exchange*, can in any way whatever be regarded as exclusively concerning the individual.

Whenever these functions are left nominally free, that is, are in the hands of individual caprice, it inevitably means the enslavement of the majority of men by a minority; in other words, the existence of an expropriating class and an expropriated class. The formal freedom of one set of individuals to expropriate and of another set to be expropriated, is a freedom the Socialists would utterly abolish, and would do so in the interest of real freedom. The Voluntaryist worships the formal, or abstract freedom of the individual; the Socialist would sacrifice this in the interests of his real, for concrete freedom. By trotting out this sounding brass and tinkling cymbal of abstract freedom, it is easy to win the applause of a certain number of thoughtless and feather-pated people, but that a thinker should be seriously deceived by it seems well-nigh incredible.

133

I have in the above taken Mr. Auberon Herbert mainly on his own lines, but to perhaps the most crucial fallacy of the whole I have not as yet referred. Emphatically society is not (*pace* Mr. Herbert) the sum of its individual units as is a heap of stones, potatoes, or cannon balls. Society is an *organism* and not an *aggregate*. Mr. Auberon Herbert might just as well talk about the human body as embodying merely the sum of the qualities of the cells of its component tissues as to talk of human society as merely the sum of its individual members. One would have thought that even a perusal of his friend Mr. Herbert Spencer's Principles of Biology would have taught him better than this. Any organised group of persons even, much more society, as a whole, presents characteristics in its nature as such that are by no means reducible to a mere sum of the characteristics of its component units; just as a living animal body is possessed of a nature which although based upon, is by no means identical with the simpler characteristics of the organic substances composing it. For myself, as I have elsewhere pointed out, I believe this consideration is capable of leading us to speculations which throw a new light on the ultimate nature of man's destiny. But with these I am not here concerned; it is sufficient for my present purpose to insist upon the bare fact and pass on.

In reading Mr. Auberon Herbert's confident appeals to reason, one can hardly refrain from exclaiming to oneself, "Oh! reason, reason, what things do they not talk in thy name?" There is a sad tendency in the present day to what I might term the degradation of certain words, to the employment of them as mere question-begging epithets to fling at an opponent's head. Thus it is with the correlates selfish and unselfish, cowardly and courageous. For example, how many a worthy person who has refused to lend some incorrigible "bounder" or sponge an additional ten pound note after repeated experiences, becomes branded by the said "bounder" or sponge as a "selfish man." How often is the man who urges measures of reasonable prudence for his own and the public welfare, branded as a "coward" by those whose interests lie in an opposite direction. Such, for example, has been the cheap weapon with which persons who, preferring their own convenience to public safety, object to dog-muzzling orders. Such a mode of controversy is, in the cases given, obviously contemptible enough, but Mr. Auberon Herbert, though doubtless without intending it, bandies about the words reason and nonsense in a similar manner. We all regard our own position as the one on which reason sheds its light, and our opponents as in the outer darkness of nonsense. Just as each man regards himself as unselfish, and his neighbour, especially if he has had a difference with him, as selfish; or himself as courageous, and the other man whose prudence annoys him, as cowardly. So I would suggest that it is best to avoid altogether the employment in controversy of question-begging epithets of this description, more especially as the persons who employ them so frequently do so in default of better weapons.

Sneers as to the "daily trough," leave our withers utterly unwrung. Socialism is certainly materialistic, in so far as it recognises that the first condition of the higher life of humanity is the soundness of its material basis, that without a full and complete satisfaction of the material wants of life for one and all, in other words, without economic equality, the pretence to "higher life" is no better than an impudent hypocrisy. Herein, Socialism differs from all the great ethical religions which have arisen during the historical period – from Christianity as much as from any other. These have one and all attempted to solve the great problem of human life and destiny, with ("not to speak it profanely"), juggling performances on the part of the individual soul, despising the "daily trough" and such like things. As Mr. Auberon Herbert very well puts it for example with Christianity: "the soul of each individual was to be the true battlefield between right and wrong; and in the soul, not in the external ordering of circumstances, was the Kingdom of God to be established. Socialism is the very antichrist, in spirit, to the teachings of the gospels, and no superficial resemblance as regards arrangements affecting property which a part of the early church made, can alter the essential differences." With the clap-trap which is sometimes talked in the supposed interest of Socialism, anent the Ananias and Sapphira incident, I have no sympathy whatever. The so-called communism of the earliest Christian church, if it ever existed, was obviously merely a voluntary arrangement to meet temporary needs.

Mr. Auberon Herbert's constructive theory that he calls Voluntaryism and which he gives at the close of his second article, scarcely needs detailed criticism from the standpoint of the present writer, after taking under review his criticism of Socialism. One is struck however with the convenient way in which he glides over certain points. For example, we are told, that two individuals under Voluntaryist conditions, are to be allowed "to settle their disputes in their own fashion;" but it does not appear what is to happen if one of the parties wishes to invoke the arbitration of the State, and the other steadily refuses to submit himself to such a vile coercive power. Would the State in this case renounce its function of enforcing contract or not? Upon this – to the Voluntaryist very important point – Mr. Auberon Herbert fails to afford us any information. Under Socialism when the institution of private property lapsed the coercive power of the State in dispute between individuals would lapse also, at least in so far as these were of a civil nature; but under Voluntaryism, where the institution of private property is to be maintained intact, it is difficult to see how the State can solve the problem of acting and not acting at the same time. Mr. Auberon Herbert tell us that the State would protect the individual whether he were a tax-paying member or not. But what would it do with the aggressive individual who is not a member? The aforesaid aggressive person, who let us suppose has forcibly deprived another Voluntaryist of his watch, might easily assert that in doing so he was merely restoring to himself property which had originally belonged to him, and that hence his action was purely defensive. Where the State interferes, such an allegation can be tested, but does any Voluntaryist suppose that our aggressor knowing himself in the wrong, would allow himself to be voluntarily drawn into the meshes of the Central Criminal Court on the principle of "Come into my parlour said the spider to the fly?" Here again we have no enlightenment as to who is to be the final arbiter as to whether the State shall be allowed to arbitrate or not. No; Socialism we know, and Anarchism we know, but Voluntaryism what are you?

The flowery peroration into which Mr. Auberon Herbert launches out contains a great deal which I can recognise as an attempted picture of a Socialist society in certain of its aspects; but on one based like Voluntaryism, on the existence of classes of propertied and propertyless, on a State which with all its limitations still implies the coercion of men, and not like the organised power of a Socialistic community, the administration of things, I fail to see any possibility of its realization. The economic impossibilities – those involved in production and distribution – of the scheme under consideration I refrain from dealing with. They are too obvious, and to attempt to set forth their nature would lead us into a labyrinth far beyond the limits assigned to the present article. The interesting point is, that Mr. Auberon Herbert would appear to be oblivious even of their mere existence. Not only does he make no attempt to afford us any explanation of how the production and distribution of the world is to be carried on under his system; but we find no reference – not so much as a passing reference – to the great economic processes, the aggregation of capital, the growth of machinery, the subdivision of labour, etc., which have given birth to the modern industrial and commercial world, and the further developments of which are again transforming that world under our very eyes. With the utmost *naiveté* he quietly ignores the exigencies of this modern world even as they now are, not to speak of the developments which are immanent in them.

What then is the sum and substance of Mr. Auberon Herbert's contention? On what is his whole argumentation based?

As we said at first it is based on the antithesis Individual and Community, the two terms converted into hard and fast abstractions. Beyond the limits of this antithesis Mr. Herbert cannot see. It dominates the whole of his intellectual horizon. The entire attitude taken up with its cut-and-dried formula and its hard inflexible categories, irresistibly impresses us with the fact that Mr. Auberon Herbert is an intellectual survival from the thought of the earlier part of the century, when propositions were set up and their validity assumed without criticism, and when the historical method and the idea of evolution in all branches of investigation were yet in their infancy. In short, Mr. Auberon Herbert belongs to the school of the Utopists. He thinks that society can be reconstructed at will on a preconceived cut-and-dried pattern. Modern Socialism is of course the very antithesis of this. It is based upon the principle that Social Systems are not made but grow. It claims, nevertheless, that the collective ownership and regulation of the means and instruments of production, distribution and exchange in the interests of all, will inaugurate a new period in the world's history in which the antagonism between Individual and Community, together with the other embodied antagonisms of civilisation shall have lost all meaning. For this reason, therefore, in Socialism alone is to be found the true Individualism – not indeed the sham, formal Individualism put forward by the theory of Voluntaryists, but a real freedom of individual development for each and all alike – as opposed to one designed merely for a propertied class. Under the Capitalist System where can we find Individuality? The character of the slave, of the economically unfree, is dwarfed and stunted where it is not destroyed. The character of those whose economic position enables them to defy circumstances is also warped. To-day we have classes but we have no true humanity. Where the liberty of becoming slave driver and becoming slave is abolished, true liberty and true individuality will emerge. True individual liberty, as Socialists maintain, is inseparable from true equality of opportunity, for all individuals. Only when men are freed from the pressure of economic necessity by Socialism – when *some* have ceased to *possess* but *all* are free to *use* – will individual liberty properly speaking begin. But so soon as this state of things is realised the, present antagonism between Individual and Community, with all the clashing interests it involves, will have disappeared for ever.

Criticism and Hypercriticism

Every social formation is concrete, that is, whilst it has its own material basis, it has also its own special world-view, its own ethical conceptions, its own political constructions, even its own aesthetic atmosphere, severally interpenetrated by the common life of the whole formation. This will be conceded by students of history generally. The most superficial view will show, for example, that tribal society in its various phases from the lower to the higher barbarism bears one general impress. The modifications which this society shows at different stages, together with local variations, are not sufficient to destroy the unity of its main features. Again let us take the period of civilisation, into which ancient tribal society developed in Western Asia and Egypt, and later in South-eastern Europe. Here, also, from the earliest beginnings of that civilisation or class-society, which we designate by the term "antiquity," we find not merely an economic organisation based on slavery with its corresponding political superstructure, but also a special conception of the universe, based on an organised system of ancestor-worship and animism, developing into definite polytheism, rooted in beliefs and world-theories ultimately derived from primitive man. In the civilisation that later on in the ancient world became dominant, the classical civilisation of Greece, and finally of Rome, substantially the same basis was present, but modified. Production was carried on mainly by a slave class. Organised polytheism still represented the speculative basis for the mass of men. Antiquity, therefore, was cut out of one block, notwithstanding the modifications it underwent during its second period. Leaving out of consideration the era of transition, the Middle Ages disclose a complete and concrete polity grounded economically on villeinage, and supplemented later by the guild-industry of the towns. Its political life is dominated by the notion of Emperor and Pope. Its speculative conceptions are

141

enclosed within the framework of the old Catholic theology, the latter developed out of the speculative syncretism of the dying ancient-world (Proklos, pseudo-Dyonisios, etc.) The period of modern Capitalism based on so-called free labour and machine-industry, has for its political side Constitutionalism, and for its speculative basis the crude interpretation of the facts of modern science with a nominal adhesion to Christian dogma.

Now, to the student the question must often arise as to the evolution of thought and practice that may be expected in coming ages. In order to obtain a world-view at all of the future, certain fundamental world-problems need to be discussed in detail. We must examine the philosophical problem in its various forms, the meaning and sanction of moral judgments, the economic structure of society, the supreme canons of life in taste and art, the significance of history, and finally, cast a glance at the ultimate ideals of human consciousness. Such a world-view must aim, that is to say, at extracting a maximum of certainty from the several departments treated, with a view of knitting together the various strands into a whole of knowledge. Thus, though not pretending to anything more than suggestion, it must yet lay claim to be constructive so far as it goes. This is, perhaps, hardly fashionable at the present day, the tendency being to cultivate destructive criticism almost exclusively, save for attempts at reactionary rehabilitations.

It behoves us, therefore, to ask, what, after all, is criticism in its best sense but the analysis of a given subject, or of a doctrine about a given subject, with a view of arriving at consistent thought with regard to it? What is the ultimate meaning of Truth in our view, *but the self-consistency of Thought*? Or, more accurately, *the self-consistency of conscious Experience as interpreted by reflective Thought*? It is needless to say that aesthetic Truth, however, or Beauty, as it is termed, represents the self-consistency of conscious experience as interpreted by pleasure-pain feeling. Now, Criticism is doubtless the first-born of intellectual progress, without which the higher life of mankind would be in a parlous state. The recognition of this fact is apt, however, on occasion to blind the mind to the further fact that Criticism may sometimes suffer from an excess of zeal and overreach itself, even to the point of becoming puerile. Historically, Criticism usually appears as a reaction from Dogmatism. There are various ways in which it may, through the aforesaid excess of zeal, defeat its legitimate function. For example, Criticism often attempts to refute a position by dint of an undue emphasis on one point, or it may run into mere verbal casuistry. But the great fallacy in the inordinate rage of modern culture for Criticism lies in the assumption that a doctrine, if it may justly claim to represent Truth, must necessarily be invulnerable to the negative weapons of Criticism at every point. The assumption that vulnerability to Criticism is a proof of Falsity rests upon the further assumption that the formulation of the Truth of a subject ought to represent a Truth that is final and absolute. This assumption is often made by persons who are keenest in their general repudiation of the claims of the older metaphysics. But if you once concede that any formulation of truth is necessarily relative, it follows that there is no intrinsic reason why any given formulation should not be able to be made to appear incorrect or even absurd from some point of view or other. That it should be obnoxious to criticism in this way certainly does not prove that it does not represent the nearest approximation to the "self-consistency of Experience as interpreted by abstract Thought." It *may* prove that it does not absolutely represent that self-consistency, or it may not even prove as much as that. It may only prove the misapplication of categories in the same way that a physicist or chemist might misapply them, when from the standpoint of his own science he criticises the theories put forward by a biologist within his own domain. But even if it did prove the theory criticised to fall short of representing absolute self-consistency of Experience as interpreted by Thought, this would by no means suffice to prove that it was not the nearest approach to such complete self-consistency as could be obtained under the given conditions, i.e., the given stage of Thought or of investigation, etc. As long as we do not hold the formula of absolute Truth in our hands, so long shall we have to content ourselves with the nearest approximation. Meanwhile, this nearest approximation, since it is only such, and not itself absolute, will be obviously vulnerable to the shafts of any criticism that may seriously set to work to overthrow it, but it is, for all that, none the less true and worthy of all acceptation. It may represent, in other words, the completest self-consistency of conscious experience as interpreted by Thought in the existing stage of the human mind, and therefore is, *quoad* that stage, the Truth. Criticism runs havoc particularly, of course, in Philosophy, where the difficulties of formulation are greater than in any other department, owing to the nature of the subject-matter.

In this connection, it may be observed that the common gibe against any formulation arrived at by philosophic analysis, that it is logomachy – with references to Mephistopheles' remarks to the student – often represents the reverse of the facts. It is the difficulty of finding words to express the very often subtle and delicate thought-distinctions arrived at in philosophic analysis that gives rise to a certain uncouthness of expression suggesting to the casual observer the notion of logomachy. The fact is that human thought in these matters has outstripped the development of speech. Modern languages, not excepting German, have made little advance upon the Greek in this respect.

It may be asked, What, then, is the test between legitimate Criticism and Criticism that is overleaping itself? The answer, I take it, is that all Criticism that as such yields no positive result is at least suspect of being mere casuistry. A positive position can, generally speaking, only be really dislodged by another positive position. The sort of Criticism which issues in mere empty scepticism, that is, in the attempt to show that all known formulations are invalid, but which at the same time does not of itself point the way to any alternative new formulation, may be a clever, brilliant, intellectual exercise, but for the rest is little better than a ploughing of the sands. As regards the problems dealt with by speculative thought, the history of Philosophy is witness to the accuracy of this statement. Yet of such Criticism is not the bulk of recent English philosophical writing made up? For in this connection I do not count the sort of positive result which does not directly issue from the Criticism itself, but which is, as it were, tacked on by the writer's prejudices or predilections. This generally takes the form of some old position long obsolete to serious thinkers, e.g., some particularly crude form of Theism, or mayhap Dualism or Pluralism. The writer brings this in by a species of rather obvious legerdemain at the end of his essay or treatise as the pretended result of what is really a purely negative Criticism. The procedure is a common one, to make a dead critical set at some philosophical formulation which, though it may be doubtless amenable to correction from Criticism, nevertheless represents as a whole the nearest approach to adequacy as yet available. This is done with the object, not of merely correcting the particular formulation in question, but of destroying it altogether. The object of destroying it is to make place for some decadent or obsolete theory infinitely less adequate, to say the least, and also, no necessary result of the previous Criticism. What is known as Parallelism, that is, the doctrine of the physical and psychical as parallel series, each having its principle of causation in itself, has been attacked in this way at the hands of critics anxious for theological reasons to restore the *influx psychicus* in some shape or form. That this involves a cruder standpoint is obvious, and for one inconsistency that Parallelism has to show this has ten. The attack on materialistic Monism often proceeds on the same lines.

To come to Metaphysics proper, here also the Monism led up to by Theory of Knowledge, that is, the investigation into the primary conditions under which Experience is possible, and hence which Experience itself presupposes, is sought to be criticised away in favour of some pluralistic or dualistic theory, which it is supposed will rehabilitate the personality of the individual as an ultimate metaphysical postulate.

Leaving questions of pure philosophy, which to many readers may be of less interest, we find the same remarks as regards the over-zeal of Criticism at the present day, apply in other departments. In the sphere of anthropology and the early history of institutions, this has been very much to the fore in the last ten or fifteen years. For instance, up to then, the fact of primitive society having been uniformly based on the Communism of land and its principal products was generally accepted by competent persons. It is, indeed, only one side of the further fact, that in early or tribal society, and in the earlier modifications evolved from it, the unit was the group and not the individual, the significance of the latter only coming into view as representing the group. The principle of primitive Communism had been recognised as established more than a generation ago by the researches of Conrad von Maurer, Nassau, Laveleve, and others, on the Continent, and in England by Sir Henry Maine. An attempt has been made to whittle down these views in recent years. In this connection, we may refer to the names of the late Fustel de Coulanges of Paris, and Professor Seebohm of Oxford, This is not the place to deal with the question in any detail, but we may briefly mention that Criticism in this particular case seems for the most part to consist in the discovery of inaccuracies in the enormous mass of detail presented by the aforesaid writers. On the basis of such Criticism, the conclusion is eagerly rushed to that the whole fabric of research establishing the existence of primitive Communism has been shattered.

A similar school of writers has taken upon itself the task of undermining the accepted conclusions of a generation past concerning primitive marriage and sexual relations. Bachofen, MacLennan, Teulon, and, above all, Morgan, had convincingly shown that early sexual relations were, like every other relation of primitive society, of a group nature, rather than of a personal nature. It was hardly to be expected that conservative criticism, on recovering from the shock received by the facts disclosed, should not attempt to rehabilitate the orthodox monogamic doctrine, and this is, in fact, precisely what happened. Professor Westermarck, of Helsingfors, and Professor Starcke, of Copenhagen, respectively wrote books with the object of demolishing the scientific results arrived at by the previous investigations. Their arguments are largely based on alleged facts concerning the higher apes. With this question is closely concerned the whole theory of the origin of political life and the beginnings of civilisation.

In the same way in Economics the various refutations of the fundamental position of the English "Classical" Economists, of which the last fifteen years have been full, and which have been eagerly seized upon as effective destructions of the Economic positions of Karl Manx, which are based upon Ricardian theory, afford good illustrations of Criticism overreaching itself in its excess of zeal.

In Ethics the best example of a Hypercriticism that has recently appeared is perhaps to be found in Mr. Taylor's **Problem of Conduct**. Every possible foundation of morals is undermined *in appearance* conclusively by Mr. Taylor without any special result being arrived at.

Again the Darwinian theory has formed a great battle-ground for Hypercriticism. The most serious attempt of this kind is contained in the doctrines put forth by Professor Weissmann. Some few years ago we were constantly hearing that Weissmann had fatally overthrown the principles of organic evolution formulated by Darwin. Since then, however, the whole Weissmann revolution has come practically to be admitted even by its supporters to involve little more than a modification of the rigidity of certain of Darwin's statements. So it is, all along the line. In every branch of thought the present generation shows a feverish eagerness, not merely to correct the details, but to upset the central conclusions of the constructive results arrived at in the preceding generation – results that constitute the second half of the nineteenth century an epoch in the history of human knowledge.

As examples of epoch-making generalisations and discoveries attacked but not destroyed, we may point (1) to the idealistic Monism which constitutes the lasting precipitate left over from the great philosophical movement in Germany from Kant to Hegel and its offshoots; (2) its pendant, the materialistic Monism of modern scientific thought; (3) the doctrine of Evolution itself as hitherto formulated; (4) the special doctrines of Darwin concerning organic development; (5) the recognition of the importance of the materialist, and especially the economic, basis of historic Evolution; and (6) the discovery of Group-Communism as the starting-point of social development. These principles, to which other subordinate ones might easily be added, the hypercritic has nibbled at unremittingly for some time past, and has been continually trumpeting forth the bankruptcy of one or other of them, but in spite of all they remain standing. We are convinced that the day is not far distant when it will be recognised that the task of the immediate future is the reconciliation of these points of vantage with each other, and the welding together of human knowledge by their aid into a unity, rather than the undermining of these positions by the quibbling methods of a hypercriticism, as is the case now.

How, then, after all is said, are we to distinguish between Criticism and Hypercriticism? Hypercriticism, where it is not purely verbal or actually dishonest quibbling, usually takes two forms. It is either an *ignoratio elenchi* or destroys itself by proving too much. In the first case, in nibbling round an established position, it may succeed in weakening or destroying minor evidence or minor contentions that had become attached to the main argument in defence of the position. In the second case, where Hypercriticism issues in mere Scepticism, it writes itself down as futile, pure Scepticism being a state of unstable intellectual equilibrium. The former kind of the hypercritical fallacy is more common in the historical sciences; the latter in philosophy, economics, and ethics – in short, in the higher

148

departments of abstract thought. As regards a generalisation found on scientifically observed data, such as those we are specially referring to, e.g., Darwinism and Group-Communism in primitive society, it must not be forgotten that these doctrines as theories are not in the position of having come down as the offsprings of a semi-conscious or unconscious tradition, or of mere naive observation, but are themselves the issue of the *conscious investigation, criticism, and testing of persons admitted to be specially competent*. Hence, we have an *a priori* right to require of the hypercritic who calls them in question a far more powerful destructive apparatus of refutation than would be necessary in the overthrow of a doctrine or dogma handed down from generations past without having been ever subjected to a testing, systematic or otherwise. To undermine the main common results of modern anthropologists is in its very nature quite a different task to that of undermining the theories or traditional opinions that these results have superseded.

Speaking generally, there are two main classes of persons who adopt the hypercritical attitude – reactionary restorationists and cynical decadents. The first seek, by bombarding the positive constructions established by modern thought, to pave the way for a despairing relapse into the pre-critical dogmatic positions of orthodoxy. The second seek, out of a spirit of apparently wanton cynicism, to overthrow the results referred to. This cynicism may be a mere pose, corresponding to the dogmatic pose of those intellectual roués who turn Catholic, or it may be a genuine cynicism bred of continual disillusionments in other departments of life. The cynic regards mere Scepticism as the goal of his criticisms, whereas the restorationist recognises the fact that Scepticism is, as before said, a position of unstable equilibrium; but for this very reason, by discrediting the constructive side of modern thought he hopes to compel a retreat upon obsolete dogmatic positions. One construction can only be effectively destroyed in supplanting it by another construction. This fact the restorationist very well knows.

The action and reaction of Dogmatism and Scepticism is a constant phenomenon in the history of the higher thought of mankind, the thought into which the speculative element enters. If an uncritical Dogmatism is a monstrosity, a constructionless Criticism is an absurdity. The difference is that an uncritical Dogmatism may have an appearance of stability sufficient to deceive the ignorant and unwary, but mere empty Scepticism, which is the outcome of a constructionless Criticism, wears an air of unreality on its face and is adopted, for the most part, as a pose.

In the antithesis between Dogmatism and Scepticism, each *per se* is alike abstract. Truth in the higher sciences and in Philosophy always implies a construction that has passed through the fire of Criticism, and is ready to challenge Criticism. All formulated Truth, that is, all formulated interpretation pertaining to the universe of things, as such, or even to man, considered at once in his deeper and more comprehensive aspects, psychological and social, is of the nature of a moving synthesis, composed of positive Construction and negative Criticism. Complete consistency of Consciousness with itself in its two aspects is unattainable. All we can expect to acquire in these higher subjects of human interest is a relative finality and an asymptotic approximation to such consistency, and the formulation which is the nearest approximation thereto up to date represents Truth, relative indeed, but nonetheless Truth. This does not mean that Criticism cannot find in it a fallacy or an unclinched position. The possibility of this is implied in the very fact that it is not absolute and complete. There are sure to be leakages and ragged edges upon which Criticism can operate. By treating these with undue emphasis where not actual exaggeration, Criticism can conclusively demonstrate the untenability of the doctrine or theory in question. Criticism, which does this, – that is, which by this means seeks to upset a well-established doctrine, a doctrine that has already been tried in the fire of Criticism, such as those we have referred to – we term *hypercriticism*, to distinguish it from the legitimate Criticism that would get rid of leakages and ragged edges, with a view of establishing the central doctrine more firmly, even at the expense of trappings hitherto associated with it. In the one case Criticism is a necessary element of progress, in the other it becomes simply an obstacle and an abuse. The reason for these remarks will be found on the perusal of much current literature on Philosophy, Ethics, Economics, and Sociology.

The tendency is unmistakable nowadays, on the part of any one who begins writing on one of the larger subjects of human interest, to think he must make a *tabula rasa* of all that has gone before him. This is easy enough to do with the aid of a little hypercritical machinery. It may either be done *apparently* by the employment of sophisms, or it may be done *really* by showing up minor defects, which will inevitably exist in any comprehensive construction. In neither case, of course, will the hypercriticism be valid, as regards its professed object of destruction; and the upshot of the whole would-be new departure amounts generally to the parturition of an insignificant and oftentimes singularly musty mouse – some comparatively unimportant innovation or a return to some old position furbished up anew for the occasion.

To sum up, what we have been endeavouring to point out is, that the Self-Consistency of Consciousness as a whole is the ultimate test of Truth; that the immediate test of Truth in any department of knowledge is the Self-Consistency of Consciousness, within that department; that Self- Consistency is never absolutely complete or perfect; that one of the great causes of the success of hypercriticism consists in the possibility for Criticism, to show the ravelled edges in even the best established formulation of ultimate problems; that every stage in the evolution of Thought gives a formulation, which, though not representing complete Truth, or perfect conscious Self-Consistency, is nevertheless *the nearest approach to adequacy* in this respect possible at a given stage of the evolution of Thought;

that such a formulation represents the Truth for us, or is, as we may say, the vice-regent of the absolute Truth at which we aim; that there are two main classes of persons who adopt hypercritical methods, the restorationist and the decadent; that the former attacks a well-established construction in the interests of obsolete or reactionary theories and dogmas, and the latter out of pure cynicism and to display his own powers of dialectic; that these criticisms may be either apparent or real, in the first case employing sophisms, usually the *ignorantio elenchi*, and in the second exaggerating actual defects, and thereby committing the fatal mistake of proving too much; that the true function of Criticism is to regulate the best-accredited construction or formulation up to date, thereby adapting it to the changes in the evolution of Thought. These include in Philosophy the basal position of "Theory of Knowledge," as elicited in the great German movement from Kant to Hegel and its offshoots, the true significance of which has only been recognised in this country during the present generation; in Cosmology the doctrine of Evolution including Darwinism in its widest sense; in Historical origins the recognition of Primitive Communism and the kinship group as the starting-point and groundwork of historical evolution, together with the results of the latest research in the development of religion and mythology, and in sociology and conception of Society as an organism, or better, superorganism – the next creation in Nature after the animal body.

Democracy and the Word of Command

There are some Socialists and Democrats to whom the bare idea of authority in any shape or form – other than that directly emanating from the decree of a majority – is monstrous. The notion of any controlling or initiative power whatever, other than this, is repugnant to them. And yet it is plain that the initiative or referendum of a democracy cannot be taken on details of executive administration, or on any matter requiring immediate decision, on a question of tactics, or with good result on matters involving special knowledge – in short, on anything other than general issues Even an elected assembly cannot deal directly with administration. In addition to this, as I have endeavoured to make clear in an article in the January number of the **Social-Democrat**, the will of the majority in itself is by no means absolutely so worthy of all acceptation as some assume. At the present time there are many considerations which ought to override it – some of which I pointed out in the article named – and even the will of the majority of an ideal democracy, a *social* democracy, must, as regards its special expressions, be subordinate to the general moral canon of a Socialist society. But if it is possible to make an idol of the will of the majority and to invest it with a quasi-sanctity and inviolability which it does not deserve, and if this is often done by Democrats, it is no less possible to make a bogey of initiative authority emanating from a dictatorial power, and this no less often happens. That in affairs of management, of tactics, of administration, or in decisions requiring special knowledge, authority, in its nature dictatorial (up to a certain point, at least), and hence, *per se*, in the current sense of the phrase, non-democratic – and this notwithstanding the original democratic sanction of election – is necessary, all must admit. In the case of a revolutionary army, military or political, on board ship, or in the factory, the workshop, &c., there must be a controlling, an authoritative voice in direction; so

153

much must be clear, one would think, to all practical or reasonable persons when once stated. The real point to determine is the nature and limits of that amount of dictatorial power which we must admit as essential in any organised community of which we can at present conceive.

Now, the type of dictatorial authority of which "the word of command" is final is furnished in the present day in military and in naval life. We all know it is the soldier's duty, under the direst pains and penalties, sometimes death itself, to obey implicitly the insanest, the most criminal order, of his commanding officer. In most military codes the penalty for disobedience must be inflicted, though the order may be subsequently admitted to have been senseless or disastrous, or even to have emanated from a man who was mad or drunk. Instances of the latter have not been uncommon in the German army. The same with the crew and the ship's captain. The command of the ship's captain is final; his power is unlimited over those on board during a voyage, i.e., on the high seas; his orders must be implicitly obeyed, although the doing so will quite obviously result in the sinking of the ship. This power is emphasised in the case of a warship, notably in that of an admiral, and was luridly illustrated by Tryon and the destruction of the Victoria some years ago. The officer in command of the other ironclad was bound to perform the evolution ordered, though knowing it must result in disaster, with the loss of hundreds of lives. Now, most practical or would-be practical persons, and not only Democrats, shake their heads over this class of dictatorial authority and its "word of command"; but the ordinary "practical" person is seldom inclined to condemn it *in toto* his attitude being to regard it as an evil, but a necessary evil. He cannot see any mean between it and a hopeless, disintegrative "democratic" control. An esteemed friend and comrade, who is strongly sensible of the evils and absurdities of the latter – i.e., of democratic control run mad or out of place – rightly argues that true democracy, *Social-Democracy*, while it means all *for* the people, does not mean the impossible absurdity that everything should be directly regulated by the people, *i.e.*, by a direct popular vote. The "people," he contends truly, should decide on all general issues by means of the ordinary count-of-heads majority; but the carrying out of measures, as well as work of administration generally, must be entrusted to suitably capable persons. In pursuance of this idea, he would not condemn the military and naval principle of passive obedience as above indicated. Anything rather than the dreaded rule of numbers in such matters. So impressed is he with this, that not even the experience he once made on a voyage with a crazy captain, who was intent on running the vessel upon rocks, in spite of the remonstrances of officers and passengers, sufficed to cure him of his devotion to the principle which nearly cost him his life. "E'en though it slay me, yet will I trust in it," said he. "I would rather, notwithstanding any day, go to sea under the auspices of a single man (a captain) with the customary absolute command than under that of a committee." Now, few of us, I fancy, will share our friend's enthusiasm for the "word of command" to this extent. If this military principle of authority were the only alternative, I imagine most persons certainly after such an experience, would decide in favour of the terrors of direct popular control. I contend, however, that it is not the only alternative. But of this more anon.

It will be observed that the special character of the military (and naval) type of dictatorial authority is that it resides in one man and that there is absolutely no appeal from the "word of command." Now, I do not hesitate to say that this form of authority is unconditionally to be condemned, for the simple reason that it is the most dangerous, and therefore the worst, that the human mind could possibly conceive. To be convinced of the latter fact, we have only to bear in mind the possibility of *insanity* or *drunkenness*, leaving out of account the effects of nervous irritation, indigestion, uncontrolled anger, and other pathological or quasi-pathological states. If we look the matter

155

fairly in the face, we can surely come to no other conclusion than that *under no circumstances whatever* ought *one* man to be entrusted with *absolute* authority, that *under no circumstances whatever* should *one* man be suffered to have the "word of command" without appeal. Any other principle of regulation, however bad, is better than this, since it is impossible for human perversity to devise one which combines within it more dangers. Every Socialist and every Democrat, I contend, should make an absolute and definite stand against the "word of command" in this sense. The man possessed of it is nothing less than a danger and a nuisance to all concerned; he is, like a "rogue" elephant in an Indian village, or a rattlesnake in a bedroom "out west," emphatically the "enemy" as such by virtue of the position he holds. But an unqualified and unconditional repudiation of the principle of dictatorial authority in the above sense by no means involves throwing oneself into the arms of the count-of-heads majority of a popular assembly or unwieldy committee.

It is to be noticed that there are two points in the existing military and naval "word of command" which constitute it what it is. The first is the fact of its absoluteness *per se*, and hence the automatic nature of its carrying out, the lack of any appeal therefrom on the part of the subordinate; and the second is the fact of its residing in one man. Now, it is especially in combination that these two elements constitute a principle than which the human mind can conceive of nothing worse. The absence of either one of them would mitigate the worst of the evils resulting therefrom. For example, the power might still reside even in the one man, but the (so-called) subordinate might *at his own risk* have the right of refusal to obey. In this case, the matter could be subsequently tried before a competent tribunal. If the "sub," had no sufficient reason for his insubordination, he would, of course, subject himself to appropriate penalties; if, on the contrary, he could show to the satisfaction of an impartial tribunal that the order given was intrinsically absurd, or that its carrying-out would have involved disastrous consequences, he could be triumphantly acquitted. But in this latter case it would be necessary that his superior should be liable to condign punishment. Had the man Tryon known that he was liable to be tried and shot for giving a bad order, he would probably have been less reckless. This, of course, would be hardly possible under the existing state of public opinion, which regards the higher functionary of the State as a little God Almighty, whom it would be rank blasphemy to punish criminally for any abuse of the powers entrusted to him, however heinous – which excuses every wrong-doing as an "error of judgment." In the future, however, when the slavish reverence for mere position shall have disappeared, it may be otherwise. But the above modification, though turning the edge of the worst evils of the "word of command" as at present understood, would not satisfactorily get rid of them. It is too cumbrous for this. Their main source lies undoubtedly in the second point referred to – viz., in the fact of the dictatorial authority being vested in one man, and even the suggested quasi-appeal from this authority would leave the root of the mischief untouched. The above-mentioned possibility of *insanity* or of *drunkenness* is alone sufficient to show the monstrous folly of entrusting one man with anything *even approaching* absolute powers where anything like serious issues are involved. And is the alternative thereto necessarily, as my friend supposed, only to be found in an unwieldy council? Surely not. It lies obviously in a committee of three, with equal voice, the casting-vote deciding in case of want of unanimity. But someone may ask how it would be if each member stood by a different opinion. The answer is, the necessity of action would force to agreement, by compromise or otherwise, of some sort. Besides, a nominal precedence might be given to a chairman on his colleagues failing to agree. This in itself would force to an agreement if the proposed order of the chairman were very preposterous. Thus, in the case before referred to, if the first and second mate of the ship had been able to override the decision of the captain, they would certainly, however divergent their views as to the correct course for the ship to take might have been, have come to some agreement to defeat the captain's suicidal intention of running it upon shoals. Similarly, if two other officers had been able to have overridden Tryon's order, they would certainly have combined to do so, however divergent their views otherwise on the proper manoeuvre to be executed. It is impossible to say how many vessels and how many lives are lost through the supreme power and responsibility being centred in one man, however capable, who may go mad or get drunk, rather than in a committee of three capable persons, as proposed. In the Social-Democratic society of the future, I am convinced that the absolute military "word of command" will be superseded by an authority carrying within itself its own check, as in that suggested; for two persons, though they might agree on a *wrong* course (being both fallible), would be not likely, to agree on a *preposterous* course, the probabilities of their both simultaneously going mad under such method as to be unanimous as to the form their delusions were to take being too remote to be worth while considering.

The case is similar *mutatis mutandis* in party leadership. The absolute direction of one man is as dangerous as the polling of a big council or assembly on points of immediate tactics might also be under many circumstances. What is wanted is the direction of a small committee of, say, three competent and trusted delegates, to render an account of their stewardship, and be re-elected (or rejected) after serving for a term.

That "a time will come" when the social organism in all its parts will work automatically, when the idea of authority in direction shall, like the State, have worked out its own contradiction, I am fully convinced. But until that time does come, authority in direction will in many departments be necessary. Were our party larger, and were we taking an effective part in politics, it would certainly be essential, to have an executive of a small number, such as that proposed, with powers to initiate such action in the name of the party as should be necessary for the carrying out or furtherance of our aims and of the immediate policy decided on. And so with a Socialist society in its earliest stages in all matters of administration, direction, and organisation, political, social, industrial, it should be recognised that there is a Scylla and Charybdis to be avoided. The first is the idolisation of the mere control of numbers – the tendency to regard the mere forms of democracy as of equal or even greater importance than the democratic end in view; and the second lies in allowing dictatorial powers, without appeal, to be in the hands of any *one* man – to wit, in the principle of the military officer's or the naval captain's uncontrolled "word of command."

A Bundle of Fallacies

In one of Aesop's fables it is related how in a congress of mice it was decided that the best way of averting the danger of capture by the cat was to hang a bell round the cat's neck as a warning of its approach. The question then was, to decide who should be the plucky mouse to bell the cat. Now this fable will bear more, than one application. There are some who plume themselves on hunting up some personal squabble to be made or some personal nastiness to be said, and doing it or saying it, and consider this a heroic form of cat-belling. But it may be pointed out that every old washerwoman (i.e., the typical old washerwoman – no disrespect to the calling or to woman in general) is fertile in this particular quality of heroism, and in fact that anybody who likes making himself a fussy and cantankerous nuisance can practise belling the cat after this fashion; in other words, can always persuade himself that something nasty has to be said or done, and say or do it. But there is another and more useful way of belling the cat, although it makes no claim to heroics. This is to expose the fallacies and misuse of language which often serve as argument with those who discuss Socialism and the public questions arising out of it both from a friendly and a hostile point of view. In this way the jingle of the fallacy may be distinguished as it is coming along, and the fore-warned become forearmed against it.

(1) First of all let us consider the "question-begging appellative" or phrase with which it is sought to damage a principle with which you disagree by calling it a "fad." Now the word "fad" means, according to Webster, "a hobby, freak, or whim," and is connected with the old word to "faddle," meaning to "fondle," or to "play with." A fad, therefore, really connotes a small or comparatively unimportant matter which engrosses a large, or at least unusual, share of attention. From this it has

readily come to mean something to which an exaggerated estimate of importance is attached. But the word has now got to be divested of all meaning whatever by being applied as a term of abuse to any doctrine or principle the user of it dislikes or finds inconvenient. For instance, to take an extreme case, we have heard Socialism itself, and Atheism and Catholicism, respectively termed "fads." Now, it is perfectly admissible to maintain that these things are all or severally either wrong or right, but in no case whatever can they be "fads." Whether they be right or wrong, true or false, they are too comprehensive, and involve too vast issues for either them or their opposites ever to be legitimately designated as "fads." An opinion zealously held may be utterly and preposterously absurd without being a "fad." On the other hand another opinion may be perfectly sound and yet a fad. Where a man devotes his whole energies to (say) anti-vaccination, and by his words or acts gives it to be understood that the entire future of the world's history depends on whether the laws as to compulsory vaccination are repealed or not, he may justly be styled a "faddist," and anti-vaccination a "fad," and this is quite irrespectively of whether we regard his views on the subject as in themselves well or ill founded.[1]

(2) Let us take another fallacy, this time traceable to a confusion of ideas, viz., the outcry against compelling a man to sever his connection with a party or organisation after he has (conscientiously, if you will) ceased to hold the principles for which it exists, or even after he has actively opposed those principles. Herr Eduard Bernstein was allowed to remain in the German Social-Democratic Party after he had denounced every Social-Democratic doctrine in turn and championed every move of capitalism *in extremis*, simply because the German Social-Democrats feared the cry of "heresy-hunter," with allusions to the Inquisition, being raised against them by the bourgeois press. The doctrine of toleration was thus stretched to the insane point that a man must be tolerated in an organisation the principles of which

he is opposing, lest those who turned him out should be accused of following the practice of the Christian Church. But, as a matter of fact, the odium attached to the heresy-hunting of the Church has its reason of being, not in the mere fact that men pronounced to be out of accord with the dogmas of the Christian Church were expelled or excommunicated from it, which was a perfectly logical and just proceeding, but in that this expulsion was made to involve pains and penalties on the part of the "secular arm." It is on the latter fact alone that the eternal infamy of the Christian Church, in its dealings with heretics, lies. I would ask those who take the conventional view, by what conceivable right a man can consider himself as hardly done by when he is formally required to leave a body with whose principles he has proclaimed himself in disagreement? If he likes to pose as a martyr on account of being subject to this very logical and obvious proceeding, let him. And surely he is welcome to the "heartfelt sympathy" of all the congenital idiots he can persuade to take his view of the case.

(3) We have all probably heard hard-put-to British champions argue, in the course of the Boer war, that because the Boers (as they express it) "stole the Transvaal from the natives," therefore, the British have a right to steal it from the Boers, not, *bien entendu*, to give it back to the natives, but to keep it for themselves. Now, without challenging the initial statement itself, utterly and absolutely false as it is, a moment's reflection shows the utter absurdity of the logic involved in the conclusion. I do not take refuge in the threadbare fallacy that "two blacks don't make a white," since, as I shall show directly, they very often do, albeit it is undeniable that for two blacks to make a white, i.e., for the second black to cancel the first, the two blacks must stand in a certain definite relation to one another, which is not the case here. But to make the absurdity at once obvious it is only necessary to state an example. *A*, a garrotter, violently robs *B*, a peaceable wayfarer, of his watch. The counsel for the defence urges as plea for acquittal that the victim (or, to make the parallel more

complete, the victim's grandfather) had at some remote date acquired the watch by sharp practice, not from the garrotter or any one connected with the garrotter but from some one with whom the garrotter has no concern whatever. I would ask the reader whether he thinks this beautiful and original defence would stand the prisoner in stead before an average British jury, or whether it would strike any one as an extenuating circumstance for the judge to take into consideration in passing sentence. The best right to stolen property, so long as the institution of private property exists, clearly rests with the original owner, but the theft from the actual possessor *by a third party* having no claim to it, is quite as much a crime as was the original theft (if we assume the actual possessor to have obtained it by theft). Forcible or covert deprivation of an *actual* possessor of property held by him, however obtained, by a person who (*ex hypothesi*) has no claim to that property, furnishes a complete case of the crime of theft. All else is purely irrelevant. Yet it is this class of windy fallacy which, incredible as it may seem, actually imposed upon some bull-headed Britons.

(4) We are all familiar with the observation applied in a reproachful tone to any one reprobating the tyranny or cruelty of one dressed in authority whether a "little" and "brief" or otherwise – "but after all he was only doing his duty!" If a man can be assumed as acting within what is called his duty, that is supposed to be sufficient to exonerate him from all blame for his action. The application of this theory reached a climax when the *Daily Telegraph*, in an indignant leader on the Homestead riots, denounced the wickedness of Mr. Carnegie's workmen in forcibly resisting the "Pinkerton detectives," and wound up with an expression of horror that the "Pinkertons" should be subjected to such treatment – men "who were doing nothing more than their duty." Now it would be interesting to know what constitutes " duty " in the eyes of this leader-writer, who evidently deems any crime committed in the performance of so-called duty as *ipso*

facto condoned. If it be the mere carrying out of functions delegated to a man by some other person or body of persons, then the Fenian who is told off by his "circle" to blow up the Houses of Parliament is doing nothing more than his duty, when he successfully carries out that, according to popular judgment, reprehensible proceeding. Similarly, the Anarchist appointed in a conclave of his party to blow up the Café Véry, was only doing his "duty" as the trusted member of his group, regarding themselves as the rightful avengers of the disinherited of the earth, when he carefully deposited his bomb under the counter. The "duty" of Torquemada was to extirpate heresy as the functionary appointed by the Church for that purpose. The Prussian sentry is doing his "duty" in firing ball-cartridge to the common danger along public thoroughfares at runaway soldiers, or at civilians who treat him with insufficient respect.

Again, is "duty" taken to mean an act performed in the ordinary course of a calling? If so, the burglar or the cut-purse, when "on the job," might be said to be only doing his duty. To the theologian, "duty" means obedience to the alleged mandates of the supernatural power that he postulates. With some persons, once more, "duty" might almost seem to be definable as an act involving unpleasant consequences to oneself or others. Now we can discriminate, I submit, in these various possible conceptions of "duty" only one element in common – that of ought, or moral obligation. But the special determination of this element always involves matter of disputation according to the particular prepossessions of the speaker; according as the latter approves or disapproves of the presupposition at its basis will be his judgment of the act as to whether it is covered by the notion of "duty" or not. The assumption underlying the proposition of the **Telegraph** leader-writer, in the case given, was that of the desirability of supporting capital against labour. The Pinkerton detectives had enrolled themselves in an association, lending itself to this desirable object, and hence, in the opinion of the **Telegraph** leader-writer and the public he writes for, in shooting down strikers at the behest of the capitalist, they were obviously "doing no more than their duty." But this same leader-writer and his public do not think the independence of Ireland a desirable object in itself, nor do they in general like to see governments representing capitalists' interests overturned in an unceremonious manner. So, in their view, the Fenian or the Anarchist is doing anything but his duty in obeying the behests of his "circle" or "group." The Fenian and Anarchist naturally take another view of the matter, and believing in their respective causes as righteous, feel they are only "doing their duty" in carrying out the mandates of their several organisations.

The result of all this is, then, that unless we are prepared to exonerate the dynamiter, it follows that the mere performing of a recognised function ought not of itself to exempt the performer from condemnation or even punishment. If so, it is undoubtedly just that the judge who is the instrument of putting a bad law in execution should be punished for so doing. The middle classes have set the example already, for the Counter-Revolution took this view in France in 1795, when, with the unanimous applause of public opinion, it guillotined Fouquier-Tinville and the judges of the "Revolutionary Tribunal," for carrying out the instructions given them by the previous government of France. It is true, as a rule, that this can only happen when the continuity of governmental life is broken by some form of revolution, but, where it is possible, I submit there is no question of the justice of making a public functionary personally responsible for his action, and refusing to permit him to shield himself behind his office. It suited the purpose of the Thermidorian reactionists to punish Fouquier-Tinville, but they did not see what a dangerous precedent for their class they were creating in so doing.

There is a mistaken conception abroad that a judge, let us say, in seeking to secure a conviction, as is the wont of most judges, is necessarily acting disinterestedly, and therefore honestly. What *personal* motive, may it be asked, can he have for doing what he does? I will tell you: *the enjoyment of the sense of power which conviction gives him over the prisoner in the dock.* It is the prospect of enjoyment of the same kind which is the incentive to small boys, who are said to be of a cruel disposition, to kill flies, spin cockchafers, and hold up cats by their tails. "Duty" is only a relative expression, and the judge who gives effect to a bad or unjust law, the executioner who gives effect to the judge's sentence, the general who "carries through" military operations of an oppressive character with the object of crushing another people or stealing their territory, are one and all criminals as much deserving of punishment (if only the opportunity occurs of inflicting it on them) as the member of the "long firm" who, in accordance with the decisions of his organisation as to "ringing the changes" or "shoplifting," feels it his "duty" to obey; or the "partner" who feels it his "duty" to save the business with which he is connected, from financial ruin, by committing a forgery. There may certainly be considerations which change the normal character of an act under special circumstances, making a "black" a "white"; but merely tacking on the epithet "duty" to a deed of blood committed by a judge, executive officer, or military commander, is no more than a specious and impudent device, designed to shield the iniquities of a governing class and its tools.

The fact is, of course, that the logic of conscience cannot sanction the thesis that social or official position makes an unethical act ethical, or robs a crime of its criminality. On the contrary, it may well even aggravate its moral heinousness by importing into it an element hypocrisy and cowardice – hypocrisy, as implied in the plea of "duty"; cowardice because the individual usually acts in conscious immunity from the natural or legal dangers to himself otherwise attending such an act. The British soldier in Transvaal could pillage and murder without fear of any police.

(5) We come now to the favourite distinction between (justifiable) sentiment and sentimentalism. When lies this distinction? Most people assume that it is to be found in *quantity*;

to wit, that sentimentalism is simply an excess of sentiment in other people over themselves. But it requires very little reflection to show that this is too personal and subjective to furnish a valid test of the distinction. If even it be extended so as to mean the average sentiment of one's day and generation, this also will not hold water, for the reason that it entirely ignores the evolutionary or dynamic element in the notion, assuming it to have a fixed value, rather than, like everything else mental and physical, to be in a state of continual progress and change. Mediaeval, or even seventeenth century, sentiment would undoubtedly have voted opposition to rack and thumbscrew as gross sentimentalism, just as an influential section of public opinion to-day votes opposition to gallows and lash to be pernicious sentimentalism, and cannot conceive that a time will come when public opinion will view these institutions with as great abhorrence as modern public opinion does rack or thumbscrew.

I assume all along the validity of the distinction, i.e., that the distinction is real. But if the distinction between sentiment and sentimentality (or sentimentalism) be real and cannot consistently be reduced to a question of mere quantity, wherein does it lie? The answer, I take it, is that it lies in the *distribution* of the sentiment, The tendency of progress is toward a raising of the standard of sentiment, an increase in its quantity, in its tending to spread over areas hitherto unoccupied by it, and it is impossible to place an effective limit and say to sentiment – i.e., to sympathy and revulsion at the idea of suffering "Thus far shalt thou go and no farther!" since such a limit would be purely arbitrary. But where the sentiment gets concentrated at one point in excess of another, other things being equal, there you have sentimentalism, not because of the absolute amount of the sentiment present, but of its distribution, i.e., of its relative amount as regards its objects. Let us take two illustrations. There are some people whose abhorrence of cruelty to animals coincides with a comparative indifference to cruel punishment of children, and still more to the torturing of convicts by treadmill and lash. Or again, they will shudder with indignant horror at the beating of a dog or the overworking of a horse, and yet will hear without wincing of the horrors of an insanitary factory, or of unwholesome manufactures. I once knew a lady who, while violently opposing vivisection of animals, was prepared to allow its practice, if necessary in the interests of science, on criminals of a certain order. Now here, I conceive, we have clearly the right to describe such sensitiveness towards animal suffering as sentimentalism, not because it is necessarily excessive in itself, but because it is altogether out of proportion to the feeling for suffering in humans. Again, the feminist sentiment is almost pure sentimentalism, inasmuch as it is sentiment which, instead of being distributed over the whole of (at least) humankind, is congested on the female sex. If a man, driven mad by jealousy, or at his wit's end for fear of blackmail, exposure, and ruin, murders his wife or mistress, scarce a voice will be raised against his being hanged; nay, the general verdict will be "Serve the brute right!" But on the occasion of Mary Ansell deliberately murdering her sister, by means of poison transmitted through the post, for the sake of her sister's insurance money; or (if possible, still worse) on that of Louisa Masset butchering with the greatest brutality, in cold blood, her little five-year-old son, in order to disembarrass herself of the expense of his maintenance, we have superhuman efforts to obtain a reprieve backed by much pathetic talk about "the poor girl!" This is true sentimentalism. By all means oppose capital punishment as much as you will, but spare a little of the sentiment you so lavishly expend over the "poor girl" for the other, the "poor fellow," who, we may imagine, just as little enjoys being hanged.

(6) There is a familiar form of fallacy which consists in attempting to smuggle in a doctrine or policy under cover of a recognised principle on the basis of a superficial appearance of such a doctrine or policy being involved in the principle in question, when it is in reality in no way connected with it. An

169

instance of this occurs to me in connection with the woman-suffrage agitation. The possession of the franchise by women may be for aught I care a postulate of eternal justice descending straight from heaven upon men, or it may be a subtle scheme to confound progress emanating direct from the bottomless pit. All I am here concerned to show is, that one argument *ad hominem* often used by woman's righters is a delusive fallacy. It is commonly represented that the political democrat or the Social-Democrat must necessarily, if he be consistent, be an advocate of woman-suffrage. Now I submit that whether right or wrong in itself, woman-suffrage is in no way whatever necessarily involved in a (political) democratic or Social-Democratic programme. Democracy, whether political or whether Socialistic, is only necessarily concerned with the abolition of class-restrictions and distinctions, in the one case political, in the other economic and social as well. This has always been the meaning of democracy up till quite recently. But now, a new question, that of sex, is sought to be introduced. It is pretended that the principle of equality involved in the democratic idea necessarily includes the acceptance of a particular version of sex-equality. Now, sex-equality may be a very good thing, but I insist that it has absolutely no connection with democracy, which has always referred to class-distinction and in no way to sex-distinction. And hence a man may be a perfectly sound political democrat or Socialist respectively and yet a vehement opponent of the extension of the franchise to women as well as certain other claims advanced by woman's rights advocates.

(7) We come finally to an important, because so very common, fallacy. I refer to the saying that "two blacks don't make a white." It is, of course, true that two actions each divorced from its surroundings and both from each other, do not affect each other – an obvious and harmless proposition enough. But in the concrete moral world furnished us by this vale of tears, things are presented in mutual connection and not in isolated

abstraction as "metaphysical entities." Viewed, then, as a part of the real world of human conduct, we find that two "blacks" very often do "make a white" – i.e., that in a world where actions possess in practice no absolute value, but are conditioned by one another, one of two actions, either of which when taken *per se* would be reprehensible, becomes just and right. Viewed as part of a connected whole, the second action, conditioned as it is by the first, loses its abstract character of wrongness or "blackness," and by the very fact of its conditioning or connection becomes "white," that is, justified. Of course, this obvious truth is recognised and acted on every day by persons who dispute it, when it suits their purpose, in controversy. The whole theory of criminal law indeed is based on its recognition. Yet there is no argument supposed to be so crushing to an opponent as flinging this utterly threadbare fallacy at his head.

As a matter of fact, in a certain sense most actions generally regarded as right are compounded of elements which, taken by themselves, would be deemed wrong. Asked in the abstract, "Is it wrong to injure a fellow creature?" one would answer "Yes." But supposing a fellow creature confronts me in a menacing attitude in a narrow passage with a revolver. It is undoubtedly wrong of him to do this, but if I raise my stick knock the revolver out of his hand I may hurt his hand, and two wrongs don't make a right, eh? Acting on the principle that two wrongs don't make a right, the Hindoo refuses to destroy the most noxious animal, snake, or a tiger, though it be working, havoc and ruin in his village. Acting on the same principle, Tolstoi would not rescue a little child from the clutches of a murderer or a drunkard as in so doing he might injure the murderer or drunkard, and, says "two wrongs don't make a right!"

Singularly enough the persons who apply this "law" against "violence" as coming from revolutionists, never dream of such an application, when one would think it would be most applicable, namely, in the case of criminals in the hands of justices They for the most part approve of torturing convicts when they are no longer in a position to do any harm, hanging murderers, and flogging other classes of offenders. Against the common criminal, unlike the logical Tolstoi, they are quite convinced apparently that two wrongs *do* make a right. It is only against Terrorists and such-like, who punish ruffians of a different stamp, that they are disposed to deprecatingly observe that however bad the latter may have been, nevertheless "two wrongs don't make a right!"

As regards this question of two wrongs making or not making a right, we may definitely assert that though two wrongs may not, as such, always make a right, yet that brought into a certain relation with each other, they *do*, in so far as the second "wrong" in annulling the first loses its original character of wrongness and becomes, *ipso facto*, right. This is the truth that enthusiasts like Tolstoi do not recognise in their abstract and unreal way of regarding human relations, and therefore for them the "saw" may have an intelligible significance. But for those who do not adopt this logical attitude of passive non-resistance, it is the baldest and most impudent piece of disingenuous question-begging. Regarding human relations from a concrete point of view, it is manifest that two wrongs often do make a right. Whether any particular "two wrongs" make a right or not, must be solely determined by the circumstances of the particular case in question.

Footnote

1. Of course, there are cases in which it may be open to discussion whether a particular clause as advocated by a particular person may be justly termed a "fad" or not, but the general principle of what constitutes a "fad" is clear enough.

The Decline of Militarism

At first sight it may seem to some a paradox to speak of the decline of militarism, in face of the much-discussed bloated armaments of the present day. But if we do but examine the matter a little, the paradox will disclose itself as an undeniable fact, and that from more than one point of view. The "bloated armaments" are in themselves no proof of the ascendancy of the military spirit, of the popularity of the military life, or of the enduring nature of militarism as a social and political force in modern civilisation, but the contrary. The very unwieldy character of the armaments are themselves a sign of the fatty degeneration of militarism, and not of its virility. The oppression of the armed peace of present-day Europe, the weight of which increases in the necessary course of its development, is fast becoming more than the economic conditions of modern civilisation can bear. This is a common observation, so common, indeed, that to many it may seem trite. Be this as it may, its true inwardness means that the end of militarism is not far off. For if the only conditions under which war can continue to exist as an institution for settling international disputes are incompatible with the economic foundation of modern society, then it is perfectly clear that war, and hence militarism, is by that very fact doomed. It is plain that it is involved in the process of working out its own contradiction from the material side at least. As soon as the armaments become too "bloated" for their continued maintenance to be possible, and that point, according to experts, is not far off, so soon the crisis will have come, and a change of some sort will be imminent. The outbreak of a European war might easily precipitate matters; or might postpone the downfall of militarism by a few years, according as its course and event turned out. But one result of the recent developments of the machinery of militarism is the dread of all responsible parties to resort to the arbitrament of these new developments in the war-industry (one can no longer term it the 'art of war'). The uncertainty of the issue is too great. There is a dread of the unknown. It is felt that the existence, political and social, of every nationality concerned is at stake, and to engage would be to hazard all on the stroke of a die. For this reason every year that passes renders the outbreak of the much-talked-of European war less probable.

Meanwhile, whatever may be the issue of the immediate future, it is interesting and instructive to note the change which has come over the war-industry and the consequent change in the character of the life of the soldier, as well as, of the way in which the military career its regarded.

Precisely the same development has taken place in war as in every industrial art. At earlier periods of the world's history fighting was a matter of skill, strength, and prowess in the individual. Just as the handicraftsman worked with his own tools, so the soldier furnished his own equipment as he pleased, rode to battle on his own horse, followed his leader of his own free will, but was under no compulsion to slavishly obey him, was his own drillmaster, if one may so say, when drilling in the modern sense was unknown – in short, was in every respect an independent craftsman who followed a particular craft, that of fighting, then regarded as the king of all crafts, and who, with his brethren-in-arms, were members of the great guild of knights or of heroes. The chief, the head of the guild, was, indeed *primus inter pares*, but had no authority independent of his comrades-in-arms. Agamemnon, king of men, had to submit to the decisions of his warriors in council. Nay, he was powerless to prevent or punish the desertion of Achilles and his myrmidons. The same with the Germanic leader, the *Herzog*, who, with his comrades, went forth to conquer the Roman world. He was simply the "eldest among many brethren," each of whom was his equal, who voluntarily followed his suggestions. William of Normandy, when, with his followers, he came to conquer Saxon England, had no independent power over them beyond the moral influence which the then but recently perfected feudal relation afforded him. Even long afterwards, at the close of the Middle Ages anal later, the new order of mercenary soldiers – the *Lanzknechte* or *Landsknechte* (the derivation is uncertain) as they were called – were subject to no discipline in the modern sense. They formed a guild of their own, usually furnished their own equipments, wore no uniform, beyond the colours of the lord or prince under whom they were serving, and whom, if he did not pay them regularly or proved otherwise not satisfactory, they unceremoniously deserted. As yet, the distinction between the common soldier and the field officer was uncertain and of comparatively little moment. Then was the time when the individual warrior could, by his personal prowess, put an enemy to flight and save a battle. Then was the time when every individual fighter had, as such, a distinct and independent value of his own.

Even as late as Charles II service in this country under the King's colours was perfectly voluntary, and the law gave the officer no power over the person of the common soldier. But this same period (the second half of the seventeenth century) was the important turning-point. It was the age when Louvois, the Minister of Louis XIV, put the French army into uniform. This was the beginning of the uniform system, and a great step towards the modern machine-army – the army which consists in an elaborately integrated bureaucratic despotism over a mass of will-less slaves, moulded to act collectively as a piece of mechanism. This is the ideal of the modern army, and the nearer to this mechanical perfection it approaches the more effectively the army fulfils its function, the better fighting machine it is. The most perfect of these war-engines of the present day is generally admitted to be the German army. But the principle is the same in all modern armies. As a consequence of this principle, the life of the modern soldier is mainly taken up with a round of purely mechanical processes – the polishing to the highest possible brilliancy of uniform buttons and metallic accoutrements generally, the keeping of the uniform in a condition in which the strongest magnifying power would fail to disclose a speck of dust. The aim of his drill is to ensure absolute uniformity of bodily position end simultaneity of movement, and even gesture. The line of the squad's or detachment's toes on parade must be mathematically perfect. As each man is, as regards dress and equipment, the exact mechanical duplicate of his neighbour, so that the whole detachment shall represent a single object, moving or stationary, so the whole congeries of boots must seem like one continuity of bootness.

The reduction of the whole army to a machine, and each separate division and sub division to parts of a machine, is the one aim of modern military organisation. In other words, its first and necessary end is the extinction of the individuality of the soldier. How far this extends may be judged from the fact that the very outward expressions of *élan* and enthusiasm have to be practiced (!) that they may be worked off with the due precision and regularity. The spontaneous war-shout of the tribesman rushing on with his people to victory or death for the glory of his kindred must be kept up as a piece of "trade finish" in modern capitalistic warfare, and correctly performed on the word of command. Only the other day a member of the German army was describing to me how, at "manoeuvres," when fagged after a hard day's march, and with parched throats, his battalion were ordered by the commanding officer to charge with hurrah. The first hurrah was not full and unvociferous enough; so the poor wretches were ordered to fall back and repeat the process; this was done till the requisite precision was attained. Fancy the Catti, the Marcomanni, the Suevi, the Goths, or the companions of Clovis having stage rehearsals of their onrush and their shout! With what contempt the free yeomen and feudal retainers of the Middle Ages would have regarded the modern soldier-slave, neither whose soul nor whose body are his own, and who is soldered into the modern army machine by "discipline" and ferocious military codes!

The fate of a conquered people in the past and present is

significant of the radical change in militarism between then and now. Formerly the man of the conquered race was forbidden the freeman's *privilege* of bearing arms. Now he is thrust into the uniform of his conquerors and has the subject's *duty* forced upon him of serving as raw material to be forged into his conqueror's army – *alias* patent war machine.

War, then; like every other craft, has become a mechanical process in which individual talent, skill, and character, play little or no part. The difference between the modern soldier and his predecessor of mediaeval times is even greater, if that were possible, than the difference between the modern proletarian and the medieval craftsmen. Hence the absurdity of those who, like that venerable humbug, the late Charles Kingsley, speak of the effects of devotion and enthusiasm on the character, effects which may conceivably, under certain circumstances, have accompanied the military conditions of an earlier age, as though they could possibly apply to the mechanical slavery of the soldier in the army of to-day. The foregoing explains the difference between the way in which the military life is regarded now, and in former times. Time was when the military career was the most popular. It was the freest of all careers. In none was a man so much his own master as when he became a soldier. As late as the Thirty Years War this is specially noticeable. The one thing that was required of him was courage and dash. The *Lanzknecht* was a boon companion who defied the world, and who, if his leader did not satisfy him, would go and serve another. Now, in this age of "scientific warfare" hardly another career is so unpopular as the military, for in no other career is a man so absolute a slave to the will of his immediate superior, and to a galling, grinding round of trivial operations, precision in the performance of which is exacted with an unyielding, rigour. The fatigues the modern soldier has to bear are not so much the old fatigues incidental to the life of the fighting man general]y, long marches under the weight of arms and armour, desperate attacks and defences, but they are the seemingly objectless fatigues exacted by the "discipline" of the modern machine army. Standing for hours rigid, without moving a muscle, covered by a tight-fitting thick cloth uniform in a broiling sun for the purposes of a "review," practice of evolutions, marching up to the top of a hill and marching down again, all to the individual concerned aimless operations, in which he is a mere mechanical unit, and the intention of which is to perfect him in this capacity. Unfortunately for him, he is, in addition, a personality with will and consciousness.

Add to this, that when war actually occurs, it is probably a war in which he has no conceivable interest, material or ideal. What enthusiasm, for example would the German Social-Democrats have in defending Alsace Lorraine against the French. What interest has the working man generally, to-day, in defending a capitalistic monarchy, empire, or even republic from destruction. If the modern man has often no ideal interest in the causes of modern warfare, still less has he any material or personal interest in its course. Time was, and not so long ago, when he could hope to gain a fortune in the sack of a single wealthy town, (not to speak of the wives and daughters of the burghers who were at his disposal if he were licentiously inclined). Limitless fortunes lay within the possibilities of the soldier. Now we have changed all that. Modern warfare is as dull and as "moral" as it is ruthless and mechanical. Of course, we shall be told that this is a triumph of civilisation, and we would not deny it. But the fact remains that the change has sapped one of the roots of the war-spirit. War has no longer aught to offer, either materially or, ideally, either in the shape of low rewards or high ideals. It has reduced the individual soldier to a cog in the wheel of the great modern war-engine; in other words, to a position which means the most abject form of slavery. Hence the life of a soldier is shunned and regarded with aversion by the enormous majority of men (even young men for whom in bygone times it was the ideal of free adventure). Charm it no longer possesses for anyone.

Militarism, all things considered, would seem, therefore, in spite of bloated armaments, in spite of the general anticipation of a European war, to be rapidly approaching its end, even within the limits of present capitalistic society. Among the first measures that would characterise the change from Capitalism to Social-Democracy, not the least conspicuous would be, of course, the definitive abolition of international warfare inaugurated by complete disarmament. And it is only by the furtherance of Social-Democracy that the certain end of militarism can be promoted. But as above said there are signs that it is possible that militarism may die out even before capitalism finally collapses, inasmuch as it is rapidly becoming a serious hindrance to the high-pressure industrial and commercial progress necessitated by the competitive conditions of Modern Capitalism. This was shown recently by the manner in which the projected Arbitration Treaty between Great Britain and the United States was hailed by the European Press. The capitalist classes would be very willing to get rid of militarism if they only knew how to do so without endangering their own position. They might conceivably come to an international understanding with each other after some little difficulty, and thus a sort of gigantic international capitalist ring, or trust might be formed, instead of, as now, cut-throat competition ruling supreme among capitalists of different nationalities. But they want an army as a reserve force against the proletariat. And never has there been a more effective weapon for crushing popular risings than is furnished by the mechanical militarism of to-day.

With militarism, moreover, are involved certain interests of the governing and feudal families of Europe, to come into conflict with which might jeopardise the whole fabric inasmuch as these feudal survivals have been accepted by European Capitalism as an integral part of its political and social system, and hence have to be reckoned with in any change which may be made. These and other minor considerations make it difficult for any decisive step to be taken towards the abolition of war as an institution, such, for example, as a universal system of arbitration-treaties involving a standing court of final appeal, and followed by general disarmament. Yet none the less, for many reasons, not so much of humanity as of self-interest, the bourgeois would like well enough to bring about such a state of things, as, except in a few industries, he has everything to lose and nothing to gain by militarism and war. He is undoubtedly beginning to see that to keep up perpetually, expensive military establishments on the chance of his being able to steal a march on his neighbour, does not pay, and that so far as international capitalistic rivalry) is concerned, it would answer better to "pool the swag" in some way than to continue a cut-throat competition involving such costly machinery for its maintenance. To perform his burglarious operations on savage races in Africa and elsewhere, all that is wanted is a small number of trained men, plenty of maxims, with, in case of need, the reserve of volunteers, the supply of which is always greater than the demand when the heroic sport of "nigger-shooting" is afoot. This would amply suffice for his "colonial" exploits in search of markets. But then, as already said, there remains the proletarian at home to be overawed! Yet, if the prospects of immediate disarmament nay not be brilliant, the handwriting on the wall is none the less clear that militarism as an institution has outlived itself and is already a "survival."

Patriotism: Its Growth and Outcome

The word patriotism, or its equivalents and derivations, is upon everyone's lips at the present time. It is a magic word which is thought by most people to cover any multitude of sins. To be patriotic in what ever cause is tantamount to being virtuous, while no worse charge can be brought against a man in popular estimation, than to say he is unpatriotic. Now I propose to examine briefly the origin and development of this sentiment of patriotism up to its present-day manifestations.

The earliest known form of human society, as you may perhaps be aware, is that which is based on kinship or blood relationship, real or supposed.

Now the first form of the sentiment which we now call "patriotism," first appears in connection with the notion of kinship or blood relationship. The tribe in its origin, and that important and often practically autonomous organ of the tribe the clan, were simply groups of kinsmen. I must here premise that modern anthropologists divide the history of human society into (1) Early or *tribal* or *group* society, which represents the first organised conditions under which men lived together at all, and (2) the later political society in which these early groups tended to become broken up and merged into centralised States. Now, the crucial distinction between these two systems of society is this: tribal society is based on the principle of association, the individual by himself being nothing, while the community to which he belongs is everything. The individual tribesman or clansman lives only as a part of the tribe or clan to which he belongs. All his morality consists in devotion to the tribal honour and glory; all his religion (this applies to tribes who have not been interfered with by missionaries) – all his religion, I say, consists in the worship of the tribal ancestors with the due ceremonies prescribed by tradition, or of certain idols or fetishes supposed to represent powers of nature capable of benefiting or injuring the tribe. Tribal society throughout all its phases is essentially communistic. The most important forms of property are held in common by the whole tribe or clan. Personal property is a casual and unimportant phenomenon applying only to objects of constant personal use. In tribal society, therefore, we have the first and most intensely real form of patriotism – a patriotism not based on territory, but on blood. To the primitive Arab tribesman that land is his country on which his tribe for the time being has hitched its tents.

2. Now, modern or political society is the precise reverse of all this. It is based essentially, not on the principle of association, but on that of individual autonomy. It is composed, not of groups of kinsmen, all supposed to be united by ties of blood-relationship to each other, but of huge agglomerations of isolated individuals living on a given area of territory. There is no essential bond of social union between these individuals which constitute the members of the modern State. Their religion is personal, their morality is personal, and their property is personal – in short, if ancient or group society may be described as *communistic*, modern or political society, with its vast centralised national systems, mast he described as *individualistic*.

The foregoing is intended to convey in a few words the crucial or salient points respectively of primitive or group society and of modern civilised or political society, considered in their most perfect and logical form. But in the real world of historic evolution these two forms overlap each other; there is a gradual transition, sometimes lasting for several centuries, from early communism to latter-day individualism, from the primitive tribe or clan to the modern State or nation. The period known as the Middle Ages represents, on certain of its sides, this transition, for universal history. The rise of the city-states of the ancient world would be the best type of the transition, were our information more complete concerning them.

Now, in considering the growth of patriotism, it is necessary to cast a brief glance at the conflict between the two principles – the two forms of human organisation, as exhibited on the arena of history.

Out of the mass of barbaric mankind organised in tribes and clans, in various stages, some tribes of nomadic herdsmen, others already settled in villages as agricultural communities, inhabiting Western Asia, Eastern Europe, and North-Eastern Africa, what we call civilisation arose in the form of the ancient city. The first beginnings of the city-state many historians would place in Egypt more than 3000 years B.C. But when and where the first beginnings of civilisation took place, remains at present a matter of speculation. Suffice it to say that the earlier forms of political society existed in Western Asia and in Northern Africa long before they did in Europe, but that before 2000 B.C. We find the beginnings of political or civilised society already established in the peninsulas of Greece and Italy. And if we examine these beginnings as represented by Sparta, Athens, Thebes, Rome, &c. (by those civic communities, i.e., of which we have the most information), we find the political, the individualistic form of society as embodied in the State – as yet confined to the precincts of the city- only very slowly making headway against the old life of the tribal societies which it contained. To give illustrations of this would take us too far. But we may quote what a great scholar has said of the Greek and Roman gens or clan: "Nothing is more closely united than the members of a gens (clan) – united in the celebration of the same sacred ceremonies, they mutually aid each other in all the needs of life. The entire gens (clan) is responsible for the debt of one of its members; it redeems the prisoner and pays the fine of one condemned. Thus the ancient city-state, the first form of civilisation which was originally nothing but the coalescence of some three or four tribes with their clans and their settlement within a walled area with a fortification in their midst – continued for long to retain the group organisations within it, with their independence largely intact. But little by little the city-state became consolidated, and in proportion as this happened, the powers and independence of the tribes and clans passed over to the central power of the city, as embodied in the united council or senate composed of the heads of the clans, who usually elected the chief magistrate or king from out of their number. Now, as the rights and powers of the smaller communities within the city became restricted and those of the city increased, the old religious patriotism – the zeal or love for tribe and clan – also gradually transferred itself to the city as such. The great temple or temples of the city-gods became the centre of city life and worship and glory, and devotion to the city, and even the ground where it stood was regarded as sacred, became the highest ideal of the citizen."

We now have to notice a further development of political society. Owing to conquest, or sometimes policy, for purposes of offence and defence, arose the federation of cities under the domination of one city and its ruler, in other words, the empire of the ancient world, such as Egypt, Babylonia, Assyria, and Phoenicia. Here a similar process went on to that within the city itself. The empire absorbed some of the city patriotism, just as the city had absorbed the old patriotism of the several tribes and their clans of which it was composed. But it did not so do to anything like the same extent. The city remained the main essential political unity of the ancient world, and hence the patriotism of the ancient world remained almost wholly a city patriotism. What broke down the city patriotism, was that great political organisation founded on conquest (of a somewhat different character to the oriental empires just referred to), viz., the Roman Empire. Rome in many cases removed the gods of the conquered cities to the seat of empire, and the Roman Empire it was that killed off the patriotism of the ancient world. But the political society of the ancient world, including Roman civilisation, owing to its economic constitution, was impotent to advance to the stage of modern capitalistic society – discovery, invention and improvement having early dried up – in short, ancient civilisation founded as it was economically on slave labour, got into a blind lane, and further progress was barred. In these circumstances it fell a prey to the Northern Barbarians with their tribal organisation and tribal patriotism mainly intact. But at this time the old city-patriotism had long been dead, and superseded by the Christian cosmopolitanism – i.e., by the idea of membership, not of a city, but of a universal church or commonwealth of the faithful. The barbarian nations, however, still retaining their tribal organisation, were also still possessed by the early patriotism of the tribe and the clan. Weakened as this was in proportion as they came in contact with Christianity and Roman civilisation, it was never quite destroyed, but lingered on till it was absorbed by the feudal notion of personal allegiance to a lord, who was, however, originally doubtless regarded in the same light as the old patriarchal lead or representative of the tribe or clan. But as medieval civilisation progressed we see the counterpart of the ancient city – patriotism asserting itself. The mediaeval township also, like the city of the ancient world, had a patriotism of its own, and throughout the Middle Ages it waged war with the feudal principle which endeavoured to crush it. In the Middle Ages thus we have local and personal or feudal patriotisms (if we may call theirs so) and at the same time the international notion of the unity of Christendom or the patriotism of the Catholic Church, But as yet there is no national or State-patriotism such as we find to-day in Britain, France, or Germany. This latter first arose as modern capitalism arose, and as the old world societies of the manor or village and of the township became broken up. It is perhaps difficult for some of you to realise how great was the independence of the village and of the township in the Middle Ages, and how they resented interference from any centralised power. One of the most cherished privileges was the right of the higher jurisdiction, which many paraphrased as the right to have a gallows and hang anybody on it who displeased the burghers or their local authorities, the symbol of independence.

On the Continent, especially in Germany and Italy, the independence of the manors and townships was virtually complete. Even in England, where it was much less so, owing to circumstances we cannot now enter into, towns such as London, Norwich, Halifax, &c., had such large measures of autonomy as would stagger the modern municipal reformer. Medieval civilisation, although not communistic like tribal society, was very imperfectly individualistic. Considerable fragments of primitive institutions clung to it. It was, as already said, through and through local, and based on the group rather than the individual – on the manor, the guild and the township. But towards the close of the mediæval period, with the new inventions that arose, the discovery of America and the Cape route, the old order began to change; capitalism and new commercial syndicates, production of wealth on a great scale, for profit, and not as before mainly for use, drove a wedge into the old society. At the same time that production began to centralise, government began to centralise – in short, the modern national State or political society based on individualism was born. As it progressed, absorbing and destroying the old institutions, or making them suborned to its own interests, the modern national patriotic sentiment developed also. At first, however, it was confined to the pride of national maintenance and defence against any form of aggression. Patriotism, in fact, to be a "patriot," meant formerly, notably during the French Revolution, to be on the side of the people of the country, not so much against a foreign enemy as against the governing classes of the country itself who were oppressing the people – in other words to be, as we should say to-day, a good democrat. But the rise and progress of modern capitalism – the capitalism of the great machine in society, of chartered commercial companies, and of modern high financial potentates and syndicates, has changed all this. The need of fresh markets, of cheap labour, of new territories to exploit for mineral and agricultural products, has altered the conditions of modern external policy, just as capitalism itself had already altered the conditions of English economic social and domestic life. The term patriotism has hence to-day acquired a changed meaning; patriotic sentiment is now an asset of capitalism. This is aided by the patriotic symbol – the national flag. Now this emblem, the flag, has become the trade mark of a certain State system. But if we look back at its evolution, we find it has passed through stages precisely corresponding to those of the sentiment of patriotism itself. At first it was represented by the totem, as it was called – that is, a symbol representing an animal or plant from which, according to the ideas of patriotism then prevalent, the tribe or clan believed itself to he descended, or at least whose preternatural protection it claimed. In the city stage the standard under which the citizen fought bore emblazoned on it the patron god of the city. During the Middle Ages we find a corresponding symbol in the patron saint of the township, or some sign supposed to represent him also inscribed on the town flag. The lord of every manor – i.e., the head of every rural community of the Middle Ages-also had the emblem representing his house, under which he fought, and which constituted his coat of arms. Now the modern nation, so soon as it became welded together as a centralised State – i.e., as the organised political whole which had destroyed the autonomy of the smaller social groups, and absorbed them – the modern nation also assumed a banner with devices taken from the arms of its royal house, or emblematic of something connected with national myth or history. The "Union Jack" of Great Britain (the two crosses), as you may know, was adopted in the reign of James I., in 1606, and in its present form (the three crosses), in that of George III., in 1801. The flag, in short, in all ages and countries has been always, in its chief aspect, a symbol of a particular form of the patriotic sentiment.

Patriotism, or the sentiment corresponding to it, out of which it sprang, has, as we have seen, its source and origin in a sentiment of solidarity with an organised group of persons supposed to have been descended from common ancestors. It had its meaning in an intimate sense of blood-kinship and the duties and privileges flowing from it. It was therefore necessarily limited in scope. Subsequently, as the social body got enlarged so as to include three or four or more tribes with their clans (a small

187

"people," in fact), often a settled community residing within walled or enclosed area round some natural stronghold, the sentiment of patriotism got enlarged too to that extent, and also became associated with a definite locality. Throughout antiquity and the Middle Ages – i.e., throughout the imperfect period, as we may call it, of State centralisation on an individualistic basis – the further extensions of the sentiment to vast aggregations of population and great extents of territory, as in modern times, were alike weak and more or less transient. Only under the influence of modern capitalism and modern State-centralisation, by which all the old group societies of whatever nature, the tribe, the clan, the village community, the trade guild or the township (as an independent political entity) have been broken up and their functions taken over by the central official organisation of the national State – in short, only since the autonomous individual has replaced the group as the unit of society can patriotism, in the modern sense, be said to have established itself.

And now the question arises in its transference and metamorphosis from the more or less limited social group, based originally on the idea of kinship, real or supposed, and later depending on local proximity, and to some extent on the possibility of mutual acquaintance, Has the sentiment of patriotism, I say, not lost all real meaning in this transference, and become a bogus and a sham sentiment no longer of any service to mankind, but on the other hand capable of being exploited by interested persons in a manner which renders it one of the most dangerous frauds at present existing?

Now let us ask ourselves what is the object which inspires modern national patriotic sentiment? It is, in the most important cases, a vast bureaucratic State-system, a huge official organisation. But, no, it will be said there is the question of race and language. In the British Islands the population consists in England of an amalgamation of various Teutonic races, the predominant being the Anglo-Saxon speaking, various dialects of the English language; in Wales we find a pure Keltic race speaking a pure Keltic language. In parts of Ireland and the north of Scotland we have another branch of the Keltic family, speaking another Keltic language. And yet Wales and even Ireland are called upon to be loyal, i.e., patriotic in the interests of the British Empire, i.e., of the domination of the Anglo-Saxon race over alien races.

Again, Switzerland, a country in which you find the strongest patriotic feeling, is mainly composed of fragments of three distinct modern nationalities with their several languages, each of which possesses outside the Swiss Confederation its own state system on a large scale. I might point out the same as regards France, Austria or Russia. It is plain therefore that neither identity of race nor language, nor, witness Germany and Austria, even a common history constitutes the essential basis of the patriotic feeling. The patriotic French Canadians have neither a common race, nor language, nor history with the Englishman. No, the only thing left then is an identity of State system, i.e., a common subjection to the same governing classes and the same official organisation.

Now this fact, we Socialists claim, is not good enough for a bond of union. We find nothing calculated to inspire a reasonable working-class in the thought that they are slaves of one governmental system run by their masters rather than another and a rival one. Hence the motto of Social-Democracy, "Proletarians of all countries unite." To-day we too often see the spectacle of the working classes uniting to applaud the crimes of their exploiters. And how is this? Because their exploiters are able to make use of the hereditary interest of slavish patriotism for their own purpose. It is related of John Huss, the reformer, that as he was being bound to the stake at Constance, he saw a feeble old woman bringing her bundle of fagots to feed the flames which were to consume him, but that the only words which escaped his lips were "Sancta Simplicitas" (Holy Innocence). I confess the same words have often come to my mind lately, as I have seen one slum vying with another more

189

squalid than itself in the number of Union jacks and royal ensigns it could display. I have endeavoured in a few words to indicate to you how the patriotic sentiment to-day has lost its old meaning, and as I maintain has lost all meaning.

If I can only persuade one among you to see how the working classes are being hoodwinked and duped in this country and elsewhere by patriotic cries, and to hasten the day, be it never so little, when the working classes of the civilised world will, with one consent, finally abandon the national flags of their masters, and range themselves under the banner of international Socialism and human brotherhood, I shall not have spoken in vain.

The "Collective Will" and Law

That the will of the majority is necessarily worthy of all acceptation is a proposition much affected by democrats in general, and is often opposed to the incoherent dreams of Anarchists, who think that in an organised society the individual will can assert its supremacy. Now, while in the main accepting the doctrine as urged against the atomistic theory of Anarchism, I am bound to enter a caveat against the too drastic, or rather uncritical, application of the formula in question. In the first place, what is the will of society, or of the majority? Is it the expressed will or the implied will, and, if so, how much of expression or of implied will goes to constitute the valid will as such? Is a *bare* majority sufficient? Is every act of a Parliament, lasting, say, for seven years, and passing measures anent questions upon which the constituencies have never been consulted, and many of which, in the hurry of modern life, are passed by unknown, unnoticed by the vast bulk of the population, to be regarded as representing the will of "society"? Then, again, is the will of the majority, even if it be really such – if, for example, it has expressed itself unmistakeably in an initiative or referendum which necessarily only reflects public opinion at a particular moment, possibly under the influence of panic – is such an expression, I ask, to be taken as a valid will, before which our deepest moral impulses as to justice and injustice must go under? I set aside such a monstrosity as decision, or judge-made law, such an important ingredient in the laws under which Englishmen live, as that is obviously a case in which society, or the "majority," is not consulted at all, though it is not so very different from the other case alluded to above of the measure passed by Parliament as to which the electors have had no voice. In either case the measure, or decision, is incorporated into the established order of things, and is allowed to remain there, not by the will expressed, or even necessarily implied, of the majority, but by the will-lessness, the apathy, of society as a whole. The majority might even disapprove, if questioned on the subject; but the law remains law, because the bulk of society is too indifferent or cannot afford time to getting it repealed. The only alternative remains, if we reject these definitions of the will of the majority, to fall back upon the arbitrary, but scarcely satisfactory, one by which everything which manages to get established is, by virtue of that circumstance, to rank as expressing the collective will.

Barring the last-mentioned solution, we are clearly confronted with more than one difficulty. We have to decide what degree of positive acceptance on the part of the majority constitutes a declaration of "will." This extends from a definite referendum or plebiscite, which, although it only expresses the will of the majority at a given moment, yet undoubtedly does so at that moment, down to a judicial decision, which probably expresses the will of only "three persons" (judges), with not even one god thrown in by way of makeweight.

If we decline to accept as authoritative anything short of a referendum, it is plain we shall rule out the enormous bulk of the laws and customs under which all civilised people live. While, on the other hand, if we accept the judge's "decision" as authoritatively representing the will of the nation, we may as well accept the ukase of any despot who by fraud, force or favour has attained to power, as being equally so. But if, once more, we refuse either alternative, and try to strike a middle course, the line we draw must, I submit, as things are to day, be purely arbitrary, not to speak of the difficulties in which we are still involved anent all laws or customs falling outside the line.

The result to which we must come would seem to be that the will or decision of the majority of the people cannot be effectively invoked in any but a few cases, that even under the most favourable circumstances it can only represent a passing phase of the will of the people, and therefore that this will, as expressed in any given manner, has no *absolute*, but only a very *relative* validity. But of what nature is this merely relative validity? It is clear that the *end* of all "just" political and social action is the welfare through progress of the whole – the commonweal. Now, to the Social-Democrat in the vast majority of issues, the verdict of the majority, fairly given, clumsy though it may be, as an instrument, is the best and indeed only possible one. But its validity can in no case be so absolute as that the individual conscience may not conceivably override it. Its verdict should be final for all democrats where it does not conflict with a deeper conviction before which the individual has the right, if he can, to make even the public opinion of the hour, bow. For example, I suppose there are few Socialists who would not be prepared to communise the means of production by force, and establish a collectivist *regime* even, against the will of the majority if that were possible. Again, there might easily be certain vindictive criminal laws in a moment of public panic receive the consent of the majority, and yet it might be the duty of the minority who disapproved of them to use every possible weapon at hand to render them inoperative. Strength of conviction in a matter seriously affecting the welfare of mankind and involving deep and decisive issues of right and wrong cannot under all circumstances bow even to the majority. For example, few would hold the judge guiltless who nowadays sentenced a witch or a heretic to be burned, notwithstanding that he might be merely carrying out the law in so doing. Yet it is held to be the correct thing to exonerate a judge on the ground of his office from blame in carrying out unjust laws, only when not so flagrant, and this is being done every day.

And here we come to an important point. Ought the "administrator and executor" of a law admitted to be against right and justice to be morally and materially exonerated on the ground of his being merely the agent for the carrying out of the collective will as supposed to be represented by that law There is no doubt that a bad law can be rendered inoperative if there is no one willing to carry it into effect. "Your majority has many faithful servants in this city of Bayonne, but not one executioner." The old theory of the English bench was that the judge was only bound to give effect to a statute if it were not against his conscience. This old theory has, of course, long lapsed in favour of the convenient doctrine that the judge can do no wrong, that his position, so far as responsibility is concerned, is that of an automaton. For those of us who decline to accept the assumption that any man can divest himself of moral responsibility for his personal actions, at will, this conventional doctrine is scarcely a satisfactory solution of the difficulty. The only logical alternative is to make the judge who puts in execution a bad law, notably where it seriously affects the life and liberty of citizens, liable, not merely morally, at the hands of public opinion, but civilly or criminally, for the act done in the performance of his so-called "duty." He is the principal agent in the wrong inflicted. "You can't indite a nation." You can seldom bring to book the makers of a law (except, of course, in the case of decision-law.) Hence it is the more urgent in the interests of true justice, that the proximate cause of the wrong, the judicial actualiser of the law, should suffer for it, where the law is subsequently recognised as unjust. If it be said that the judge himself may have honestly believed in the justice of the law and of his sentence I reply that that does not alter the criminality of his act. The Anarchist may conscientiously believe that all statesmen and police functionaries are scoundrels whose blood justice demands. Yet if he proceeds to mete out to them the just penalties of their crimes as he and his fellows conceive them, he is, nevertheless, in spite of his conscientious belief in the righteousness of what he has done, deemed fairly amenable to punishment. So with the judge. The recognition of the injustice of a criminal law ought to carry with it, in the minds of those who do so recognise it, the demand of merely for its abolition but for the punishment of those who from the secure position of the judicial bench have carried its provisions into effect. The middle-classes of France after the "terror" guillotined Fouquier Tinville and the jurors of the "Revolutionary tribunal" for having given effect in their official capacities to a law passed by the Convention, i.e., established by the then Government of France, thereby recognising the principle here put forward. That they were justified in so doing is to me perfectly clear. The right of no man ought to be admitted to divest himself of the personal responsibility attaching to his personal acts. No man is compelled to be a judge or executioner against his will, or being such, to remain a judge or executioner. He personally elects to put a law into execution, and as such ought to be prepared to abide by the possible consequences to his own person of his own act. There is no special sanctity in "law" merely as law, which may indeed be the expression of a lasting public opinion, but also may not. The administrator of the law in refusing to execute a bad law involving injury to his fellow citizens is performing a great public service. It at least gives "pause." If the administrator has been mistaken in his refusal others will undoubtedly be found to execute it, but in any case he himself is exonerated. If time shows he is right he may well have been the means of rendering an unjust law nugatory.

In conclusion, we may ask ourselves, is there any case in which the expressed will of a majority, certainly a large proportional majority, if not a final arbiter of right, would at least approach to this condition in an infinitely greater degree than any majority that does, or is supposed to, impose its will on the world in the present day. I think there is, and that it is to he found, and found only in a democracy where certain well-defined general principles are universally recognised as lying at the basis of all social life as to the reciprocal rights and duties of individual and community. This condition, it is scarcely necessary to say, has never been realised as yet. It can only obtain in anything approaching a complete form under a Social-Democracy, in which a self consistent theory of moral and social life has grown up, and in which any intrenchment on its principles in the old direction of personal coercion will be impossible. In these circumstances the will of the majority as expressed in a referendum or initiative in matters lying outside the moral and social "canon," as we may term it, would be (for practical purposes), *absolutely* binding on all citizens.

The Bourgeois Radical Movement and Socialism

We often hear the observation made by Socialists in a deprecating manner respecting some theory or agitation forming part of the party programme, "Oh, that as been taken over from the old middle-class Radicalism." The implication is, of course, that the position in questions is a superstition which ought to be got rid of by Socialists, or which at best has no particular connection with Socialism. The persons who use this argument, ignore the fact that there are many points in the programme of the old Radicalism which Socialism presupposes, but which have as yet never been realised. We too often forget that the middle classes have only very imperfectly fulfilled the task assigned to them by their historical function, and that reforms unfulfilled, or at least only half-fulfilled by the middle-class naturally fall to the lot of social-democracy to carry through. These are the points of contact between Radicalism and Socialism. The only difference is that Socialism consistently regards them merely parts of a whole, whereas radicalism commonly conceives them as independent ends in themselves. But this is no reason why Socialists should not treat such aims as an essential part of their programme and why they should not energetically work for them.

The relation of the ideas of the old middle-class revolutionary movement with regard to the modern revolutionary movement of Socialism is really threefold – (1) There are the ideas and objects which especially concern the former, and which have been long since *generally* adopted or realised; (2) there are the ideas and objects which in themselves more intimately concern both movements, but which, owing to their civilly been *in the main* adopted or realised, have lost the practical importance they once had; (3) theme are the ideas and objects which concern both movements, but which have not as yet won a complete victory even in essentials, and hence which still retain their practical importance. We will consider these three categories for a moment. To the first class belong all suffrage movements based on property – i.e. short of the universal suffrage movement – freedom of domicile, abolition of restrictions on combination, together with Malthusianism, the attack on luxury as such, stale gibes on aristocratic vices and bad habits, the view that a Republican is necessarily a democrat, and generally the revolt against the old-fashioned and direct forms of political tyranny whose poetical expression is to be best found in Shelley; and last, but not least, nationalist movements. The second comprises most fiscal and currency reforms, also the universal suffrage movement, payment of members, Republicanism, *viewed as a burning question*, Disestablishment, and the attack on the classes privileged by *status*, such as noblemen, apart from the general capitalistic class), the Prince of Wales, and so on. Finally, the third category is represented by the movement for secular education, for freeing the individual from oppressive laws relating to marriage, for the assertion of the principle of sexual freedom before the law and public opinion, for the repeal of other laws wantonly hindering the individual from living his own life, which are based, not on economic or political necessity but on old conventions that have lost all their meaning, if they ever had any, or on bald moral prepossessions or theological superstitions, and this despite the attempt which will probably he made to justify them on grounds of social expediency as a last resort.

If we once distinguish between these various classes of questions we shall see that the vague allegation one hears sometimes from Socialists to the effect that so-and-so "belongs to the old bourgeois Radicalism," with the derogatory implication that the theory or agitation in question is a superstition no longer worthy of the attention of Socialists, is utterly empty and stupid. That there is some such superstitions one would not deny. But an agitation may have been taken over from the old political Radicalism, and yet may be a most important ingredient in the modern Social-Democratic movement. Modern Socialism, as already said, presupposes all or most of the reforms championed by the middle-class movement of the last century, and the earlier decades of this. And in so far as this movement has not fulfilled its function, in so far as it has not carried these reforms through, the said function necessarily passes on to the movement which succeeds it in the scale of historical progress. As already said, there are some points striven for by the earlier Radicalism which, although they have not been completely realised, have nevertheless made such headway that their importance effectively gives place to that of other more urgent points of agitation. But there are none the less, on the other hand, objects equally common to the modern and the older movement, which it is just as necessary to urge forward parallel with the directly economical objects immediately concerning the working-class struggle of to day.

For example, anti-militarism in Germany is a "plank" common alike to Herr Richter and to the Social Democrats. Similarly the onslaught on police-bureaucracy. Yet again, the attack on a monarchical veto. All those things are essential to Social-Democracy, and, being as yet unrealised by the old Radicalism whence they sprung, must necessarily loom big in the Social-Democratic agitation. Before deciding whether a doctrine or aim of the old Radicalism should constitute a living part of our programme, or not, we must judge the particular point in question on its merits, The fact of its belonging to the old Radicalism is not in itself against it. Let us take two instances of ideas for which the old middle-class Radicalism strove. The first is the idea of "nationality." This implies that the political "unity" and "independence" of a certain territorial aggregate (by no means always conterminous with race or language, but which in a more or less vague way aims at being so) should be a primary aim of the party of progress. Now this was certainly very essential to the development of modern capitalism in more ways than one. Small states with a diversity of laws affecting industry and commerce, with no uniformity of coinage, with different customs arrangements, and with Governments none of them stable, as centralised Governments are, but of various degrees of instability, were obviously awkward factors in an expansive capitalism which required a free world-market for its continued existence, not to say development. Hence small independent feudal states had to go, the process being gilded over by the sentimental humbug of "patriotism."

The movement associated with the year 1848 which aimed at the establishment of centralised governments on a national basis was the high-water mark of the bourgeois ideal of nationality. In so far as nationalism, i.e. the independence and unification of nationalities was essential to progress, it was accomplished by the movement named, which reached its climax in the foundation of the German Empire. Socialism, as such, has, I contend, nothing to do with the aspirations of struggling nationalities towards independence and the attainment of "national consciousness," and a national existence – with the endeavours of Greece to enlarge her boundaries for the purpose of floating a new loan with Armenian independence or with Polish patriotism. If a partial exception be made in the case of Ireland, it is only because English rule in Ireland is s intimately bound up with the question of absentee landlordism, and the whole Irish agrarian problem. Nationalism, with its corresponding ideological expressions covered by the word patriotism, may have had its historical justification, but with its further realisation Socialism has no interest or concern. However necessary it may have been, dynamically considered, as an element in the capitalist phase of social development, like every other essential element in that phase, it has *per se* been an unmitigated curse. The material fact of national unity and independence, whether in the case of Germany, Hungary, or Italy, has never brought any good to the working classes of the countries in question. The moral spirit engendered by it, the idiotic self-glorification of every nationality at the expense of every other, has been fruitful in nothing but obstruction to

200

progress, delay in the Socialist movement, and a whole shoal of red-herrings of every description.

It is quite true that Socialism will have to take over the accursed legacy of existing national frontiers from the bourgeois world-order, but Socialism will take it over merely with the view of killing it off and burying it at the earliest possible moment. Here Socialism is at a disadvantage as compared with Christianity. The latter found the old local patriotisms sapped and undermined by the Roman imperial system. Unfortunately we have no international power, even though that power were despotic, to do us the service of treading under its iron heel the sham sentiment evoked by the amorphous aggregates of population embodied in the modern centralised nation or state. The ancient "city" was, at least, an organically rounded-off social entity of manageable size. The modern nation or centralised state is a hideous monstrosity, the offspring of capitalism in its various phases, in its present shape the outcome of the developed capitalism of the great industry. We quite admit that in form it may, and probably will, survive the earlier stages of Socialism, but its ultimate disappearance is none. the loss certain. The sentiment of national patriotism will then, let is hope, be reduced to its last expression the holding of annual dinners, or some harmless festivity of this sort, such as is affected by the natives of certain English counties resident in the metropolis. The Nationalist movement, therefore, is an old Radical "plank", which clearly no longer belongs to us as Socialists.

We will now take an opposite example. We not unfrequently hear that the attack on the old theological systems, as enslaving the human mind to-day, is a matter with which we have no special concern. This is, however, on quite a different footing to the foregoing. Secular education, of course, forms part of the Social Democratic programme in all countries. But, weakened though it has been, it would be rash to say that clericalism, in the shape of theological dogma, has ceased to be a danger, and hence is no longer to be regarded as an active enemy.

The weapons of the old Radical Free Thought movement in the popular attack on this evil may have been largely superseded by the weapons of modern science and criticism; and the direct onslaught may have become less necessary since the flank movement has, so to say, taken the enemy in the rear. This admission by no means says that a direct attack is even now never the right tactics to pursue. It does not exonerate us from the obligation of making such a direct attack whenever the occasion presents itself. (Religion may be a "private matter", as the German programme has it, in many case, but it ceases to be a private matter when it stands in the way of popular intellectual progress and especially when it tends to interfere with a scientific insight into historical and social problems. The allegation that Socialism has no opinions on such questions must be taken in a somewhat Pickwickian sense. What is really meant thereby is that among persons whose theological belief is practically dead, but who may or may not have a certain sentimental affection for the old formulae embodying that belief it is not worth while stirring up dying dogs by unnecessarily gibbeting of these formulae. But, on the other hand, let any socialist agitator try and bring home the truths of Socialism to a body of persons possessed of any serious belief in theology, and he will soon have the necessity of taking up a determined attitude on these questions brought home to him. The practical good sense of Socialists in such cases generally gets the better of their rigid shibboleth, and their anti-theological (not merely non-theological) attitude becomes as robust and aggressive as that of an old Voltairean. In this case it, is clear, therefore, that talk about aggressive atheism or aggressive freethought as belonging exclusively to the old radicalism is nonsensical where it is not actually disingenuous. In fact, in face of the active campaign of the Roman Catholic Church among peasants and workmen in many parts of the continent of Europe, as well as in some of the States of North America, the notion of maintaining that religion is at purely private matter, and Socialism has no concern with ii, if it is a pretence is a dishonest farce, and if it were no pretence would mean treachery to the party.

It were surely a much better policy while always insisting on the avoidance of barren theological controversies or the unnecessary irritation of smouldering religious sentiment to candidly admit that Socialism, like every other system of society, has its own *Weltanschaung*, or conception of the universe, and that, rash as it would undoubtedly be at present to attempt to confine it within the four corners of any formula or set of formulae – that nevertheless, it is, if nothing else, incompatible with the supernaturalism and with much of the ethics of the old religious systems. It is, of course, perfectly true that a man may favour any particular "planks" of the immediate party programme and vote for them while remaining a strict Catholic or Calvinist or Jew or Moslem; the present writer would be the last in the world to choke off such extraneous aid – aid which is not merely desirable or advantageous, but, in the present position of affairs at least, is in most countries absolutely essential to the formation of a Parliamentary Socialist Party. All that is sought to be urged here merely points to a distinction between such "proselytes of the gate" and those who definitely recognised as members of the Socialist Party. The profession of dogmatic theological beliefs by the latter can but mean one of two things – either deliberate deception, or such a hopeless nebulosity of mind as to suggest that the personas in question are extremely undesirable members of an organisation where sincerity, outspokeness of conviction and clearness of intention are of the first importance.

Treacherous Toleration and Faddist Fanaticism

Social-Democracy has been unwearied in the affirmation of its principles not only against the present order of society and its supporters, but also against those who, while on one side professing the same ultimate end as Social-Democrats, nevertheless on another repudiate alike the programme of Social-Democracy and its method and policy. I refer to the various groups of "Communist-Anarchists" and "non-Parliamentarian Socialists." There is, of course, a type of Anarchist who, by his very principles, cuts himself off from Socialism altogether. But those Anarchists who label themselves as above, whatever they may do or feel, however illogical they may be in theory, at least do not definitely detach themselves from Socialism. And the latter type, to which the majority of persons calling themselves Anarchists belong, is nevertheless regarded by Social-Democrats as the greatest danger to the party when hanging on to its skirts. Now there is, I conceive, a dangerous tendency everywhere, at the present time, that the movement, having religiously expelled all elements that could be suspected of Anarchism in any form or shape, denouncing the "toleration" certain comrades would have extended to such misguided persons as of the devil – there seems; I say, a grave danger of its developing a limitless toleration in the opposite direction. While to doubt the efficacy of Parliamentary action is anathema, to doubt or to express open disbelief in the root-principles of Socialism is deemed quite consistent with continued membership of the party. The very self-same persons who would give a Nieuwenhuis and a Landauer short shrift, grow eloquent upon the undesirability of "making a martyr of" a Bernstein or a Blatchford or of anyone who under cover of the name of Socialist preaches anti-Socialistic reaction, be it music-hall jingoism or the doctrine that the proximate end of Socialism is municipal tramways and its highest ideal improved factory legislation. The Socialist body as a whole, it is said, is sound and does not sympathise with, indeed, utterly repudiates, these views. But it would be a mistake, it is further said, to expel these persons or to refuse to recognise them as comrades! (Oh Socialism, Socialism, what queer fish they would have us assimilate in thy name!) For do they not believe in municipal tramways, lighting, water, and even sewage; nay, have they not intimated their willingness, under certain circumstances, to consider legislative interference with the conditions of adult labour? How can one refuse to recognise such a man as this as a full-blown Socialist, even though in other matters of secondary importance – such, for example, as war, internationalism, foreign policy, belief in and work for the transformation of society by the communisation of the instruments of production, &c. – he is not as sound as we could wish? No, we are told if we want a big party, or even a party at all, we must count all as fish (however "queer" it may be) that comes to our net – all men as comrades who adopt our label, and consent to swallow, say, a little municipal sewage by way of credentials. The way in which men, who, if they only happen to depart from Socialism on the reactionary side, are tolerated, gives pause indeed to consider, when we think of the promptness with which men who talked too "revolutionary" have been given their party-quietus in the recent past. Talking too revolutionary may be silly, it may be waste of time, and do no good; but reactionary doctrine, jingoism, gas-and-water Socialism, factory legislation as panacea, these things sap the foundation of Socialist theory and disintegrate the party. The weak-kneed toleration which shudders with horror at the idea of not regarding as a "comrade" a Blatchford, a Bland, or a Bernstein, because they have done – what? Merely set at nought what are elsewhere acknowledged as fundamental doctrines of Socialism, that is all – is surely a sign of decadence in a party, not of strength. If those who hold such views as the above-mentioned "comrades" (?) are not aware that they have, *ipso facto* ceased to be Socialists, surely it is the duty of the party, as such, to point it out to them. That good Social-Democrats can take up this attitude over "differences of opinion" of such wide-reaching importance as those referred to, and yet be prepared to unceremoniously eject a comrade who happens to disagree with the rest of the party as to the value of Parliamentary action (important though this latter may also be), must surely have ideas of party logic which are decidedly peculiar, and hence require an explanation which we have as yet waited for in vain.

But where are you to draw the line, it will be said? You cannot have unity of opinion on every question. This is perfectly true, and no one would suggest making a test point of vaccination or anti-vaccination, teetotalism, or moderate drinking, of a belief or disbelief in "occult phenomena," of any point of metaphysic or of more opinion. But let us remember that Socialist principle is definite and not to be played fast and loose with by Socialists, if the name is to retain any significance whatever. Hence the question of the soundness or unsoundness of any individual opinion often turns on the way it is held. Thus a Socialist may express an admiration for an ascetic life (say) or for exclusive fruit-eating, or for top-hats, and prefer those things to their opposites without any violence to his Socialism. But if he preaches asceticism, fruit-eating or top-hats as the great panacea for social ills, then he, *ipso facto*, ceases to belong to the Socialist Party, and to tolerate him as a "comrade" is simple idiocy. What is vital in Socialism? In the first line, I take it, comes the (1) Collectivisation of *all* the instruments of production by *any* effective means ; (2) The doctrine of the class war as the general historical method of realising the new form of society ; (3) The principle of internationalism, the recognition, i.e., that distinction of nationality sinks into nothingness before the idea of the union of all progressive races in the effort to realise the ideal of true society, as understood by the Social Democratic Party; (1) The utmost freedom of physical, moral and intellectual development for each and all consistent with the bare necessities of an organised social State.

For the rest, the question turns upon the consistency or inconsistency of any theory, with those positions. It is commonly asked whether dogmatic theological belief is consistent with Socialist principle. I take it that the promulgation of the thesis that the acceptance of any dogma which primarily has any other basis whatever except reason (i.e., a logical process resting on given matter-of-fact) is essential to personal or social salvation or well being, is anti-Socialistic, and that the man who promulgates it can no longer claim to belong to the Socialist Party. This is why the Socialist Party as such can never be Christian. Christianity requires an act of faith on the part of its votary. He may prop his faith up by reason afterwards, if he will, but his first duty as a Christian is faith in a divine revelation. The doctrines of Socialism are held by Socialists on the ground of a conviction arrived at by reason, observation and evidence, and they are prepared to stand or fall by this test.

Another point. The mere repetition of an abstract Socialist formula is not of itself sufficient to constitute a man a Socialist. He must be prepared to adopt and act upon the implications which the formula directly involves. Thus his adhesion to the doctrine of the class war involves his opposition to all measures subserving the interest of any section of capitalism. This, coupled with his Internationalism, leaves him no choice but to be the enemy of "his country" and the friend of his country's enemies whenever "his country" (which means, of course, the dominant classes of his country, who always are, for that matter, his enemies) plays the game of the capitalist. Let us have no humbug. The man who cannot on occasion be (if need be) the declared and active enemy of that doubtful entity "his country" is no Social-Democrat. Again, a man may call himself and be called a Socialist because he is willing to nationalise or municipalise certain branches of industry on the ground of their peculiar monopolistic nature rendering nationalisation or municipalisation desirable and feasible in his opinion, while at the same time repudiating the desirability or feasibility of the socialising of other branches of industry, where these peculiar conditions do not obtain. This exceptional Socialism represents the attitude of the average Fabian, the Webbite, though not, I believe, of all Fabians. Now are we, I ask, to be condemned to hug such a man as this to our bosoms as a "comrade" because, forsooth, he can in a contain sense repeat that he favours the "socialisation of the means, &c."

The Socialist Party ought to come to a clear understanding as to what amount of divergence from principle and declared policy can be tolerated from professed members of the party. Let us hope the next international congress will deal with it. At present we find ourselves in the anomalous position of having persons (few I admit) nominally in our ranks, who are positively less socialistic or even more anti-socialistic than many who still claim to be no more than Liberals or Radicals.

Factitious Unity

There is an unmistakeable tendency in the present, day among political parties claiming to represent advanced principles to erect party unity into a fetish before which everything else must bow. The integrity of principles is quite a secondary consideration provided that the unity of the party be maintained. Anything to avoid a split – that is the motto of the practical politician of the dawning twentieth century. Now, it would surely be well for some of the enthusiastic advocates of unity at any price to ask themselves occasionally for what their party exists, about the integrity of whose unity they are so zealous? Is unity, then, for the sake of the party, or the party for the sake of unity? Wherein lies the raison d'etre of the party? Is the object of the part y the realisation of certain principles, or do the principles exist for the sake of the party in such wise as the, green dragon, the name, and the painted signboard exists for the sake of the publican or the wholesale brewer behind him? The green dragon plainly has no reason for its existence apart from beer and profits, and since a patch of red or a patch of yellow on the dragon's tail, nay the metamorphosis of the dragon itself into a sea-serpent, is unlikely to seriously affect either beer or profits, such changes as above may well be regarded with comparative indifference by the eye of the publican, provided the licence remains intact. In the same way, if the principles of a party are like the signboard depicting the green dragon, the unity of the party, like the integrity of the publican's licence, is obviously the one thing needful. . If the end and object is money, office, or power for its own sake, then clearly the solicitude of the practical politician, as he is called, to avoid a split in the party, is justified in its day and generation. If, on the contrary, party organisation itself is subservient to certain definite ideals, and has no abject or significance apart from such, then equally clearly, whenever those ideals are threatened by the unity of the party, that unity must go by the board.

But, it will be said, a split in a party can hardly fail to impair its efficiency as an instrument for the realisation of its ideals. Moreover, a party cannot afford to lose, maybe, able and energetic men. Hence it is surely much better to patch up differences of opinion that may exist, and unite on the basis of same vague and general formula on which all can agree. To this it may be replied, as concerns the first point, that the realisation of the ideals of a party is less likely to be effectuated by the attenuation of those ideals for the sake of mere numerical strength than by the surrender of certain amount of such strength on behalf of the vigorous maintenance intact of the principles for the sake of which the party avowedly exists. What may be gained by the sacrifice of the integrity of principle is at most the gain or partial gain of some temporary success. For example, by throwing everything else overboard, the S.D.F. might possibly succeed by a coalition with other bodies in realising, say, payment of members or such an undoubted social reform as the eight hours day in all Government departments. But the S.D.F. would see greater things than these. It is not for these things, or such as these, desirable as they undoubtedly are in themselves, that twenty years of unceasing work and sacrifice have been offered up. It is for something else that well-nigh a whole generation of Socialists in Great Britain has learned to labour and to wait.

Then as to the second point. It is alleged, by practical politicians, so called, as a reason for toleration or compromise, that a party cannot afford to lose an able man or men, merely because they happen to be shaky on some vital point of principle. To this it may be replied that the ability of doubtful members cuts both ways. It may be of more danger to party principles when inside the party organisation than it is of advantage to the enemy when working against it outside. A party having any regard for its principles should, surely look to it that its able men – those, therefore, most powerful for leading – should be straight even

212

more than the ordinary rank and file – and, hence, if they go wrong, should be the more inexorably expelled. A party that is worth its salt can always afford to lose a man or two without collapsing, but it cannot always afford to have a powerful leader inside incessantly pulling the wrong way. Here, again, we ask, is the object of the party to hold together solely for the sake of office, emoluments, or party tranquillity, or for the sake of its avowed aims.

One illustration of the tendency of the practical politician to sacrifice all to avoid "splitting the party" is afforded by the British Radicals of the present time, and another by the German Social Democrats. Whatever we may think of English radicalism as a political creed, it has certainly in the past represented some definite principles. Those principles were those of the rising middle classes while they were still revolutionary. They involved the negation of nearly everything that modem Imperialism champions. The Peace, Retrenchment, and Reform doctrine meant attention to home affairs, hence anti-expansion, anti-militarism, enthusiasm for the rights of small and weaker nations, and all-round general political rectitude. Now, modern Imperialism, as just said, whether it call itself Liberal or other, means ruthless disregard of all other nations and races where their rights conflict with your own, reckless expenditure or military and naval matters, and a postponement of the domestic reforms, so, dear to the heart of the old Liberal, to the Greek Kalends. All this is admitted in so many words in platform speeches by the leaders of the Liberal Party. And yet we find these very same leaders, from Campbell-Bannerman to Lloyd George, literally grovelling on their bellies before a man like Lord Rosebery, the very incarnation of the Imperialism they otherwise denounce, eagerly catching at every insidious phrase let fall by their oracle for the purpose of twisting it into the semblance of a modification of the view the speaker is otherwise known to hold. And all for what? That the Liberal party organisation may reap the temporal advantages believed to ensue from a man of Lord Rosebery's position and influence deigning to reenter its ranks. The Liberal leaders know well enough that Lord Rosebery at heart has no sympathy with the views hitherto connoted by the term Liberalism, views which they themselves, in general, profess to still hold. But what of that? If Liberal principles lose the Liberal organisation gains, as they think.

We Socialists of the S.D.F. justly pour contempt on the English Liberal Party for its inconsistency and time-serving. We must not, however, permit ourselves to be too self-righteous. The glorification of mere unity as such, however false and factitious it, may be, is unfortunately not confined to Liberalism. It seems, unhappily, a pestilence which dogs the steps of every party that has grown to any considerable proportions in wealth and influence. We see much the same thing at the present time among our comrades of the German Social Democratic Party. It has been of late crucially manifested in the, Bernstein controversy. Mr. Bernstein repudiates almost every principle hitherto regarded as of "faith" in Social Democracy. He champions every form and well-nigh every abuse of capitalism. The politico financial schemes, of Messrs. Rhodes, Beit, and the cosmopolitan financiers of the Rand generally have found in him their warmest advocate. English misrule in India he also takes under his aegis. He has systematically attacked every Social Democratic doctrine in turn, to the delight of reactionary readers and hearers. In a, word, Mr. Bernstein is incomparably less friendly. to Socialism, if any meaning is to be attached to the word at all, than the mildest English Radical. To judge from his expressed opinions, in fact, Mr. Bernstein has no more sympathy with the recognised principles of Social Democracy, and perhaps rather less than Count von Bulow himself. And yet, wonderful to relate, for fear of causing a split in the party, for fear of jeopardising party unity, the German Social Democrats could not muster up sufficient courage to exclude Mr Bernstein from their ranks. In this case the mere desire of preserving a formal unity must be alone in question, since it can hardly be alleged that there is any extraordinary ability at stake.

One must admit, of course, the difficulties a large party has to contend with. Differences of opinion on matters of tactics, on minor and outlying points of theory, or even, it may be, in one or two items of the immediate progamme – that such must be we fully recognise. But whatever may be said, it is not difficult to distinguish between this and unsoundness of fundamental principle. Social Democrats, at least, of all lands, need to pull themselves together, and wage a war to the knife, against the modern accursed tendency to the glorification of Factitious Unity.

Down With the Pioneer!

The greatest foe of all progress is the superannuated pioneer. The man, or the party, or the society, or the public body, which in its time has played a conspicuous part in a particular phase of the progressive movement, and especially if he or it has succeeded in materially helping to realise the particular phase in question, is, almost invariably, an obstacle in the path of further progress. After us the deluge, so far as progress is concerned, is the attitude of the pioneer who has done his work. That progress should have any further phase beyond the one which has made his own reputation, or which he has been instrumental in achieving, never seems to occur to the pioneer. But unfortunately he does not always confine himself to passive opposition, only too frequently misusing the influence or name he has acquired through his previous exploits by throwing it into the scales on the side of reaction.

Illustrations of the above thesis are to be had galore. What more worthless politicians from a democratic point of view, or more hopeless reactionaries, than are to be found among the survivors of the '48 movement? Your Kossuths, your Crispis, your Mazzinis, what did they later become? Kossuth declared the greatest danger of the age to be Socialism, Crispi developed into the notorious premier of Umberto, Mazzini into the cowardly denouncer of the Commune while the corpses of its martyrs still strewed the streets of Paris. The contemptible nationalist ideal for which the men of '48 mostly fought was miserable enough, it is true, but it is supposed to represent a stage in the development of modern capitalism from feudal conditions, and as such could be conceived in its day and generation as a progressive idea. Yet the anti-Socialism of most of its former apostles is notorious.

Again, take our own trade unions. The notion of the modern workman's combination was looked upon as revolutionary in early part of the nineteenth century – nay, later than the middle of the century the defence of trade unionism was counted to Professor Beesly for a righteousness entitling him to rank among the boldest of advanced social thinkers for all time. The feeling of the governing classes towards it, until quite recently, may be measured by the fact that it is scarcely a generation since the last of its legal disabilities was abolished – by no means without opposition. Yet what is the greatest obstacle to the formation of a solid Socialist party in this country? Precisely this very trade unionism, the erstwhile pioneer of working-class emancipation! Just those very men who, in their day, valiantly championed the cause of working-class organisation to attain limited economic ends against the capitalist and official reactionists of that time, are the men who to-day are most eager to block the way toward that organisation for political purposes, which has for its goal the complete emancipation of labour, economic, political and social.

To descend from great issues to a comparatively small one. A great authority in sanitation was telling me the other day, that the two most backward provincial towns of England, in matters sanitary, now, are precisely the two which were the first to adopt modern principles of sanitation at all. Having arrived at this stage, no power has yet been able to induce them to make those further improvements which other towns, many of which have only within the last few years had any sanitation in any form or shape, are now enjoying.

Once more. What country has the stiffest and most illiberal system of divorce in the present day? None other than England, the country which was the first to adopt the modern principle of the legal dissolution of the legal status of marriage under any conditions. While on the Continent, where divorce has been recently introduced, and in most of the States of North America, a marriage can be dissolved on any reasonable grounds, incompatibility of temper and the like, in Great Britain our judges and legists have steadfastly and systematically set their faces against any reform of the old English statute which makes

218

adultery the sole ground for divorce. Not only have they striven against reform by legislation, but they have done their utmost by decision to accentuate the principle of the indissolubility of marriage on any other than the ground named.

Everywhere, and on all hands, we find illustrations of the truth that the greatest foes of progress are its pioneers. Be it the man, the nation, or the public body which has been the most active in fighting successfully for a reform or a progressive idea, he, she or it, there are ten chances to one, will be the greatest obstacle and often the bitterest foe of all further reform. Explain it as you will, fact it remains. Oh! if the average man would but learn to rule the opinion of the pioneer out in all issues of progress!

Natural history tells us of orders of living beings (e.g., insects) who die after having laid their eggs or otherwise accomplished their reproductive functions. Unfortunately the pioneer does not generally die after having accomplished *his* function. On the contrary, he has a way of hanging on a long time – be he man, institution, or national mode of thought. I am not in the habit of quoting the Bible, or seasoning my Socialism with Christian sentiment, but I must say that there is one passage in the epistle to the Galatians (chap.v), which appeals to me in this connection. "I would that they were even cut off that trouble you," writes St. Paul anent his Petrine rivals, who seem to have been giving trouble in his newly founded "branch." Now, here I feel inclined to echo the spirit of the aspiration expressed by the great "Apostle of the Gentiles." Would indeed that the pioneer were cut off as soon as his work were done, or, at least, on his first symptoms of "troubling"!

Imperial Extension and Colonial Enterprise

What Imperial extension, what the blessings of our beneficent rule, what the opening up of new territories *are supposed* to mean we all know. What these high-sounding terms really mean, few of us distinctly realise. The working-class at home see that they are not materially benefited by the expansion of Greater Britain, as it is called. But they are assured by their pastors and masters that it is a necessary and glorious thing, and as this thought affords them some amusement now and then at the music halls, in the shape of refrains and cheers, they are content to let the matter slide. They do not see that the question concerns their interests one way or the other, otherwise than sentimentally in the capacity of subjects of that glorious Empire upon which the sun never sets. Yet it unquestionably does concern them. It may not immediately influence wages or hours, but it affects something more vital to them than wages or hours, it affects the system upon which wages and hours are based.

The capitalist system of the Old World, as we often say, is breaking down by its own weight, i.e., the system of the exploitation of labour by the monopoly of the means of production has reached a stage at which it cannot control the means of exchange. The home markets of every country are exhausted, and the foreign markets hitherto open are becoming rapidly exhausted too. Even where this is not the case, the ceaseless expansion of competitive production of itself necessitates the continuous opening-up of new markets. Add to this the advantages as to cheapness in the employment of native as against European labour in many important branches of production which follows in the wake of the conquest or "civilisation" or annexation of new countries. The various mining companies of South Africa have already practically got rid of white labour altogether. Hence the Chinese slavery which has scandalised all decent persons.

Here, then, we have the true meaning of modern foreign policy, the real aim behind that philanthropy which is so anxious for the spread of civilisation, for the christianising of the negro, and for the suppression of the slave trade. What the governing classes and their catspaws, the philanthropists, really want is to open-up markets into which to "shoot" the shoddy products of their factories and to acquire fresh fields and pastures new wherein to start fresh profit-grinding operations. The sole benefit of Imperial expansion accrues in the long run to the large capitalist. That he may be glad to "shoot" certain portions of the surplus population of these islands into new lands is quite true, and even that he may be willing to grant free passages for the necessitous unemployed who are willing to be "shot" there. And for a very good reason. By so doing he kills two birds with one stone. He gets rid of dangerous elements at home, and he plants the nucleus of a new reserve army of labour in the fresh territories to be exploited. All this is gilded by the talk of the "chances" by which a few out of the thousands of emigrants sent out rise by land-grabbing to become rich exploiters in their turn. Emigration, we repeat, is only a subtle device to prevent a revolution at home by which a radical change in the present system might be effected, and to extend the operations of that system.

Whether the working-classes of Great Britain or of any other country desire an indefinite prolongation of present conditions it is, of course, for them to say. But it cannot be sufficiently impressed upon them that such is the effect, say, of the successful opening-up of Africa to capitalist exploitation, or, as it is speciously termed, to the "influences of civilisation," by the European Powers. And this is the case, no matter which "Power" or "Powers" are engaged in the operations of conquest and annexation. How important is the opening-up of Africa for the growth and even the continued existence of capitalism, is shown by the fact that even where there is otherwise a rivalry among civilised nations, their governing classes will stand in together against the barbarian just as they will against the proletarian. Frenchmen will assist Italians, Germans Britishers when it is a question of the "nigger" asserting his claim to independence, and to live his own life in peace and freedom, just as German assisted Frenchman at the time of the Commune, when it was a question of the workman asserting his claim to independence. Whatever be the squabbles, national or sectional, of capitalists with each other, they will always close in their ranks when capitalists, as a whole, and capitalism itself, are threatened, whether by barbarians or proletarians. The insurgent barbarian attacks the invading capitalist civilisation in the interests of a pre-capitalist form of human society, the insurgent proletarian attacks it in the interest of a post-capitalist form of society. The savage or the barbarian fights for his independence, in order that he may live on in his old, crude, primitive, semi-communistic life of the past. The workman, the proletarian, in so far as he rebels against the power of capital, is fighting, unconsciously though it may be, for the higher, the fully-developed, communistic life of the future.

This higher Communism, in which the work of the world will be carried on by all in the interest of all, and not by one class in the interest of another class, is what modern civilisation has before it as its inevitable outcome, but the result may be retarded, the present system of exploitation and wage-slavery may be maintained for a generation or longer yet, by the sweeping away of the independence of the savage and barbaric peoples of the earth and the opening up of their territories to European commerce and industry. Just as the one hope of the slave-holding states of North America of maintaining the system of negro slavery lay in the formation of new slave-states out of the fresh territories that were being opened up on the eve of the American civil war, so the one hope of maintaining the present system of wage-slavery is to extend its sphere of operations. In order to continue to exist it must destroy primitive societies all the world over, together with earlier methods of the exploitation of human labour – above all, chattel slavery. Hence its sham humanitarian zeal! Its enemies, therefore, are two, one in the rear and one in the front – Barbarism and Socialism. This being so, it is clearly the interest of Socialists, and of the working-class movement generally, to make common cause with these primitive peoples – barbarian or savage, as we term them – who are resisting the invasion of their ancestral tribal lands and the overturning of their old social customs and constitution by hordes of hired ruffians and buccaneers sent by European Governments to clear the way for capitalism with maxims and new pattern rifles. There are many ways in which a spoke may be put in the wheels of these forces of aggressive capitalism. Those of an adventurous turn, instead of joining the hordes of chartered companies, might do good service in the organisation of native resistance in drilling, and in teaching the effective use of firearms. Those who remain at home can similarly do good service in stirring up working-class public opinion, till it becomes as much as a Cabinet's place is worth to engage in "military operations" of this description.

The "Monstrous Regiment" of Womanhood

All parties, all sorts and conditions of politicians, from the fashionable and Conservative west-end philanthropist to the Radical working-men's clubbite, seem (or seemed until lately) to have come to an unanimous conclusion on one point – to wit, that the female sex is grievously groaning under the weight of male oppression. Editors of newspapers, keen to scent out every drift of public fancy with the object of regaling their "constant readers" with what is tickling to their palates, will greedily print, in prominent positions and in large type letters expressive of the view in question, whilst they will boycott or, at best, publish in obscure corners any communication that ventures to criticise the popular theory or that adduces facts that tell against it. Were I to pen an impassioned diatribe, tending to prove the villainy of man towards woman, and painting in glowing terms the poor, weak victim of his despotism, my description would be received with sympathetic approval. Not so, I fear, my simple statement of the unvarnished truth.

Now, I think it will be admitted, as a general principle at least, by all parties in the present day, that equality before the law, as it is termed, is the first condition of liberty, and that where you have respect of persons in this connection, you are destitute of the primal elements of personal freedom. According to the popular theory just indicated, respecting the position of women, we might expect to find every law framed in such a way that women should invariably come off less than second best in any dispute with men: in short, that law would be enacted and administered solely to the advantage of men. Is this so in actual fact?

Let us first take our existing marriage laws. We shall find that in England whilst the woman is practically relieved of all responsibility for the maintenance of her husband, he can be compelled by poor law to maintain her under a penalty of three months' hard labour for leaving her without provision, should she choose to apply to the parish. On anything that by latitude of interpretation can be deemed ill-usage or neglect, she can, if rich, obtain judicial separation with alimony from the divorce court, or, if poor, a magisterial order for separation with weekly maintenance from the police court. Jackson versus Jackson has decided that a wife can leave her husband at will, that he cannot raise a finger to compel her to remain with him or to come back, neither can she be imprisoned for contempt of court for refusing to obey an order for restitution of conjugal rights; in other words, it is decided that the contract of marriage is the single case of a contract which one of the contracting parties is at liberty to break without reason given, and without compensating the other party. But it is well to remember that it is only one of the parties that has this liberty, for Bunhill *versus* Bunhill gives the wife the right to follow an absconding husband and break into his house, if necessary, for the purpose of compelling cohabitation. He, on his part, is precluded by the decision in Weldon *versus* Weldon from obtaining restitution of conjugal rights even by way of action; he is liable, however, for his wife's postnuptial torts, so that she has only to slander or libel some person without his knowledge or consent, and whilst she comes off scot free, even though possessed of property, the husband can be cast in damages. Trespass to land, trespass to goods, injuries done through negligence, all these actions coming under the legal definition of "torts," render the husband liable, no matter what private wealth the wife may possess.

Now, let us take the single instance on the opposite side – the perennial grievance of the woman's-righter which is deemed sufficient, apparently, to swallow up everything else. How often do we hear it said in tones of intense indignation, as conclusively proving the vile tyranny of man, that while the husband can obtain a divorce from his wife on the ground of adultery alone, the wife, in order to obtain such relief, has to prove an additional charge of cruelty. I think that there is no greater evidence of the bogus character of the sentiment talked on this question than the fact that this trumpery argument is the only one its votaries can adduce. Apart from the circumstance, well known to students of the Divorce Court, that it is the uniform practice of judges to twist every act of impoliteness or trivial ill-temper on the part of the husband into "legal cruelty," the reason of the distinction must be obvious to any one not blinded by his or her prepossessions on the subject. I am certainly the last to advocate any binding on either side, and would gladly see divorce obtainable by the properly formulated demand of either party, but it is quite clear that under our present conditions of society with its bases of individual property-holding, whilst it would be grossly unfair to continue to enforce marital responsibility on a man for a woman whose offspring was of doubtful paternity, the grievance on the side of the woman against the man in case of adultery has no more than a sentimental significance: Even then, when the case becomes gross, as where a strange woman is introduced under the common roof, the wife can obtain relief on the elastic plea of technical or legal "cruelty." One would think that if the bewailers of the pretended oppression of woman do not want to make themselves ridiculous, they would drop this preposterously "manufactured" grievance, since it is obvious that the distinction made in this case is entirely owing to the economical liabilities of the husband from which the wife has the good luck to be exempt. Looking at the matter all round, I think, then, no one can deny that the existing marriage laws are simply a "plant" to enable the woman to swindle and oppress the man.[1]

Turning now from the civil law to the criminal law, we find a similar – or even greater – disparity of treatment. From the beginning of the nineteenth century, of course, whilst flogging, the tread-mill, and other brutal forms of punishment have been retained for male offenders, they have been abolished for females, so that though a man may be subjected to torture and degradation for mere breaches of prison discipline, a woman is exempted from them for the most heinous crimes. As happened a few years ago in Ireland, a woman may torture her children to death and there is no outcry for the lash, yet surely if you do not flog the female child-torturer you have no right to flog any other human being. The sex-favouritism of modern penal law is made more conspicuous by the ever-recurring howl of the "base, bloody, and brutal" grand juror for the lash to be applied to new classes of offences (for men of course). But the most atrocious instances of sex-privilege occur in connection with the Criminal Law Amendment Act of 1885. Whilst the abduction of a girl under eighteen, or the seduction of one under sixteen, involves the man concerned in serious penalties, the girl or the woman gets off scot free, and this even though she may have been the inciting party. This is carried to the extent that a young boy of fourteen may be himself induced to commit a sexual offence by a girl just under sixteen – that is to say, nearly two years his senior – and he can be sentenced to imprisonment, followed by several years in a reformatory, whilst the law holds the inciting girl absolutely guiltless. The villainy of such an enactment is unparalleled, more particularly when one considers that a girl approaching sixteen is often practically a woman, whilst a boy of fourteen is seldom more than a child.

If we turn from the law itself to the administration of the law, we find, if anything, still more startling enormities. I do not propose to give many instances, or any, at length, inasmuch as my readers may find such galore by consulting any daily paper. I may, however, refer to a case tried a few months back in which a woman killed her husband by throwing a lighted paraffin lamp at him in the course of a quarrel. Will it be believed that this woman was – not convicted of murder and recommended to mercy, not even convicted of manslaughter – but acquitted in flying colours, because, forsooth, she whined and alleged in her defence that the act was done on the spur of the moment when she did not fully realise the inflammable nature of paraffin oil This was the flimsy rubbish that judge and jury complacently accepted from the mouth of a woman. Every one knows that, had the husband in a fit of exasperation suddenly forgotten the properties of paraffin, and had let the lamp fly at the head of some drunken virago of a spouse – every one knows how the judge would have pointed out how, according to the law of England, this was a clear case of wilful murder, how the jury's verdict would have been in accordance with his summing-up, accompanied, perhaps, with a recommendation to mercy, which the Home Secretary would have "carefully considered," announcing after a few days, that on a thorough review of the facts of the case he regretted "he saw no reason for interfering with the course of the law," and how the wretched victim of sex-injustice would have been consigned to the tender mercies of the hangman, probably after having, like the witches of old, "admitted the justice of his sentence" – the unjustly condemned always do that! A similar case was heard on the 23rd of May 1894, at the Middlesex sessions. A woman who had stabbed her husband so that he was lying in a dangerous condition in the hospital was released on her own recognisances. Her excuse was that she was drunk at the time. The husband was condemned, however, to pay 5s. a week for her support, at which she grumbled, alleging that he could well afford £1 a week. A short time after she came back and again assaulted the husband. She was this time fined a trifling sum with the alternative of fourteen days' imprisonment!

The case of the constable, Cooke, at Wormwood Scrubbs, may still be remembered by some of my readers. If ever there was a case of provocation reducing the crime of murder to one of excusable homicide, surely this was one, and the jury, who convicted Cooke of murder on the technical point of law, showed that they thought so, by the rider to their verdict. But Cooke, having the misfortune to be born a man, is, in spite of the recommendation, promptly hanged by Mr. Asquith. A still more recent case is that of the young workman, Walter Smith, at Nottingham, whom Mr. Asquith similarly hanged, in this case, even in the teeth of local public opinion, with the moral certainty that the shooting was, if not a pure accident, as some thought, the act of an insane person. Take again, the infamous trial of Mr. Noel of Ramsgate. Here was a man, who, without a tittle of evidence, was kept in gaol with a capital charge hanging over him for weeks. Yet so far was local public opinion from showing any sympathy for the unfortunate victim that this rabble of small shop-keepers and lodging-letters thought it necessary to reward the agent who had worked up the charge against him. with the public presentation of a purse of sixty guineas. Take, again, the case of Hogg of Hampstead. This man, it is well known, after the police had done their best to connect him with the charge in the Piercey murder, was able to prove so conclusive an *alibi* that his impeachment could not even be entertained. Yet, in spite of this, public opinion of the baser sort was not to be baulked of its prey, and on the date of his late wife's funeral, Hogg narrowly escaped being lynched at the hands of a mob. For what? For having had the misfortune to be the husband of Mrs. Hogg, who had been murdered by some one else – and that a woman. Given the case of a woman found murdered, the method of policemen on the look-out for promotion is to fix upon some wretched man who has known the woman (anyone will do). This is called a "clue." The finger is pointed at this man and public opinion thus worked up into the requisite state with regard to him. The manufacture of "circumstantial" evidence is then easy. Say the woman had been murdered with a knife. A carving knife is found in the back kitchen of the murderer designate! a circumstance scarcely compatible with innocence! Say the woman has been shot. The bullet found in the deceased fits the bore of a revolver known to be in the possession of the murderer as by Treasury fixed upon. (N.B. – The fact that two million of this sized revolver bullet are turned out annually makes no difference.) Conclusive evidence of guilt!!! Is she poisoned? Some supposed lover of hers, or her sister's, or her cousin's is proved to have an empty bottle of vermin-killer in the recesses of his scullery cupboard. – Evidence which no jury under the sway of current sentiment could resist.

Mr. Noel of Ramsgate was kept in durance and brought up before the bench to make a seaside holiday week by week, on not even as much evidence as this. James Canham Read was condemned and hanged on admittedly perjured evidence (for which, of course, the Treasury never dreamt of prosecuting), and on that of three mutually self-contradictory witnesses. The very attitude of public opinion towards a man accused of the murder of a woman is significant. If he is confident, it is said he is trying to brazen it out. If he is despondent, it is conclusive proof of a sense of guilt. One would like to know what manner a man, charged with the murder of a woman, ought to assume in order to set himself right with public opinion.

It only requires any one to read his newspaper carefully to see that if the law is designed with the object of favouring women, the administration of the law is worked ten times more to this end. I need only allude to breach of promise cases. Here the woman is allowed to plunder the man at her will as a punishment for a refusal to wreck his own life, and possibly her: as well, in a marriage which he feels would be unhappy. This is a scandal which has been often enough discussed, but which, nevertheless, chiefly affects the well-to-do classes. But the instances already given show the grossest and most flagrant inequality before the law, not in civil but in criminal accusations. Can any one deny that in all cases where a man has been instrumental in causing the death of a woman, the coroner, the magistrate, the judge, the jury will do their utmost to twist and wrench the act into a murder charge? But when a woman has been instrumental in causing the death of a man, in how many cases will a verdict of "wilful murder" be returned? One requires only to read one's paper with a critical and unbiased mind in this respect, and one can only come to one conclusion – that there is a steady, unconscious sex-prejudice at work in public opinion against the man because he is man and in favour of the woman because she is woman.

Woe betide the luckless husband or paramour of a woman who has come to a violent end. As in the cases quoted of Noel at

231

Ramsgate and Hogg at Hampstead, a perfect blood-lust infects the public mind. A bestial sentimentalism, which flings aside every consideration of common justice, seems to spread over the whole community. Contrast this with the sentiment evoked by the sweet female poisoner – Mrs. Maybrick, for instance, and others that I must not name, because, having only poisoned men, they have, of course, been acquitted. For the tender-hearted British small middle-class juryman, above all things, holds "Womanhood" in honour, even where associated with homicidal proclivities.

Compare the case of the excitement and adjournment of Parliament over Miss Cass some years ago, who was said to have been wrongfully arrested for solicitation, with the perfect equanimity with which arbitrary police arrests of men in the street nightly take place without attracting notice. The difference in the value put upon the life and liberty of the sexes by public sentiment is sometimes not without a grim humour. About a year ago a paragraph went the round of the papers headed *Cannibalism on the Niger*. It stated that a recrudescence of cannibalism had shown itself in the Niger territory, narrated how a man had been killed and eaten in spite of the protests of European residents, but that no steps to punish the delinquents were taken. A few days afterwards, it went on to say, a woman was killed and eaten, and this time, we were told, "the authorities felt bound to interfere." Accordingly the two negroes concerned were seized and promptly hanged. Now I contend that however much the Western European may have become convinced of the superior sanctity of the female over the male sex, it is unfair to allow this dogma to play a part in administering justice to negroes who know nothing whatever about it. The poor ignorant negro, who finds that the killing and eating of a man evokes a simple remonstrance and knows nothing of the deification of womanhood, naturally thinks that what is sauce for the gander is sauce for the goose, and kills and eats accordingly. And surely before you hang him, you ought to give him instruction in the new *cultus*.

The way in which public opinion is hocused over the whole question is significant. As already stated, the ear of the average man is open on the one side and deaf on the other, and as a consequence the newspapers are open on the one side only. Hence out of twenty cases, civil or criminal, into which the sex question enters, nineteen of which will probably represent flagrant injustice to men, and flagrant partiality to women, but the twentieth may have the semblance of pressing a little hardly on the woman – out of these twenty cases, while the nineteen will be passed by without remark, the twentieth, the exception, will be seized upon with a hawk-like grip, trumpeted forth in every paper, exaggerated and commented upon in every key of indignation as illustrating the habitual tyranny of vile truculent man towards downtrodden woman and the calculated injustice of the courts to women. That's the way the "trick" is done, and public opinion artificially and sedulously kept in its present course.

It can hardly have failed to be observed by everyone, how vast a difference exists between the energy with which any injustice to men is protested against as compared with a corresponding injustice to women, and a still greater difference in the results of the protest. Injustice towards men is perhaps protested against but in nine cases out of ten the protest is tame and remains barren, but a protest against any assumed harshness in the case of women, however trifling, is invariably and immediately effective. Again, a wrong which touches both sexes, let us say, is protested against. It is remedied as far as women are concerned and the protest dies out, even though men may suffer more than before from it. As an instance of this, take the outcry anent the flogging of women in Russia, and the protect raised by a meeting in Hyde Park, not against the general ill-treatment of Russian political prisoners, not against flogging, altogether, but a protest embodied in a resolution taking women out of the category of common humanity, and exclusively denouncing

233

cruelties exercised towards female prisoners, thereby implicitly countenancing such cruelties when perpetrated on men. The "advanced" women present on the occasion referred to, to their shame be it said, did not insist on making the resolution apply to both sexes. And these are the persons who are so eloquent on the subject of "equality." Again, take Mr. Labouchere. Mr. Labouchere made it his business in **Truth** to hunt up every obscure case of girl-flogging in the country, and to trumpet it forth in his journal as though it were a crime compared to which common murder were a venial affair. But now, had Mr. Labouchere one word for the brutal floggings of boys, not by private individuals, but in national institutions, such as reformatories and training ships? Not one. What he expressly denounced was not flogging, but girl-flogging.

Again British public opinion is dissolved with indignation at the notion of the solitary woman being taken liberties with in a railway carriage, and demands the heaviest punishment for the offender. But what has either the law or public opinion to say to the female blackmailer? She for years plied her trade on the Metropolitan Railway unmolested by the police. She is never prosecuted, and the law gives her every facility for bringing false charges whilst public opinion treats the matter as a joke, or as of no importance. The late judge Baron Huddleston stated that in his opinion men stood in much greater need of protection against women than women against men.[2]

I think on a survey of the facts given, every unbiased person must admit that women, so far from being oppressed, are steeped up to the teeth in sex-prerogative. In short, if their position is called one of oppression, I can only say that this new-fashioned oppression is to me absolutely indistinguishable from old-fashioned privilege! But if this be so we have to ask ourselves the reasons given for some of these privileges, at least. A considerable section of them are undoubtedly based on the traditional "weakness" of women, as compared with men. Now as regards this point, I would suggest that though women are unquestionably as a rule, weaker *muscularly* than men, yet there are circumstances under which, for practical purposes, the strongest man is as helpless as the weakest woman. In an age when disputes were generally determined by individual prowess, this argument may have had some point. But I submit that in the hands of the law, the policeman, the gaoler or the hangman, the relative difference of muscle between the sexes has absolutely no significance whatever. The strong man about to be flogged or hanged, even though a Samson, is in no better case than the weakest girl. Again, the invention of fire-arms has, on another side, obliterated the importance of the difference in muscular strength between the two sexes. A weak woman armed with a revolver can hold a Hercules well in check.

This point of the muscular inferiority of women to men is often confounded with another point in reality quite distinct – that of constitutional vigour. Now, although as already stated, women are undoubtedly, as a rule, inferior in muscular strength to men, the opposite is true as regards their vitality and physical endurance, although popular opinion credits them with a greater weakness here also. It is well known to the medical profession that a woman can pass through a physical strain and recover herself in a manner and to an extent that no man can. I do not propose dwelling on this point, as it is generally admitted by all medical authorities and has been often enough conceded by opponents in this very controversy. It is illustrated by the excess of the adult female over the adult male population in this country (about a million) notwithstanding that male births are considerably in excess of female. In addition to this, Lombroso and other competent authorities have recently discovered that the nerve-sensibility of women, and hence their susceptibility to pain, is much less than that of men. This being the state of the case, I maintain that any argument based on the "weakness of women" in favour of a different treatment of women to that accorded to men falls completely to the ground. Women, at the present day, so far as their "weakness" is concerned, have exactly the same claim to considerate treatment at the hands of the law and of public opinion, as men have, neither more nor less.

I may as well take the opportunity of dealing with an objection which is almost sure to crop up as regards favouritism to women in the matter of criminal punishment. It is undeniable that imprisonment for women means a very different thing from what it does for men – its sting being for them completely taken out. So true is this that women prisoners have only got to make a firm stand against any regulation to get it altered. A little while ago fifty women refused to carry out an order made by the Governor of Wormwood Scrubbs for bringing coke into the laundry. If men had refused to obey any regulation they would most probably have got the lash till they yielded. But what was the lot of these women. The Governor at once politely cancelled his regulation and "order was restored"!! Such is the farce of penal discipline in the case of women. Now, in any demand that may be made for equality in this matter, I am met by this argument – "Are you not in favour of abolishing all forms of brutal punishment?" I say yes, in common with most Socialists and Democrats, I am in favour of all forms of corporal and of capital punishment whatsoever being abolished and of reducing imprisonment to simple reclusion. It is then argued: – "But surely the abolition of these things in the case of women is better than nothing"; it is at least a step. My answer is that in the first place it is *not* a step, but generally a shirking of the whole question. And further I reply by putting another case. Supposing that it were proposed for certain forms of punishment to be abolished for persons possessing incomes over £300 a year, but retained for all whose incomes fell below that figure. Precisely the same argument might be applied. "It is better than nothing!" – "it is a step." Yet, you know that all with one consent would protest that if (say) capital punishment is to be retained at all, it would be monstrous to let a murderer off because he possessed over £300 a year and hang another who had been working on £50 a year. All would say this and properly so, however strong might be their

236

opposition to capital punishment in itself. The protest would be in the name of equality before the law. Now this is precisely my case. In both instances you are punishing the criminal for what he cannot help and not for his crime. Every increment of penalty you inflict upon a man over and above what you inflict upon a woman for the same or an equal crime, I maintain is a legal infamy. *It is a punishment not for the offence but for the crime of having been born male.*

Now let us take the other side of this woman question. Let us consider the alleged disabilities of women. I have already disposed of one of the alleged injustices to women in discussing the marriage laws; it is, therefore, not necessary to allude to it here. First and foremost, then, comes the question of the franchise. The Woman's Rights advocate is, of course, ever shrieking over the fact that the female sex has not got the suffrage. On the monstrous iniquity of this, she will expatiate in press or on platform by the column or by the hour. (She ignores the fact that a legally privileged body – the Royal Family for example – commonly does not possess the suffrage and yet is not counted "oppressed.") Now let it be granted as an abstract proposition that women ought to have the suffrage and that the vote is a necessary condition of equality between the sexes. Conceding this, for argument's sake, I contend that, as far as the rights of women are concerned, (1) the want of the suffrage is altogether unimportant, and (2) the granting of the suffrage *immediately and without conditions* could not possibly accord with the principle of equality between the sexes. As to the first point, when you find that every law relating to sex-questions and specially touching women is constructed with a view to giving women prerogatives as against men, as has been the case with the recent laws respecting marriage, and other matters, and when you find that the administration is even more partial to women than the laws themselves, I think one may fairly say that the case for women having direct control over legislation and administration is, even from the point of view of women's rights, not a pressing one. I think it will be admitted that supposing *per impossibile* that parsons and landlords invariably administered the law, not in the interests of their own class but of the agricultural labourer – I say, I think if this were so – the case for appointing working-men justices, though theoretically as strong as before, would at least lose much of the urgency that it has now. Yet so it is with the legislators and administrators of law, as far as women are concerned. In this country, in North America and in the British colonies, at least, men make and administer laws not in favour of their own but of the other sex.

Let us turn to the second point, that the immediate and unconditional granting of the suffrage to women would be incompatible with equality between the sexes and give rise to a sex-tyranny exercised by women upon men, not, it is true, directly, but through and by means of men themselves. Such would be the case for the following reasons. Firstly, there is the question of population. I assume, of course, universal suffrage, for both sexes, which is the only principle worth discussing in this, connection. The population of women exceeds that of men in these and most other countries – very considerably indeed in Great Britain. Now, the result of this on the basis of Universal Adult Suffrage, if conceded directly and unconditionally, is obvious. We should simply have the complete domination of the female vote. This would be moreover reinforced by, at the very least, a large minority of the male vote. For it is important to bear in mind, that whilst chivalry, gallantry, etc., forbids men to side against women[3], it is a point of honour amongst female upholders of woman's rights that they shall back up their own sex, right or wrong. Universal female suffrage, therefore, under present conditions, might easily come to mean *the despotism of one sex*.

But it is sometimes alleged that the *great bulk* of women would not vote solid with their sex, inasmuch as they are not "political women." In reply to this I have only to point to the case of Wyoming and other places in America, where, as I am informed, every public office is filled by a woman, except, mark you, that of police constable, and where a man can perform no legal act without the consent of his wife, as also more recently in New Zealand. Again it is alleged that just as men on juries judge women leniently, so women on juries would judge men leniently, more especially, it is said, as the quality of mercy is stronger in women than in men. I can only answer that this also is not confirmed by experience. In the case of Wyoming the verdicts brought by the female juries against male offenders have been often of so vindictive a ferocity as to have amounted to a public scandal.

Once more, it is alleged that with the removal of the so-called disabilities under which women at present labour i.e., the lack of the franchise, the closing of one or two of the professions, etc. – the prerogatives, the chivalry now accorded to and claimed for women, would disappear, leaving the sexes really equal before the law. I again answer that experience does not lend colour to this forecast. For it would almost seem that, *in exact proportion to the removal of any real grievances that may once have existed, has the number of female privileges increased*. At the present day, women have infinitely more advantages as against men than at the beginning of the nineteenth century, let us say, when they were suffering under one or two genuine disabilities (e.g., the laws regarding the earnings of the married woman now long since repealed). Then, before a law-court, a man-party in a suit had at least some chance of fair play against a woman opponent. It is not so now. Then, a female criminal had not, as now, any assurance of practical immunity from the severities of the penal law.

The other chief grievance in addition to the want of the suffrage is that some of the professions are closed to women. I ask, "What profession?" In the United States no trade or profession whatever, that I am aware of, is closed to women as such. In this country the medical profession, the one most sought after by women, is open, and, as far as I know, the law and the church are the only important callings, at all likely to be adopted

239

by women, that are closed to them. And why is this so? Simply, because there has been no movement on the part of women for opening them. The moment women begin to agitate for admission to the legal profession. there is not the least doubt whatsoever that they will obtain it within a year or two. At all events this terrible hardship sinks down to the fact that one or two callings are legally closed. Moreover, as a set-off even against this, you have the enormous reputation, literary and otherwise, which a woman can acquire with slender means. The ability and industry utterly insufficient to raise a man out of the level of mediocrity is often adequate to furnish a woman with a name and fame equal to an income for life. I do not wish to mention individuals, but some instances will probably occur to many of my readers.

Such is the present state of the woman question – a steady determination on the part of public opinion to believe that women are oppressed – a steady determination on the part of women to pose as victims – in the teeth of facts of every description showing the contrary; a further determination to heap upon them privilege on the top of privilege at the expense of men under the impudent pretence of "equality between the sexes." The grievances that women labour under as women resolve themselves into three the fact (1) that the wife has to prove technical cruelty in addition to adultery on the part of her husband (a very easy thing to do) in order to obtain a divorce; (2) that women have not as yet the parliamentary franchise (although without it they succeed in getting nearly every law framed and administered in their favour), and (3) that one or two callings are closed to them (albeit in most branches of intellectual work it is far easier for them to make a profitable reputation with moderate ability than for men). These are the three main grievances existing in this country at present and usually quoted to show the burdens under which divine Womanhood (with a big W) is groaning. Is it too much to ask my readers for ever to clear their minds of cant on the matter and to honestly say whether these disabilities, such as they are, counterbalance the enormous prerogatives which women otherwise possess on all hands. Defend these prerogatives if you will, but do not deny that they exist and pretend that the possessors of them are oppressed.[4]

The foregoing, then, I repeat, is the present state of the woman question – as it exists in our latter-day class society, based on capitalistic production. The last point that we have to consider is as to the relation of this sex-question to Socialism. Some years ago, on its first appearance, I took up, my esteemed friend August Bebel's book **Die Frau** in the hope of gaining some valuable hints or at least some interesting speculations on the probable future of sex-relations under Socialism. I was considerably disgusted, therefore, that for the "halfpennyworth of bread" in the form of real suggestion I had to wade through a painfully considerable quantity of very old "sack" in the shape of stale declamation on the intrinsic perfection of woman and the utter vileness of man, on the horrible oppression the divine creature suffered at the hands of her tyrant and ogre – in short, I found two-thirds of the book filled up with a second-hand hash-up of Mill's **Subjection of Women** and with the usual demagogic rant I had been long accustomed to from the ordinary bourgeois woman's-rights advocate. It was the reading of the book in question that induced me to take up this problem, and to make some attempt to prick the bladder of humbug to which I was sorry to see that Bebel had lent his name.

In doing this I of course acquired the reputation of a misogynist. This is the natural fate of any one who attempts to expose that most shamelessly impudent fraud (the so-called woman's-rights movement) which was ever supported by rotten arguments, unblushing misrepresentations, and false analogies. I have given some instances of the former in the course of this chapter. I will give one instance of a transparently false analogy which is common among Socialists and Radicals. It is a favourite device to treat the relation between man and woman as on all fours with the relation between capitalist and workman. But a moment's consideration will show that there is no parallel at all between the two cases. The reason on which we as Socialists base our persistent attack on the class-privileged man or woman – on the capitalist – is because we maintain that as an economical, political, and social entity he or she has no right to exist. We say that the capitalist is a mere parasite, who ought to and who eventually will disappear. If it were not so, if the capitalist were a necessary and permanent factor in society, the attitude often adopted by Socialists (say, over trade disputes) would be as unfair and one-sided as the bourgeois represents it to be. Now, I wish to point out that the first thing for the woman's-rights advocates to do, if they want to make good the analogy, is to declare openly for the abolition of the male sex. For until they do this, there is not one tittle of resemblance between the two cases. It is further forgotten that the distinction between men and women as to intellectual and moral capacity is radically different from that between classes. The one is a difference based on *organic structure*; the other on *economic circumstance*, educational advantage and social convention. That such a flimsy analogy as the above should ever have passed muster shows that the blind infatuation of public opinion on this question extends even to some Socialists.

It will be observed that I have not discussed the question of the intellectual and moral superiority, equality, or inferiority of women to men. I am content to concede this point for the sake of argument and take the plainer issue. What does Socialism, at least, profess to demand and to involve? Relative economic and social equality between the sexes. What does the woman's-rights movement demand? Female privilege, and when possible, female domination. It asks that women shall have all the rights of men with privileges thrown in (but no disagreeable duties, oh dear no!), and apparently be subject to no discipline but that of their own arbitrary wills. To exclude women on the ground of incapacity from any honourable, lucrative, or agreeable social function whatever, is a hideous injustice to be fulminated against from platform and in press – to treat them on the same footing as

242

men in the matter of subordination to organised control or discipline is not to be thought of – is ungentlemanly ungallant, unchivalrous! We had an illustration of this recently. At a meeting held not long since, the chairman declared that all interrupters of speakers should be promptly put out. A man at the back of the hall did interrupt a speaker and was summarily ejected, Subsequently a woman not only interrupted, but grossly insulted another speaker, but the chairman declared that he could not turn a woman out. So it is. A woman is to be allowed, of course, full liberty of being present and of speaking at a public meeting, but is not to be subject to any of the regulation to which men are subject for the maintenance of order. And this is what woman's-rights advocates and apparently some Socialists term equality between the sexes!! Advanced women and their male supporters in demanding all that is lucrative, honourable, and agreeable in the position of men take their stand on the dogma of sex-equality. No sooner, however, is the question one of disagreeable duties than "equality" goes by the board and they slink behind the old sex-immunity.

This sentiment also plays a part in the franchise controversy. Let women have the franchise by all means, provided two things, first of all: provided you can get rid of their present practical immunity from the operation of the criminal law for all offences committed against men and of the gallantry and shoddy chivalry that now hedges a woman in all relations of life[5]; and secondly, provided you can obviate the unfairness arising from the excess of women over men in the population – an excess attributable not only to the superior constitutional strength of women, but still more, perhaps, to the fact that men are exposed to dangers in their daily work from which women benefit, but from which women are exempt, inasmuch as they are, and claim to be, jealously protected from all perilous and unhealthy occupations. Now, surely it is rather rough to punish men for their services to society by placing them under the thumb of a female majority which exists largely because of these services.

Of course all the economic side of the question which for this very reason I have touched upon more or less lightly falls away under Socialism. Many Socialists, indeed, believe that the sex-question altogether is so entirely bound up with the economic question that it will immediately solve itself on the establishment of a collectivist order of society. I can only say that I do not myself share this belief. It would seem there is something in the sex-question, notably, the love of power and control involved, which is more than merely economic. I hold rather, on the contrary, that the class-struggle to-day over-shadows or dwarfs the importance of this sex-question, and that though in some aspects it will undoubtedly disappear, in others it may very possibly become more burning after the class-struggle has passed away than it is now. Speaking personally, I am firmly convinced that it will be the first question that a Socialist society will have to solve, once it has acquired a firm economic basis and the danger of reaction has sensibly diminished or disappeared.

Nowadays any one who protests against injustice to men in the interests of women is either abused as an unfeeling brute or sneered at as a crank. Perhaps in that day of a future society, my protest may be unearthed by some enterprising archaeological inquirer, and used as evidence that the question was already burning at the end of the nineteenth century. Now, this would certainly not be quite true, since I am well aware that most are either hostile or indifferent to the views set forth here on this question. In conclusion, I may say that I do not flatter myself that I am going to convert many of my readers from their darling belief in "woman the victim." I know their will is in question here, that they have made up their minds to hold one view and one only, through thick and thin, and hence that in the teeth of all the canons of evidence they would employ in other matters, most of them will continue canting on upon the orthodox lines, ferreting out the twentieth case that presents an apparent harshness to woman, and ignoring the nineteen of real injustice to man; misrepresenting the marriage laws as an engine of male, rather than of female, tyranny; and the non-possession of the suffrage by women as an infamy without a parallel, studiously saying nothing as to the more than compensating privileges of women in other directions. Working-women suffer to-day equally with working-men the oppression of the capitalist system, while middle-class women enjoy together with middle-class men the material benefits derived from a position of class-advantage. But in either case, as I have shown, as women, they enjoy a privileged position as against men as men. Only the will not to recognise the truth on this question can be proof against the evidence adduced.

Footnotes

1. Since the above was written, an act has been passed practically freeing the woman from the obligation of fidelity. She may now commit adultery and still retain her claim on the man if she allege "neglect" or "cruelty." The courts will probably consider "neglect" proved if she showed that her husband has not taken her out when she wished to go, or has refused her a silk dress, or has occasionally stayed too late at night from home. As for cruelty, the wife has only to smash her husband over the head with a poker while a witness is in the room. The husband may be tempted to observe that his wife has a bad temper. On a proof of his having thus abused his wife before strangers the court would doubtless hold a charge of "cruelty" to be "fully made out."

2. In this as in most other cases of this kind, we may observe, the allegation is considered a mere joke, that men are in danger from women, because forsooth, the courts are administered by men. just as if this mattered when, though they are administered by men it is true, yet in all cases where the sex-question enters they are "worked" so exclusively in the interest of the other sex, that no barrister dare suggest that a swindling, blackmailing woman is anything worse than a poor, hysterical creature, on pain of losing his case.

3. So much is this the fact, that, as before pointed out, in the worst blackmailing cases, the defendant's counsel is bound in the interests of his client to pretend that he doesn't wish to imply anything against the female witness except that she was liable to hysterical delusions. In another connection, it is seen in cases of infant-murder, when the indignation of modern public opinion is turned not against the mother who has committed the murder, but against the putative father who has had nothing to do with it; truly a new and improved conception of justice, though a trifle vicarious, which the

new Feminist cultess has the merit of having originated.

4. Before leaving this side of the question, I may allude to a quasi-argument, supposed to be crushing, which is sometimes brought forward when it is suggested that in view of the fact that all women are not angels, they should not be allowed to work their undisputed will with the men they come in contact with. "Women," it is pleaded, "are what men have made them." My answer to this is, that women are just as much what men have made them as men are what women have made them – nay, if there is a difference it is against women, since in the nursery, during the impressionable period of childhood, boys are entirely under their control.

5. A friend of mine is fond of arguing that the privileges of women are simply the obverse side of laws for the protection of the weaker. On this principle I would observe that any system of tyrannical privilege can be condoned. For example, it might be urged that the power of the Southern state planter over his slaves was necessary to the protection of the physically and numerically weaker white race against the ferocious negro. A similar argument is, in fact, used to-day to justify the action of negro-lynching mobs. Any system of oppression may be explained away, if one chooses, as being designed for the "necessary protection" of the oppressor against the oppressed.

Some Current Fallacies on the Woman Question

In the following remarks on the above subject, I should premise that my intention is only to appeal to those persons whose minds are warped in favour of Feminism[1] by certain plausible-sounding arguments, which they have been in all sincerity accepting because their fallacy has never been pointed out to them. The rack of hysterical molluscs, who are imposed upon by hollow sentimental whines anent their "mothers and their sisters" (why not their grandmothers, their aunts, their female cousins, or their mothers-in-law?), may be fairly left to stew in their own rather thin juice. As for myself, when I hear of injustice, say, of prison brutalities practised on men (brutalities from which women are exempt), my indignation, I say, is intensified, when I think it is the sex to which my father and my brother belong (or did belong) who are their victims. But I should never think of trotting out this purely personal sentiment as an argument for the special favouring of men in this connection, in any discussion on the relative treatment of men and women. I therefore propose confining myself to certain popular statements which one commonly hears and which are supposed to make for the views promulgated by women's rights advocates – statements which, if they were true, or if the implication conveyed in them were true, world undoubtedly afford some grounds for a serious consideration of the conventional view of this question put forward by the aforesaid advocates. They are, in fact, the only semblance of argument which the latter seem able to produce.

These argumentative statements consist very largely of variations on two main contentions – both of them, as I maintain, in the nature of false analogies. The first is the assumption that the relative position of the sexes bears some analogy (it is commonly represented as a very close analogy) with the relation between employer and workman – the employer representing the man and the workman the woman. The talk about "the proletarian in the household" is founded on this assumption. Now, as I have often pointed out before, the very basis of an analogy is wanting in this case. The difference between man and woman is not all economical or social one: it is an organic or biological distinction from which, as contended by non-Feminists, is deducible the difference in capacity between men and woman, both as to quantity and quality. The distinction between capitalist and proletarian is, on the other hand, *not* biological, but purely social, being simply one of class, based on economical circumstance. But what is further amusing is the way in which this preposterous analogy is worked, so that the woman is represented as the oppressed side of the equation in the case. Now, it is quite clear that if we are to fake up an analogy at all between sexes and classes, it is the man whose labour is exploited and not the women. It is the duty of the husband to *maintain* his wife, not the wife her husband. The husband is compelled, by custom and by law, to do *corvée*, or to yield up such portion of his earnings as may enable his wife to live in comfort – just as the villein was compelled to do *corvée*, or to pay his lord a proportion of the produce of the fields worked by his labour. The lord had the practical monopoly of the villein's means of existence – the land. Under the most favourable circumstances, he exacted from him a toll, in the shape of rent in kind or money, and other dues, for the privilege of working the land. The woman possesses the monopoly of what is, if not a primary, at least a secondary necessary of life to the great majority of men – the means of sexual satisfaction, her body; and for allowing him access to which the law entitles her to demand a rent and dues in the shape of food, clothes, shelter – in short, provision in accordance with the station of life occupied by her "villein," the husband, without any exertion on her part. But, it may be said, she has her duties to perform in the household, which may sometimes involve not inconsiderable labour. But so had the feudal lord *his* duties to perform. He had to go out to battle to protect his tenants against foes from without – an operation which might easily cost him his life – and to see that justice was administered on his estate. It is true there was often no adequate power to prevent the lord from neglecting the welfare of his tenants, but there is no power at all in modern English law to prevent the wife from neglecting her duties to her husband and family. The husband remains even more hopelessly the slave of a worthless wife than the mediaeval serf was of a tyrannical and rapacious baron. I do not press the foregoing parallel myself, as I consider the whole attempt to establish an analogy between class and sex-opposition to be fallacious, *ab initio*. But I think I have sufficiently shown that if we are to have the analogy forced upon us at all, it will work out in quite a different sense to the "proletarian-in-the-home" theory.

Yet it is in the class of argumentation of which this theory is a specimen that it is considered incumbent upon all democrats to champion the pitch-forking of women into every sphere of activity which, from its lucrative or honour-bearing character, happens to excite their envy, quite irrespective of their suitability therefor. As against this, all that is contended by myself, and other democrats and Socialists who think with me, is that the cumulative experience of the human race through at least three thousand years establishes a case for what is termed, in legal phraseology, a "presumption" that the woman is less capable than the man in those spheres of activity in which she has hitherto not shone. It is true that this presumption is rebuttable, and has in individual cases been rebutted. But the onus of rebuttal, it is contended, rests with the individual woman who aspires to the post or occupation in question. If she has given clear and unmistakable proof of her capacity, it would be absurd to exclude her on the ground of her sex alone.

But, on the other hand, one swallow does not make a summer, and the fact that an occasional woman is to be found to which the presumption will not apply is not by any means sufficient to rebut it as a general principle. Therefore, it is insisted, such isolated cases ought not to be regarded as establishing a precedent for reversing a practice resting on such a widely established induction as that of the inferiority of women to men in so many departments of executive and directive activity. The induction referred to is strengthened rather than weakened by the theory, so dear to woman's rights advocates, that gyneocracy (the supremacy of the female) was universal in the earliest stages of human society. There is, of course, another theory, that the so-called gyneocracy was peculiar to certain races, and hence cannot be regarded like other institutions belonging to the same period as forming an essential stage in social evolution generally. But, assuming the former theory to be right, it is obvious that women in primitive times enjoyed a governmental and executive authority which they were unable to maintain, presumably owing to inherent incapacity, since the fall of gyneocracy wherever it has existed, is too widespread a phenomenon to be accounted for by local or special causes and the hypothesis that the victory of private over tribal or communal property-fielding had anything to do with it is manifestly absurd when we consider that personal property holding and inheritance is just as possible through females as through males, a state of things which actually obtained concurrently with other gyneocratic institutions, in some cases long after the ancient primitive communism had broken down (e.g., in Lykia, as also to a large extent in Egypt), and yet that, in spite of all, either the gyneocratic institutions perished, or the races subjected to them went under before non-gyneocratic civilisations. If the above be in any way admitted, it follows that the appeal to democratic sentiment and democratic analogies in support of the so called "claims" of women is entirely beside the mark. It yet remains to be proved that women have any "claim" at all to the exercise, say, of the suffrage, or of any other responsible function. It may be an open question if you like, but it cannot be decided off hand on the basis of "natural rights," "social equality," or any of those grounds which are urged in the case of classes, or of nations on approximately the same level of development.

Would people but abstain from quite going off their heads,

in considering this question, they would be compelled to admit that women have never been oppressed as subject classes have been by dominant classes, or even as subject races have been by dominant races. The superficial disabilities to which women have been subject have always been more than compensated by other privileges. The woman has always been queen in her own sphere. She has always had very substantial rights, and exercised authority in a very substantial manner. The distinction of rights between the sexes has always been more as between spheres of influence rather than as between domination and subjection. Nevertheless, that an *organically* inferior being should not be in certain matters subject to the relatively superior, is a proposition which I for one am not prepared to endorse off-hand. But the inferiority of women has not been proved, it will be said! True, but as already pointed out, the course of history, from primitive times upward, makes out a strong case of presumption in favour of the inferiority. And that presumption has certainly never been, as such, rebutted. Those who doubt this may be referred to the painfully-laboured special-pleadings of Bebel in a certain chapter of **Die Frau**. The forlorn defence of an able advocate is always the best indictment of all untenable position.

As things are, women, by considering themselves in the light of a class, and agitating, not for equality, but for supremacy (the "equality" is a mere pretence) in class-fashion, are really creating a sex-antagonism which ultimately means the sacrifice of their strongest weapons. They are flinging away that moral power by which they have hitherto, for good or for evil, swayed men, wholly unchallenged, for the sake of a brute force wielded by men in their favour, which they may lose at any time. They are resigning the psychological magic by which they have bent men to their will for the privilege of being allowed to invoke the brute force of the policeman, the prison warder, the judge, and the bailiff. The fact would seem to indicate a female degeneracy, if that were possible, since the exchange, one would think, could only benefit women who united in their persons the attributes of badness, ugliness, and stupidity. The absence of any one of these qualities has generally sufficed, hitherto, to enable them to work the oracle themselves. They have now invoked the phantom of the brute force of the state to settle their quarrels with men, thereby calling into existence a sex-hostility which will one day recoil on them as sure as men are men and women are women.

Meanwhile, middle-class public opinion still continues in favour of the oppression of men, and the immunity of women from all control. It is a "revolting injustice" to subject public women to sanitary measures. It is perfectly in order to mutilate men who have contracted disease from these unexamined women. It is a monstrous iniquity that a man should exercise any power over his wife's property or earnings. The latest "right" claimed by the "advanced" political women of New Zealand is the confiscation for the wife's exclusive use of half the husband's property on marriage! Sir John Bridge, doubtless, aptly expresses public sentiment when, in discharging a young man against whom a bogus charge had been brought by a prostitute, after she had first of all assaulted him, admonishes the young man – that he give the sweet creature ten shillings compensation! Truly a nice way of fulfilling a police magistrate's duty of protecting harmless citizens on their way home at night! Another police magistrate, Mr. Francis, is severely hauled over the coals by certain hysterical Feminist organs for not passing a vindictive sentence on a husband charged with administering to his wife what, for aught they knew, may have been a thoroughly well-deserved thrashing. As the same magistrate said, when dealing with another similar case, if all husbands were sent to gaol for trivial assaults on their wives, there would not be enough prisons to contain then. Yet this is exactly what our Feminists are aiming at. The chief function of the magistrate, according to them, ought to be to act as assistant-bully to brow-beating wives. We have already got some way in this direction. A friend of mine heard a manifestly bogus charge – of indecently assaulting a daughter – tried (the prisoner apparently being only convicted owing to a misunderstanding of the jury), where the judge put it to the wife whether it would not inconvenience her to be deprived of the labour of her husband-slave, and, on the creature answering in the negative, sentenced him to a month's "hard."

The second main-root of a number of fallacies as to the possible capacities of women, both as regards quantity and quality, in various departments where they have not hitherto distinguished themselves, is expressed in the view that modern woman is the product of "centuries of oppression," and hence cannot be expected, at present, to show forth the latent glories of her intellectual and moral character. Now, for my own part, I should certainly demur to the fact of the centuries of oppression, but the granting of them does not help the Feminist case. In the first false analogy we had the confusion between sex and class; here we have the confusion between sex and race. For the advocates of the theory forgot that, were it true that women have suffered under a special oppression as women, the effects of such oppression would necessarily, on the average, be divided equally between both sexes of their descendants, and could not possibly be inherited after the manner of what someone has called a "hent-ail," in the female line only, and hence could not affect women more than men. Women no more constitute a race or species by themselves than they do a class by themselves. Nevertheless, this preposterous argument has been repeated over and over again, until to many people it is an unassailable truth upon which it is perfectly safe to base speculation as to an infinite vista of untold feminine achievements. Really Feminists would do well to drop argument, and confine themselves to blithering about "mothers and sisters"! It is so touching!

In addition to the foregoing sources of fallacy, there is a fooling among Socialists, in itself perfectly natural and legitimate, to the effect that the change from Capitalism to Socialism must involve considerable alteration in the condition of women. So it certainly will, but it by no means follows that the changes involved will he along the lines of the modern Feminist movement, as so many take for granted. That the position of women must change is obvious; but to assume that it must take the form of the female prerogative prevailing in. the more advanced capitalist states of to dry, or even of a mechanical equality which takes no account of organic differences, is a mere assumption which the wave of Feminist sentiment has hitherto allowed to pass unchallenged within the ranks of our party on the Continent as well as here. It is this assumption which will have, in the future, to be subjected to a rigorous criticism, a criticism very different from the one-sided *plaidoyer* for the Feminist position contained in the, in other respects, excellent book of August Bebel, **Die Frau und der Sozialismus**. Men will perhaps learn in time to approach this woman question with an open mind, unbiassed by that blind hatred of their own, and blind worship of the other sex, which at present characterises Rebel as well as so many other writers on the subject.

Footnote

1. It seems to be decided now by the usage of the majority that the above, and not "Femininism," is the correct form of this word.

Female Suffrage and its Implications

It is impossible to separate the question of the suffrage from the woman question in general, which is as much as to say, the suffrage opens up the whole question as to whether women as a whole are to perform the same functions in society as men and hence to have the same rights. The question, it may be observed, mainly concerns political rights (in the widest sense), *i.e.*, rights of sharing in the direction and administration of society – equal economical rights are, of course, conceded in general, equal advantages from equal labour in some form or other being a fundamental demand of Socialism. While as regards social and legal rights, as we shall point out presently, women are already in a position of privilege as regards men. It is, then, with legal and administrative rights that we are primarily concerned.

Now, it seems to me, that the question we are dealing with resolves itself into three: (1) Are we justified in barring any section of human beings as a whole, which, through general intellectual inferiority or otherwise, is recognised as relatively incompetent to fulfil certain functions, from those functions? (2) Have we the right to conclude that women are, in general, intellectually inferior to men, or otherwise incompetent to have a voice in legislation and administration? (3) Admitting them to be sufficiently competent, are there other grounds, justifying their exclusion at present from public life in this sense? As regards the first point, first let us examine what the conception "justice" means.

It may be quite true that concrete justice always implies a definite content, but nevertheless, all concrete and particular justice presupposes an abstract and general justice by which the former can be measured. Now, the abstract principle of justice is covered, I take it, by the notion of *equality*, as Aristotle found out long ago. But when closer viewed this "equality," it is seen, must be a relative equality. It must be an equality determined by the total circumstances of a particular case and not merely by one or two of its most obvious and superficial aspects. It is this last consideration which decides its character or determines its content in any particular instance.

Judged by this standard, then, I take it there exists a right to debar in general the unfit from the exercise of certain functions within a given society – provided that the unfitness results from organic causes and is not merely the temporary and direct outcome of defective economic and social conditions within the society itself. This is generally recognised even as regards the franchise. For example, children, *i.e.,* young persons up to a certain age, are by common consent excluded from the right to exercise the suffrage as being unfit by reason of immaturity. Even the most suffrage-thirsting democrat limits his demands to adult suffrage. Then, again, where you have within a society an alien population of an intrinsically lower race the right to exclude such a population from interfering in the regulation and administration of such a society by its votes or otherwise, would be admitted at least by many thoroughgoing democrats. And the more so now that the experience of this particular application of the man-and-the-brother doctrine in the United States has proved its unworkability. The reason is obvious – lower races stand in the same relation to higher races that children do to adults. Their minds are so far different from the former, that there is no basis of organic equality between the two. In this case, of course, of lower and higher races, while the attempt to amalgamate them in one commonwealth can only be productive of mischief, the true solution is that the organically lower race should be left to itself to work out its own social destiny. For instance, my solution of the negro question in America would be, while excluding the negro from the franchise in the white States, in those of the Southern States where he was in an overwhelming majority to hand over the government of the State entirely to the negro, to the exclusion, for that matter, of such white population as there might happen to be. The white American might not like this, but it would be the only just way out of the difficulty which his ancestor has created by forcibly importing the negro out of Africa. This, however, by the way. I have only wanted to show that the exclusion from political influence in the society, whether by vote or otherwise, of elements organically inferior, or, if you will, organically different, from that which has hitherto constituted the society, is not necessarily inconsistent with a democratic attitude which would level, in politics, all distinctions [apart] from economic differences; in other words, on class in the ordinary sense of the word.

Between fundamentally disparate things there can be at least no *direct* relation of equality. Now Socialism is a doctrine proclaiming the fundamental identity for a common socio-political life of the men of the progressive races, the apparent diversities being non-fundamental to such a common life. These diversities it traces mainly to economic and political causes – in the case of classes to economical causes solely; in the case of races within the circle of modern civilisation (with which, as above said, Socialism is alone directly concerned), largely to political causes, as well as to economical causes, the organic differences between these races, if we assume such to exist, being so slight as to be non-fundamental from the point of view concerned. But Socialism does not affirm that the negroid branch of the human family (say) is in the same case. For here we clearly have to do with an organic difference of a deep-lying, if not fundamental, character. The mind of the savage, of the Bushman, or even of the Kaffir, is to that of the progressive races as the mind of a civilised child to that of a civilised adult. There is plainly, therefore, here not even the basis of a common politico-social life. This fact alone (we observe, by the way) ought to bring home to us the cruelty and criminality of the imperialistic enslaving of such races, thereby destroying their own social forms-forms which are alone suited to them. It is, I say, a false conception of justice which demands for such races the franchise in an alien social organisation. True justice insists upon the duty of "hands off," i.e., of freedom and development for them from within, along their own lines. For where deep-seated organic disunction obtains, justice must have a different content to where no such distinction obtains.

Again, as already said, within every community you have an order of human beings who by common consent are unfitted for the functions of regulating and administering the community, viz., children or young persons under age. Here also there is no basis of direct equality, the immaturity constitutes an organic distinction which in this case also gives justice with regard to them a different content to what it would have if this distinction were not present. There is a justice, of course, in their case, because there is a form of equality to be arrived at, but it is an indirect justice because the equality is indirect. There is justice, for that matter, for all living beings, for animals as well as human beings, but it does not consist in giving them all the franchise. I think it is clear, therefore, that we are justified in debarring any order of persons from the franchise if they, as a class, indicate an inferiority based on an organic difference which is likely to render their co-operation in political or administrative life a danger or disadvantage to the community as a whole. For let us make no mistake, the active franchise (so-called) means the first step towards the passive; and this again is the step to all other political functions; just as the Bar is the first step towards the Bench, and this again towards the highest administrative functions in the existing State. You cannot practically limit any order of persons to the first step alone, with a "thus far shalt thou go and no farther." from the right of election to a legislative body, to the right of membership of that body, for instance, there is no logical halting-place.

Now the question arises, are we to regard women as possessing a deep-lying organic difference, involving inferiority, to men? If so, we shall be *eo ipso* justified in opposing woman-suffrage on the ground that the well-being of the community as a whole would be endangered thereby. "Equality in a reasonable

258

sense," as Möbius says, "can only mean that injustice is done to no one, that there is equal reward for equal achievements." It does not mean necessarily, as above pointed out, that every one, irrespective of vital differences, should have the *same* rights. Have we, then, the indications of mental inferiority in woman? I must here enter a protest against the trick of certain Feminists in attempting to belittle the difference between men as a sex-class and women as a sex-class. The immense *difference* (I do not say, mind, inferiority) between the mind of woman and the mind of man is patent and obvious to all who have no interest in denying it. An attempt to ignore this self-evident fact – a fact open to the observation of everyone – seems to me waste of time to discuss. Deny the *inferiority* if you will, but do not deny the *difference.* Talk about there being no greater difference between the sexes than between one man and another and one woman and another, we can hardly regard as seriously meant.

References to the comparatively slight distinction between the sexes in animals does not affect the question. It would seem that the sex-distinction in man approaches the relative magnitude of the specific or variational distinction in the lower animals. Möbius explains this greater differentiation of the sexes in the human species than in animals by the long period of helplessness in the human offspring. Whether this is so or not I am not prepared to say. The point really at issue is, I take it: Does this distinction involve either general inferiority or inferiority in certain directions? Both those points I think must be answered in the affirmative. Of course, I cannot here argue the case in detail. The main line of proof for the general inferiority of women is given at length in the introduction to the well known work of Lombroso and Ferrero on the **Female Criminal**. To take the physical indications of inferiority first. I will not dwell upon the inferiority as regards size and development of physique generally, though this might also have its significance, but would point out that according to the researches of Bischoff and Rüdinger not merely is the female brain absolutely smaller than that of the man, but relatively smaller allowing for the difference of size in the organism. Rüdinger has dealt with the matter, and gives a series of plates and tables showing from a large number of instances that the important parts of the brain are themselves relatively smaller; and not only so, but what perhaps is more important, that the convolutions even in the new-born child are much simpler and cruder in the female than in the male. The differences are vastly accentuated in the adult, the formation of important parts of the brain presenting quite a different appearance in this respect between the sexes, approaching, as regards proportions, in the female to the pre-human type. The inferior sensibility to pain discovered by Lombroso in women is a well-known fact. The special character of the female sexual system and its functions by the amount of vital energy they absorb would, apart from anything else, naturally lead us to expect an inferior development. The same conclusion is pointed to by the earlier ripeness of the human female organism.

Now, let us look at another group of facts not referring directly to the structure of the female sex, but to its intellectual functioning. Where and when throughout history can we discern in any branch of original thought or imagination or emotional activity, women that have achieved anything noteworthy – in science, in philosophy, in political practice, in invention, in the fine arts (painting, poetry, music)? The few exceptions in one or two of these departments in which women have approached the achievements of third-rate men, only suffice to prove the rule. Now, how do you explain this? Oh, it is said, women have been repressed, and have had no opportunity of showing their latent capacities! But it is forgotten that they have by no means been discouraged in all departments; on the contrary, rather the reverse in the fine arts and certain lines of literature. Furthermore, male genius has shown itself, where it existed, in the teeth of the most adverse circumstances. "Ah, but," it will be replied, "how many among men are not geniuses, and yet you don't deny them the franchise on the ground of inferiority on that account!" This is to mistake the argument, which is only designed as a test. From the heights of the summits one may gauge that of the table-land beneath them. If one order of human beings produces a continuous crop of geniuses in every – the most divergent – departments, and another order does not, we may fairly conclude that the average of the order that produces few or no geniuses is also, as an average, inferior to the order that produces many. Again, as regards the undoubtedly considerable memory capacity of women when specially cultivated, a capacity which enables them to compete with men in cram-examinations, Möbius (**Die Physiologische Schwachsinn des Weibes**) points out that even this form of intellectual power is rapidly lost in women, especially after a few years of married life. He observes the same in every other form of mental activity in the case of women. However brilliant in the girl, it has no durability. These things, however, I admit, though undoubtedly indicating inferiority, might not be taken as sufficient to exclude women from public functions.

We will, therefore, pass on to a more serious form of inferiority. I refer to the special tendency of women to hysteria. In common language, the word hysteria (hysterical, &c.) is often used to designate any form of mental excitement or strong emotion. This, of course, is a misuse of words. I have heard it said that men "get hysterical" over political issues, over Parliamentary candidatures in this country, Presidential elections in the United States, &c. Such talk, however, is merely synonymous with saying that they get excited, but mere excitement of the passions or emotions does not necessarily imply hysteria.[1] The symptoms of true hysteria, in women, the exaggeration of trifles into issues of absorbing importance, the flushing, the stertorous breathing, &c., are familiar to common observation, and may be found detailed in any medical treatise on the subject. Now this form of nervous and mental disturbance, is, I submit, almost wholly confined to women. It is not to be denied, of course, that men, or rather boys, occasionally exhibit hysterical symptoms of the genuine type. But these cases are always comparatively rare. With women, on the contrary, hysteria is the commonest disorder. It varies, of course, enormously in degree, from being a mere tendency exhibiting itself in slight and unimportant nervous symptoms to cases in which it becomes positive insanity and even acute mania. It has been calculated, I believe, that at the lowest estimate one woman out of every four or five is more or less subject to hysteria in one or other of its forms. The Government report, published in Germany in 1902, on the employment of women in post offices and other public departments, shows how heavily this form of nervous and mental disease handicaps women in the exercise of very simple administrative duties in that country. I am not aware whether a similar report on the subject has been issued in Great Britain. The very word hysteria, from [ύζτερα] (womb), is a proof that the disease has been from time immemorial associated with the female sex; and this is none the less significant, whether or no we accept the opinion that the womb itself has an exclusive connection with it. Hysteria, then, being a form of mental disturbance especially affecting women, and by no means to be confounded with mere emotional excitement, which may exist and proceed from a variety of causes equally in both sexes, surely it would be advisable for those impartial male persons who clamour for the admission of women to all political functions to suspend their enthusiasm at least until they have looked this subject up in recent medical treatises.

Scarcely less important is the characteristic in women often remarked upon, namely, the curious absence so frequently seen of a sense of justice, as such.[2] This, which so often vitiates their moral character (using the phrase in its true and widest sense), is, I think, itself deducible from their inability to appreciate abstract considerations generally, or, indeed, to interest themselves in any subject which does not centre in an individual. They care, not for principles, but for persons; they hate and love, not causes, but men. That, under certain circumstances, a defective moral sense is very liable to be engendered by this tendency, is obvious – for the simple reason that a moral principle is a universal and abstract rule and no respecter of persons.

In concluding this portion of the subject, I will call attention to one singular inconsistency in Feminists. The physical weakness of woman is commonly held a sufficient ground for the possession of certain privileges and exemptions, but the mental weakness of woman, which may or may not exist, but of which there is at least prima facie evidence, is held to be no valid ground for denying her access to functions involving grave responsibilities. Now this is an instance of the strange perversity which feminist sentimentalism engenders. (When I use the word sentimentalism, I must remind you, I intend not as most people do, to denote an excess of sentiment beyond what I like myself, but a *one-sided* sentiment whatever its amount may be.) The Feminist cannot see that granted that he admits the first he is ethico-logically bound to admit the second. However, I know there are some who are prepared to adopt a logical attitude. A dear friend of mine, one of the most prominent English Socialists, observed to me recently that while he was absolutely convinced of the physical, intellectual, and moral inferiority of woman to man he was nevertheless in favour not only of political but of all other equality between the sexes, which for that reason he thought would do no harm. I am afraid we cannot all be quite so sanguine on this head. However, this is at least a consistent point of view.

And now let us deal with our last heading for discussion, which turns mainly upon this last point. I have sketched out very briefly a few of the grounds which might lead us to think that the organic difference between man and woman is of a very deep lying character and does involve the mental inferiority of the female sex, of a kind and degree justifying exclusion from political functions.

This, however, is a matter difficult to prove to everybody's satisfaction. Let us, then, for the sake of argument, concede the point of intrinsic unsuitability, and enquire whether, even though a case were not made out on this ground justifying exclusion from the franchise, there might yet be other grounds which, at the present time at least, would render the concession of political functions to women unjust or undesirable.

In the **Legal Subjection of Men** (Twentieth Century Press, 1896) the privileges of women over men in the matter of law and its administration in this country will be found described in detail. These inequalities exist. But that is not all. Feminists only claim equality with men in so far as it has agreeable consequences for women. And this applies all along the line. Did you ever hear of "advanced" women clamouring for equality in the matter of military service or even for the right to become police constables? One often hears the Feminists' wail over the economic inequality between men and women. They claim, and justly claim, equal wages for equal work, no preference to men over women. With this we are all agreed. *But have you ever heard of a Feminist demanding equal penalty for equal crime?* Because I never have. Oh, no! Here comes in the "poor weak woman" whine. The muscular weakness of women (in spite of, as is admitted, a greater constitutional vigour than in man) is held to be sufficient to relieve the woman of the larger part of the responsibility for her actions in so far as criminal law is concerned, and yet no protest against injustice is made by those whose voice is so loud otherwise in denouncing sex-inequality. As Mr. Collinson, of the Humanitarian League, has pointed out, one great difficulty in getting rid of brutality in punishments is the one-sided sexual nature of such brutality, viz., that it affects the male sex only.

The Feminists, in their eagerness to admit muscular inferiority in women, with a view to justifying sex-privilege before the law, forget that they are giving away part of their own case. The inferiority in the matter of muscular strength of the female sex, if it be conceded, must imply a strong presumption of mental inferiority. Oh! exclaims someone, physical and mental strength are seldom united in the same individual. Quite right, I answer. This holds between individuals of the same sex but not between one sex and another, and for the following reason. The sex-class Man, say, possesses a certain measure of inherent vital force (if you like), a certain average of potential; as energy, capacity, or power. This power may realise itself in any given individual as physical at the expense of mental, or as mental at the expense of physical, but, over the whole range of the male sex both balance one another. If, however, you admit in the case of women a consistent average inferiority in power over the whole sex, on one side of its manifestation, viz., the physical, the presumption is obviously strong that this expresses an inferiority in the total sex-capacity, mental as well as physical. The argument from the individual member of a class cannot be applied to the class as such, any more than the single instance can subvert the rule. For the above reasons I would advise woman's-righters to choose the one side or the other. If they stick to the weakness of woman physically as ground for woman's privileges and immunities, let them give up prating of equality otherwise. If they contend for equality let it at least be an even equality all round.

We come now to a last and very important fact, and that is that if we take our stand on universal adult suffrage, there being a vast majority of women in the population, we are simply handing over the whole administration of affairs to the female sex. At any time if the female sex chooses to vote solid it can upset the entire male vote. Now, I ask, are you prepared for this? And I think I need hardly say more on this point.

The conclusion I draw from the above facts alone, and apart from all other considerations, such as those previously indicated, is, that setting aside the question of the intrinsic suitability or unsuitability of the female sex for the exercise of political functions it is at least not just or equitable that women should exercise such functions – even the suffrage – (1) So long as women possess sex privileges as against men, or so long as they are not prepared to accept the whole duties and responsibilities of life in an equal degree with men; (2) That it is undesirable they should be given the franchise at all so long as the acquirement of the vote by women would possibly mean the political subjection of man, owing to the excess of the female population. I contend that so long as women have special privileges at criminal law, special favouritism at civil law, special exemption from military service, the right of maintenance, when married, by the husband, &c., it is neither just nor expedient that they should, in addition, by the concession of the franchise, be placed in a position to dominate men politically by sheer weight of numbers.

Footnote

1. The mere shedding of tears *per se*, an ebullition of temper, a display of enthusiasm, however unusual in intensity, a wave of emotional sentiment (started, as so often happens, by collective suggestion), a one-sided or even "cranky" insistence upon a particular aim; all these things have usually no connection what ever with the special pathological condition termed hysteria. Excitement is only one symptom of hysteria. As well say that every person with a flushed face is suffering from scarlet fever as that every person who gets excited is therefore hysterical. Of course, as we all know, all the above symptoms are commonly stigmatised as "hysterical," which in such cases is merely a term of abuse by those who are annoyed by them. Where there is any approximatively or even conceivably adequate external cause for the display of an emotion, recourse to a pathological explanation is unwarranted and gratuitous. Besides, there are many pathological mental conditions other than hysteria. If I am not mistaken, Hippocrates was the first medical authority to whom a description of true hysteria was attributed, and which is, I believe, surprisingly accurate even when compared with present-day manifestations of the malady.

2. Of course, on saying this, one is fairly bombarded with irrelevant insistence on the fact that men can act unjustly, a proposition which, of course, no one denies. The point here is that women, as a rule, cannot even *understand* the principle of justice as such, or irrespective of their liking or disliking for individuals concerned in a particular application of it. Many men are sometimes swayed by personal prejudice, but women seem almost invariably to be so.

Briton or Socialist?

The dominant political impulse has been for well nigh two decades past what at present is known under the name of Imperial Expansion. This impulse is not confined to Great Britain, nor even to Europe, for the United States have within the last few years been seized with the same craving or mania (if you will). To Socialists the significance of Imperial Expansion is perfectly clear. It means the latest and most developed form of the capitalist craving for new spheres of activity, for new markets, cheap labour, and the command of fresh sources of mineral wealth, besides new berths for the hangers-on of capitalism, the official classes. In this last connection it is worthy of remark that (as recently pointed out by our comrade Karl Kautsky), while at the time of Cobden the leading great capitalistic industry was the cotton industry, now it is the iron industry which is the dominating, or, at least, the foremost branch of capitalist production.

At an earlier stage the policy of Free Trade sufficed as an outlet for that expansion which is as necessary to the continued existence of the capitalist system as breathing space is to that of the animal body. This is now no longer the case. Since the great industry in its most developed forms has taken possession of well-nigh the entire Continent of Europe, the, until a generation ago, outlying states and territories of North America together with the older European and especially British colonies, the competition between the various national groups of capitalists has become too keen. Earlier markets have ceased to suffice or to be available, or, still worse, have become the hot-beds of competition in their turn. Hence it has become essential for capitalists to organise nationally and to employ the political power of the state directly for the purpose of obtaining for their capital fresh outlets in which they (the capitalists of the particular state in question) shall have a monopoly, or, at least the power of constituting one if they choose, against those of other states. Now, this means the bringing of all the barbarous and savage countries of the earth, together with all the weaker civilised states that possess anything worth having, under the political control of the great capitalist states; in other words, their absorption by the latter. This process has been going on unceasingly of late years, the instance of it on the largest scale being what is known as the "scramble for Africa." The rapid absorption of that ever-diminishing portion of the earth's surface which has not already been brought under the dominion of capitalism – where the factory with its machinery is unknown, and whose inhabitants remain unblessed by the wares of the Great Industry – into the world market and under the sway of modern production, is not merely essential, but of pressing urgency if the present system of society with its great capitalist syndicates on the one side and its army of wage-slaves on the other is to be maintained. Under the old conditions this is impossible. Those interested in the maintenance of capitalism are well aware that if the expansion does not take place fast enough, the system by which their class profits will dissolve in revolution. Hence their eagerness to leave no stone unturned to force annexation at a hot-house pace.

In order to effect this they are obliged to have recourse to various tricks. Among others, the "patriotic" swindle is the most effective for bamboozling the lower middle and certain sections of the working classes. And this brings us to the important question as to the relative position occupied by the several modern capitalist states in the scramble for new territory, from the point of view of the international Social-Democracy. It is needless to say, the Social-Democrat, in so far as he sees modern patriotism to be simply a stalking-horse of modern capitalism, will tend to regard the respective merits as between the claims of one state and another as a case of the proverbial tweedledum and tweedledee. In general he will be right in this attitude. But here, as elsewhere, we have to judge according to the circumstances as they present themselves, and cannot rest satisfied with a merely general view. And if we take the concrete situation into account we cannot fail to notice that it is not indifferent whether one capitalist Power or another obtains a position of advantage in the near future. For instance, any increase in the power of Russia is justly regarded with apprehension by many, owing to infamous character of the Russian Government. Germany, in a lesser degree, is also regarded with dread, owing to its quasi-absolutism and the semi-despotic power of its military and feudal-bureaucratic oligarchy. All this is true. But what is not often recognised is that from the Socialist point of view the most dangerous power of all is not Russia or Germany but Great Britain. The foregoing seems a paradox. Britain, it is often said, is the freest country – a proposition which, if it simply means that as compared with Russia, Germany, or even Italy, there is less direct coercion of the expression of opinion in Britain than elsewhere may be conceded up to a certain point, though, since the imperialist idea has seized the British public the force of this proposition has been very much weakened. But for the Socialist the question of mere political reaction must be subordinate to more far-reaching economical considerations. Governments may change or be overthrown from one year to another, a great economic movement makes itself felt through generations. Just at the present time we are at a turning-point in human history. It probably depends upon the course taken by politico-international events in the immediate future whether capitalism is to have a new lease of life, lasting, it may be, for generations, or whether the transformation of society shall take place within measurable time.

Let the present expansion of the sphere of action of the capitalist system go on unchecked or receive a further impulse, and the hopes of Socialism must be indefinitely postponed. Karl Marx has pointed out how a social system never becomes obsolete until it has exhausted all the forms under which it can function. Marx and Engels fell into the error, as they afterwards confessed, of thinking that already in 1848 the capitalist system had come to the end of its tether, notwithstanding that its most advanced form, that of the great machine industry, had at that time, in many parts of the continent, scarcely got a foothold. More than two generations have passed since then, and capitalism, with its "machine industry," having exhausted itself in the old countries, feels compelled to make haste to go forth and conquer fresh fields on pain of its collapse as an economic system. This expansive movement makes itself throughout the whole capitalist world to-day, but the typical, because up to date most successful, representative of it is Great Britain. The Briton has the faculty of "opening up" new countries – possessed by no other nationality. The Frenchman, the Italian, even the German, are not "in it" in this respect compared with the Anglo-Saxon. Hence we may fairly conclude, in view of the pressing necessity of expansion evinced by modern capitalism, that the chances of a new lease of life for the present economic system of society largely depend upon the success of Great Britain in pursuing the imperial policy so popular recently. This is, it would seem, instinctively felt by the other capitalist Powers, who, much as they would like to get the game into their own hands, shrink from combining to destroy that great stronghold of the capitalist system, the British Imperial power.

It is sometimes alleged as a palliation of the successful attempt on the part of England to rob the South African Dutch Republics of their independence – and that, too, by disinterested persons who ought to know better – that it meant, after all, the substitution of a higher civilisation for a lower. Whether a civilisation of Stock Exchange gamblers and speculative mining agents is "higher" than a civilisation of peasant-farmers living in a semi-patriarchal condition, I will not stop at length to inquire. There seems to be a confusion here between "higher" and "more advanced." That modern mining and financial capitalism represents a more advanced stage of civilisation than peasant-farming of the patriarchal type is obvious. But whether with any appropriateness it can bear the appellation "higher" may fairly be doubted. That those nations in the van of historical development have to pass through all the crucial phases of Capitalism before Socialism is possible, is true enough. But as we have before pointed out, the bringing of races and countries *in the rear* of historical development into the direct sphere of the capitalist world, is not an essential part of the historical process at all, but conduces to one end solely, the *prolongation* of the capitalist system by securing it a wider area of operation; in other words, consolidating it on a broader basis. Now, apart from the actual capitalistic issues for which the British directly fought in the late Boer war -the substitution of a twelve- for an eight-hour working-day in the mines, a seven-day working week, the replacement of white labour by the thinly disguised slavery of coloured labour, the raising of the dividends of the mining companies by £4,800,000 – apart from these I say, and even supposing the annexation of the peasant Republics to the British Empire, had been the sole point at stake, as it was the ultimate aim, the attitude of Socialists towards the late war (in so far as their Socialism is not a mere fair-weather sham) was necessarily on the side of the Republics. For the Boer States were admittedly the great thorn in the side of capitalist development in South Africa generally. Once get your Cape-to-Cairo British Empire fairly under way and the capitalist system will be rescued from the imminent danger which at present threatens it of internal collapse, and the advent of Socialism correspondingly postponed.

Socialism and Bourgeois Culture

The influence, whether directly conscious or otherwise, of class-prejudice and class-interests in determining, in whole or in part, current opinion among our dominant intellectual lights forms a noteworthy commentary on the economic interpretation of history, first formulated by Marx. According to the popular tradition of the fitness of things, the man of science, the philosopher, even the political economist, must necessarily occupy a higher region than that in which the atmosphere of material considerations and low class-interest prevails. An examination, however, of the latest developments of modern thought, especially in the departments in Economics, Anthropology, and the early history of Institutions, does not exactly tend to inspire our confidence in the "objectivity," as the Germans would say, of the point of view of certain prominent university professors and writers on the above subjects.

Let us turn our attention for a moment to that central question in political economy, the theory of what constitutes the basis of value in an economical sense. Well up to the middle of the nineteenth century the doctrine laid down by the so-called classical economists on this point, the doctrine of Adam Smith, Ricardo, etc. was accepted by writers on Political Economy with hardly a dissentient voice, and indeed almost as a matter of course. The theory in question formulated the, to the unsophisticated mind, obvious fact, that the basis of Exchange-Value consists in the quantum of labour embodied in commodities. This is as much as to say that commodities, in the last resort, must always exchange with each other on the basis of the relative quanta, of labour they severally embody. This doctrine was never intended to imply that special circumstances might not modify the operation of the principle laid down, in any given case. By the old economists it was never intended to mean more than that the tendency of all operations of exchange was necessarily to gravitate towards the exchange of equal quantities of labour as embodied in objects of social utility.

Now seeing that, given the existing psychological constitution of the human animal, it is unthinkable that (other things equal) a given quantum of labour should exchange for more or less than an equal quantum of labour of the same or of a different kind, one would scarcely have thought that any one would have ventured to call in question the principle as such. But thereby hangs a tale. The sting of this very simple, and obvious doctrine in Political Economy lay in the ethical implication it was supposed to contain. Time was when this ethical implication seemed to suit the book of the middle-classes very well. As against the feudal landholder whose wealth was inherited and was moreover, founded directly on the soil itself, and hence not so obviously due to labour, it was very convenient, namely for the rising capitalist to point to labour as the basis of the wealth of the community, and as the central pivot on which all exchange in an open market must ultimately turn. But in the fulness of time arose one Marx, who, taking his stand on the fundamental principles (the doctrine of value among them) laid down by the recognised economists, was prepared to show that the capitalist system itself was not, any more than the system of feudal landlordism, built upon ultimate facts of human nature, justice, morality, etc., and that the means of production that were *upon* the land, were no more the result of the capitalists' labour than the land itself was of the landlords. The originally economic doctrine pure and simple, that labour is the basis of value, henceforth acquired a new ethical colouring, which was by no means so agreeable to the latterday capitalist as the former had been to his predecessor. The ethical-economical conclusion that labour being the source and basis of value, all wealth of right belongs to labour, this was a very inconvenient doctrine for the upholders of a system of society based on the exploitation of labour by capital. It was necessary, therefore, in the interests of social order and political stability, to seek to undermine the simple and harmless economic doctrine itself, now that it seemed to lead to such untoward consequences. Accordingly, an English Economist, William Stanley Jevons, was found to try and prove that labour was not the substance of value at all, but that value in exchange was a superficial accident or label, as it were, affixed to the commodity by the fluctuation of supply and demand – or, as it is termed, by the "Final Utility" of the commodity in question. This theory has been taken up and worked for all its worth by the so-called "Austrian School of Political Economists," of whom, Böhm-Bawerk is perhaps the most eminent. The "final futility of final utility" has been well exposed by Hyndman his little book, **The Economics of Socialism**. That any one could possibly imagine that to the long run and in an open market exchange-value could mean anything else than the amounts of labour severally embodied in the world of commodities, would indeed be incredible did we not know otherwise of the effect of class-prejudice in blinding men's minds to the obvious.

But it is not only in political economy that modern culture is twisted to subserve class-interests, and to pander to class-prejudice. One of the great achievements of the mid-nineteenth century and the decades immediately succeeding was the discovery by students of the early history of institutions, notably by Conrad von Maurer in Germany, by Sir Henry Maine in England, and by Emile de Laveleye in Belgium, that early human society is based on Communism, a crude and limited Communism it may be, but a Communism in which the land, at that stage practically the sole source of wealth, was in some way possessed in common by a kinship group; it was worked in common, and its produce enjoyed in common; that in this early tribal society, represented to-day by existing savage and barbaric peoples, the tie of blood, real or imaginary, is the strongest of all bonds, so much so, that the individual has no *locus standi*, no recognised existence even, apart from his clan or tribe. Now the scholars who discovered these principles had no *arrière-pensée* in the matter. They followed whither their researches led them without, a thought of consequences; but here again the upholders of the established order of society in the declining years of the nineteenth century began to get nervous lest the above theory, which had been hitherto universally accepted, might prove of dangerous tendency. They saw the above accepted doctrine being used by Socialist thinkers as the corner stone a new theory of historic evolution. Hence what happened may be imagined. Writers appeared who made it their business to attempt to undermine the old positions. Monsieur Fustel de Coulanges in France undertook to upset the huge bulwark of facts, going to prove the existence of primitive communism as a universal stage in the development of human society. What he did succeed in proving, was that the earlier writers in sifting the immense mass of material their disposal had made some mistakes; also that certain documents and customs quoted by them as referring to primitive communistic institutions were possibly susceptible of a different interpretation. Other writers have followed in the same strain. But the great body of evidence on the subject of primitive communism collected by the scholars of the previous generation remains in any case intact. It has nevertheless become the fashion with the students of the present generation at our universities to pretend to view primitive communism at best as a theory that has been very seriously "blown upon" indeed. This, notwithstanding that the facts on which the conclusion that group-communism was the economic basis of early society remain the same to-day as they were thirty years ago, and the majority of them, at least, do not admit of any other interpretation than that given them by the scholars of the last generation.

Once more researches of anthropologists of a generation back, at the head of whom was the late Lewis H. Morgan, arrived at the conclusion that with primitive man promiscuity was the earliest form of the sexual relation; that this, however, soon became modified into group-marriage with its to us complicated rules excluding sexual relations within the *gens*, the totem-kindred, etc. Morgan inferred that group-marriage was a salient

276

stage in the evolution of the marriage-relation from his studies of the classificatory system of relation-ship he discovered among the Indian tribes of North America, and among other barbaric races. The principle of group-marriage, by which, it should be explained, all the males of one group are husbands to all the females of another group, and vice versa has been quite recently shown by Messrs. Spencer and Gillen to be still in actual operation among the Arunta-tribes of the interior of Australia. Now, as we may imagine, the discovery that polygamy and monogamy, the only two forms of marriage officially recognised during the period of civilisation, were themselves preceded by, and arose from, earlier forms of a very different character was not agreeable to the devotee of existing marriage law and custom. The respectable bourgeois would have felt more comfortable if it could have been shown that monogamy was the earliest and only normal form of the marriage relation.. And there were not wanting men of learned e to endeavour to satisfy the respectable bourgeois. In 1889, Dr. Westermark's book, **The History of Human Marriage**, appeared, in which he undertook to prove something like the above position. What he did prove amounted to establishing the fact that in the majority of barbaric and savage races existing at the present time some form of individual marriage, or at least of pairing co-habitation, has superseded the institution of group-marriage, a fact which Morgan himself had never disputed. To Westermarck have associated themselves other recent anthropologists. In one of the latest books on the subject, by Mr. Ernest Crawley, entitled, **The Mystic Rose**, the anti-promiscuity, anti-group-marriage theory of Westermarck is adopted. The shifts to which Mr. Crawley is put in his attempt to explain away the evidence afforded by custom for the once prevalence of the institution of group-marriage, are instructive, if not always edifying. Mr. Crawley, like others of his school, is very anxious to paint primitive man in the character of a smug British bourgeois. In his efforts to do this, he sometimes endeavours to prove too much. For instance, on p.484 of his book, we come across the statement that "one is struck by the high morality of primitive man." Now, far be it from me to asperse the moral character in general of our primitive ancestors. But if Mr. Crawley means sexual morality in the current bourgeois sense, then I submit: that the statement not only goes in the teeth of all available evidence, but is flatly contradicted by many of the customs dealt with by Mr. Crawley himself, in the course of his book (e.g., "exchange of wives," "sexual hospitality," "sacred prostitution," etc.). But it is not only in sexual matters that Mr. Crawley would be sponsor for the integrity of primitive man's bourgeois moral character. On p.233, speaking of the varied and elaborate practices – exchange of garments, eating together, mutual feastings, etc. – instituted as pledges of social union and harmony, Mr. Crawley urges that they tend to prove the individualism of early man and the weakness of the tie of clan, tribe or kin. "Why," asks he, "these anxious methods of welding together the body politic, if the 'tie of blood' was instinctively so strong?" The answer is clear. All these ceremonies refer, originally at least, to persons outside the given group. They are emphatically inter-tribal, inter-clannish ceremonies, symbolising the bridging-over of the social division in question, either as a whole, or by the adoption by one group of an individual member of another group. They only confirm the strength and importance of the of blood or kin with early man and certainly (*pace* Mr. Crawley) do not throw any doubt upon it.[1] So much for Mr. Crawley's attempt to show that our primitive ancestors were good individualists.

Following on the lines of Mr. Crawley, we find the well-known. writer, Mr. Andrew Lang, in his **Social Origins** equally anxious to maintain the reputation of primitive man for bourgeois respectability. This gentleman, if we mistake not, has before given proofs of his zeal for the established order, spiritual as well as temporal. We believe we are not wrong in stating that some years ago, in an address to the students of one of the Scotch universities, he warned his hearers against applying the results attained by comparative mythology to the dogmas and myths *of* *their own religion*!!

We have given here only a few instances of the influence of capitalist class-consciousness upon scientific thought and research, in view of the approaching struggle for proletarian emancipation with all that that connotes. In this way is science coloured by the class-interests of its time We may refer those who are interested in seeing how this works out in other departments, to the supplementary volumes, or the so-called "tenth edition," of the **Encyclopaedia Britannica**, recently issued by the **Times**. Among other productions to be found there we would commend to students of philosophy the article *Metaphysic,*' by Mr. Thomas Case of Oxford, for a crude vindication of the crudest form of the old orthodox dualism in philosophy and psychology.

We do not accuse all these writers of consciously pandering to views associated with the interests, real or supposed, of the dominant. classes, for there is such a thing as unconscious or subconscious, personal, as well as class-interest, and this works in mysterious ways its wonders, to perform. But it would seem clear that, whether consciously or unconsciously, workers in the fair fields of science are not altogether to be trusted in the present day as to the pure "objectivity" of their conclusions. They have a tendency to turn the edge of the latter when that edge is in danger of penetrating the epidermis of cherished bourgeois interests and prejudices. For are not the dominant classes the material patrons and monopolists of learning, and therefore have they not a claim to "call the tune" of the conclusions learning shall put forth?

Footnote

1. We may observe that the very complexity of the rules to which Mr. Crawley refers is presumptive evidence of their early origin, just as human speech in its earlier phases shows a complexity of structure which is simplified in later developments.

2.